WAR AND INTERNATIONAL ETHICS

Tradition and Today

W.L. LaCroix, S.J.

UNIVERSITY
PRESS OF
AMERICA

Lanham •

Copyright © **1988** by

University Press of America,® Inc.

4720 Boston Way
Lanham, MD 20706

3 Henrietta Street
London WC2E 8LU England

British Cataloging in Publication Information Available

Library of Congress Cataloging-in-Publication Data

LaCroix, W. L. (Wilfred Lawrence), 1933-
War and international ethics : tradition and today / W.L. LaCroix.
p.   cm.
Includes index.
1. War—Moral and ethical aspects.   I. Title.
U22.L33   1988
172'.42—dc19   87-28053
                                                    CIP
ISBN: 0-8191-6708-8 (pbk. alk. paper)
ISBN: 0-8191-6707-X (alk. paper)

All University Press of America books are produced on acid-free
paper which exceeds the minimum standards set by the National
Historical Publications and Records Commission.

DEDICATION

To my mother

and my father

ACKNOWLEDGMENTS

The author thanks the following publishers and copyright holders for permission to use the excerpts printed in this book.

Michael Glazier, Inc., for Louis J. Swift, THE EARLY FATHERS ON WAR AND MILITARY SERVICE.

Princeton University Press for Carl von Clausewitz, ON WAR, ed. and trans. Michael Howard and Peter Paret. Copyright (c) 1976 by Princeton University Press.

Sheed and Ward for John Courtney Murray, WE HOLD THESE TRUTHS. Used with permission of Sheed and Ward, Kansas City, Missouri.

Theology Digest for John C. Ford, "The Hydrogen Bombing of Cities."

CONTENTS

INTRODUCTION TO

INTERNATIONAL ETHICS

> One must know that war is everywhere and
> justice is contention, and that all things
> happen by battle and necessity.
>   Heraclitus, Frag. 80

Examining the ethics of war might seem an incongruously bloodless academic exercise. But it must be done and done ahead of time. Once war has begun, calm reflection is rare and we seldom are virtuous enough to rely on insight alone to guide us.

Moreover, it has continuously been done. From the time of the ancient Greeks, people have examined the appeals made by state leaders which they set forth to justify the state going to war, appeals which claimed to make reasonable the deliberate destruction of lives, property, and political systems.

The examination of these appeals has continuously been done because people have always been uncomfortable with claims that the bloody agony called war could be a reasonable thing to do. What could ever be so important as to justify the killing and the havoc of war? Must one go back to the metaphysical necessity of things, as Heraclitus did? Or might one call on such a simple thing as righting a situational wrong? Or preventing one?

It is interesting that there is a long history in Western thought for the general position that war can make sense if certain conditions were present. What is more interesting to the ethician is that there has been a remarkable homogeneity throughout this history in which appeals have been made. Even if those who made them were hypocritical in doing so, that they made the appeals, and made them in terms of the same ideals, says something important.

It is a theme of this work that this history, and especially these homogeneous appeals, often referred to as the tradition of the Just War, will be helpful, but not decisive, as we try to find what sense there is today in war and other international ethical problems. To support this theme, the methodology herein will be to find and examine the ethical standards and the arguments used in this tradition by those who have thought that war could be a justifiable act of a state.

This history of Just War thinking is not a story of a single theory handed down intact from age to age and consisting in precise moral rules _from_ _which_ particular decisions about war were made. Rather it is a story of a living tradition of values and attitudes _according_ _to_ _which_ specific moral principles were formulated in response to new international circumstances. This means that the tradition itself requires we study it using a methodology that can handle changes as well as continuity.

Appreciation of this tradition of the Just War diminished in the first half of the twentieth century, apparently because of the conviction that the tradition was incorrigibly subjective and anachronistic. But recently, and especially after the Second World War, it has enjoyed renewed approval, at least as one among many viable approaches to international ethics.

It is in this spirit that I offer this study of the positions of the past, tracing not only what people held but why they did so, and tracing how, as time went on, they changed and developed what they held. The hope is that such a study may enable us to make valuable contributions to contemporary thought.

To test this methodology, after a survey of the tradition of the Just War, I will offer some specific applications to the contemporary questions of nuclear weapons, intervention, revolution, and terrorism.

CHAPTER ONE

A METHODOLOGY
AND SOME PREDISPOSING ATTITUDES

"Men seem obstinately to reject the view
that state behavior is not at some point a
fit subject for moral judgment. One sign
that this principle is accepted as relevant
is the compulsion of political actors to
justify their deeds in moral terms."[1]

Leaders of democratic nations find they cannot
long follow a policy in international dealings unless
the majority of their own citizens are convinced it is
virtuous. Likewise, judging from their writings and
speeches, totalitarian rulers need to convince their
people, those in other nations, and perhaps even
themselves of the same thing. In their public
pronouncements, leaders employ appeals to those moral
terms that, by consensus, are significant for the
international milieu: "assisting friends", "stopping
aggression", "territorial security", "protecting the
freedom of individuals", and the like.

When France went to war against various European
countries in the early 1800's, Napoleon spoke of the
actions as a "revolution on horseback" to assist the
different peoples gain their liberty from archaic
political and social aristocracies. When Austria went
to war against Serbia in 1914, its leaders stated that
Serbia had been carrying out operations urging Serbs
and other Slavic peoples within Austria-Hungary to
start a separatist revolt. Germany and Russia soon
joined in the war, each claiming it had to assist its
friend (Germany for Austria, Russia for Serbia).
Lenin wrote in 1916 that socialists always side with
the oppressed and will, when necessary, carry on war
with them against international imperialism. When
Germany attacked Poland in 1939, Hitler claimed it was
not only to eliminate the continuous insecurity of
Germany's eastern frontier but also to protect the
German minorities in Danzig and the Polish Corridor
against the "war" on them by the Polish government.

La Rouchefoucauld long ago suggested that
"Hypocrisy is an homage vice pays to virtue." [Maxims,
#218] Could state leaders' proclamations of virtuous

1

motives be hypocrisy on an international scale? That, of course, would depend on the subjective disposition of the several leaders. But the appropriateness itself of the appeals (the "homage") would have to be presumed before the hypocrisy could make any sense. I shall call this appropriateness of appeals to virtuous motives the "hypocritical imperative". It perhaps accounts for much of the evidence we have that there is an ethics germane to war and other international relations. Because leaders make such appeals to justify state actions, we know that certain values and certain standards are morally operative, whether the particular actions are truly instances of them or not. It is with this kind of evidence that we properly begin an ethical study.

I. A Methodology for the Use of a Tradition

Since the ethician has no privileged source of information, the way to start a study in any specific area is to investigate what are taken to be the rules of moral behavior by those in that area. Only later should come validation or a theory how the rules fit together. For international ethics, we must start with the appeals to principles and values made by state leaders and others to justify their dealings. These appeals indicate what in the consensus of the time are the norms for such international activity. The hypocritical imperative would underwrite the connection between the appeals and the operative norms. There is, in this part of the methodology, the assumption that state decision makers in any consensus will gravitate toward morally significant norms.

It is not enough to discover and analyze only current moral decisions. The ethician must also recall and analyze the past moral decisions in similar matters, in order to see how the present decisions differ and whether they have reason to differ.[2] For one wants to do an ethics, not an historical or sociological study, and it would be important to establish whether there has been a continuity in appeals for justification over changes in time. (We will see there is evidence of a remarkable homogeneity, a "tradition", in these appeals.) Moreover, this comparison process opens us to the possibility of an induction to new substantive ethical principles precisely by being part of the critique of what we have now. If the wisdom of the past is not

2

part of our present efforts, we cannot be ourselves wise.

On the one hand, this strategy can avoid anachronism. Today's problems in international relations are contextually unique and not mere repetitions of past problems. But they still have perennial elements, and often show an ancestry that makes it wise to identify what elements from the past are involved in order to identify what is being modified and why. There is need of new ethical standards, new substantive principles, but these should come from decisions that use the earlier principles even though they are not bound by them.

On the other hand, this historical comparison need not imply that there are no principles that go across barriers of culture and historical periods. All that is implied is that one only understands a principle from the tradition when one appreciates the set of decisions from which it was originally formulated. This set may or may not have included situations essentially like the ones needing moral decision today, but that cannot be decided before some examination.

An historical moral tradition in international ethics consequently could be significant even though it cannot validly give us those types of principles from which we can then directly deduce principles for today's problems. Today's problems are not merely instances of uniformly recurring situations. Henry Kissinger has suggested, "History teaches by analogy, not by maxims."[3] The use of "analogy" is quite apt here. Since the earlier principles came by inductions from the decisions of those who tried to express certain values in their historical circumstances, we may think of those principles as indices of certain fundamental values germane to certain international problems. We can then compare problems today that are similar to those that provoked those earlier decisions and principles to test the adequacy of our attention to those values.[4]

Most past thinking on the morality of international practices has grown out of thinking upon practices in times of war. Therefore, any study of international ethics must go through some of the history of what has counted as morally justified behavior in war and examine the reasoning involved.

3

We will take some time to investigate the origins and evolution of this "Just War" tradition. How something came about is a clue, but not a conclusion, to its meaning for us today.

Before starting with this investigation, two preliminary items need to be treated: one on the makeup itself of those moral principles that are to be studied; another on the danger of having certain subjective attitudes that predispose those who do such a study. The reason for the first item is that, as noted earlier, the methodology requires an accounting both for changes and for continuity in the moral standards. The second item is needed to distinguish this study from what today might be called "advocacy" philosophy.

II. The Kind of Ethical Principles We Find in the Tradition

The methodology herein assumes that ethical principles are complex things. That is a necessary assumption if we are to consider them as connected in a tradition in which those that apply to the same problem area are analogous, somewhat similar and somewhat different in their historical expressions. Consequently, we need a concept of principles that will allow us to talk about a tradition that has continuity as well as change.

The concept I have adopted is one that also helps us understand how different ethical standards that are operative for state leaders can still be considered experressions of those moral values we have in our private lives. To explain this concept, it will be convenient to imagine any moral principle as a complex of two levels, each of which has its special characteristics.

First-level, or formal, principles (e.g., "be honest," "be fair," "insure domestic tranquillity," "there must be a proportionate cause to make it reasonable to go to war") primarily are attitudinal, or procedural, and express ultimate values and virtues. These principles are empty of content that would direct someone to concretely specific actions. They instead indicate values according to which specific moral directives are to be formulated. Any individual acting on one of these principles would make a judgment how to balance well all the values

4

involved in the specific circumstances.

Second-level, or substantive, principles dictate exactly what in the concrete situation counts as the honest, the fair, the insuring action, or the proportionate cause for war. These are the standards from which particular decisions and actions are to be judged. From early on there has been the tradition that these second-level principles come by inductive procedures using the individual judgments of people expressing the first-level values in particular social contexts.

This induction to second-level principles helps us understand the difference we find between moral standards that pertain to decisions for personal action and decisions for actions in reference to one's office. For example, people decide in the social relations of the time what counts as virtuous action as a parent, teacher, business manager, citizen, judge, senator, president. Depending upon one's office, one has a distinctive set of values for which one is morally accountable. What would count as "being fair" as an individual among equals has always differed, at least in certain matters, from what counts as "being fair" as a parent or a president. Accordingly, the second-level moral standards to which people have appealed have differed according to their institutional role even though in the standards they tried to express the same first-level moral attitudes.

An example from history would be the physical act that deliberately takes the life of another human being. For the private individual, the standard has generally been that killing another is moral only in a situation where such an action is immediately necessary for self-defense or the defense of another. However, for one who has public office, or is an agent of society, say as a soldier or as a public executioner, it may be moral to order such an action or to carry out the order to do such an action at times other than those of immediate self-defense.

This concept of two levels in ethical principles also helps make sense out of the changes in the Just War tradition during its history. Since each comes by induction, any second-level standard is only as applicable as was the extent of the individual decisions from which it is drawn. But each of these particular decisions phrases problems and emphasizes values in ways at least somewhat special to the times. Consequently, the generation of standards is never over. In every decision, there is potentially a tension between the immediate standard as it now exists and the fundamental values and virtues it expresses.

Such a tension becomes most noticeable when there are major changes in the historical circumstances, changes which often involve the new appreciation of some human value (such as the respect for some political right). At one time people thought that care for the common weal justified taking violent action against a group within one's society that held to a different religion. But after the European "wars of religion" in the early modern era, people in the North Atlantic community came to think that care for the common weal should involve religious freedom as a political right.

At one time people thought that it was a duty for the more advanced nations to assist "backward" nations on the road to higher standards of civilization. But today there is a general conviction that, even if outside control might help raise the standard of living of these countries, their control over their own political fate is more important.

As changes in standards occurred in history, quite often for a time there have existed two or more apparently incompatible second-level principles. (For example: "Intervention for cultural enhancement is what counts as justice in one nation's involvement in the political affairs of another nation." "No, total nonintervention is what counts.") During these times, people trying to express fundamental values have made inductions from sets of decisions that differ precisely in how they join various values with the historical circumstances. For the time being, there is the lack of ethical consensus.

This lack of consensus could last for some time, as it has with the case of whether a use of nuclear weapons would risk morally disproportionate damage. Confronted with this lack of ethical consensus, how is the office-holder of good will to make decisions? May the President and members of Congress push forward the construction of nuclear weapons? During such times of ethical uncertainty about the proposed action, the tradition suggests that people may employ a procedural

6

principle for deciding about the morality of performing an action (the "doing" of the action), the decision for which could not be postponed.[5] From such a procedural principle, one might argue that it is moral to go ahead and manufacture nuclear weapons, if there is a time constraint, even when there is no consensus whether the damage they would cause would be morally proportionate.

III. Ethics and the State Leaders

To find that the social office as well as circumstances affect ethical standards implies that substantive ethical principles are not determined simply by a description of the physical acts involved. Holding others against their will, taking their property against their will, or taking their life against their will would usually be morally wrong for a private individual to do: kidnapping, robbery, murder. But if a government did them "with due process," they might be understood as legal imprisonment; taxes, fines, or seizure by eminent domain; capital punishment or war. The "same physical act" takes different ethical interpretations because of the obligations of office. From head of family to governmental leader, the one who holds an office must make decisions appropriate to the values that are germane to the group which requires the office for its common good. There is long and continuous historical testimony that there are significant differences in the ethical standards for private individuals and for those in societal offices.[6]

Ethical standards for state leaders making decisions in international affairs blend fundamental values, obligations of office, and the contemporary international circumstances. As we intend to study these standards, there are several circumstances of the international scene that we might profitably keep in mind.

First, there are no international institutions acknowledged by all nations (1) by which to decide distribution of benefits and burdens coming from whatever international cooperation takes place, (2) by which to call for loyal contribution of effort, or (3) by which to effect distribution of sacrifice of national self-interest.

As an example to highlight the difference between the international lack of such institutions and the situation within a society, let us take the assertion: "We could solve the world's (hunger, arms) problems if we were willing to make the necessary commitment." Numerically, the "we" refers to each and every human being. But so taken individually, the statement is false. The individuals as individuals could not solve any one of the world's problems. That is why the individuals feel frustrated. What if the "we" referred to the several world states? If the problem were contained within one political society, there would be an organization, or one could be formed, to deal with problems that require continuous group attention. But internationally no organizational "we" exists that by an enforceable commitment could effect solutions. (In 1986 the leaders of Ethiopia showed scant interest in resolving that country's hunger problem despite the willingness of other nations to assist.) Yet the original statement sounds plausible; it makes us feel guilty that we are not solving the problems. But it contains a fallacy of equivocation. There is no referent for the "we" that would make the claim true.

Second, there is not a social cooperative basis internationally as there is within a society. Rather, there is a spectrum along which are varying mixtures of competition and cooperation because states act not in the context of shared moral and civil values but in the context of national goals pursued by various means. The sovereign and independent states are a system of states and not a society of states. In times of international competition, power takes on prominence. Of course, there are many levels of power internationally, and what levels a state will use should depend on the many interests it has at stake. But each state has a bedrock interest in its own survival, for only then can its institutions serve its own societal common good.[7]

George Washington proposed that state leaders keep in mind the prudential rule that "No nation is to be trusted farther than it is bound by its interest."[8] Such a rule would, for example, affect where one drew reasonable lines in what counted as "honesty" between nations. It seems reasonable to hold that what counts as honesty in diplomatic dealings between countries would involve less complete revelation than honesty between a governmental office-holder and the people who elected the officer to serve them.

Finally, there are certain international practices, recognized by consensus, that draw presumptive lines of responsibility. These are designated as (1) the principle of self-help, (2) the principle of independence, and (3) the principle of sovereignty. Self-help is the principle whereby the state has the right to act to advance its legitimate interests and to employ such measures as it may deem necessary to protect those interests. Independence is the principle whereby the state is not answerable to other states for its actions. Sovereignty is the principle whereby the state has the right to make its own final decision as to its overall interests and societal procedures.

Sovereignty as a category of international thought first entered as a theory to explain the locus of "finality" in matters of authority in international dealings. There had been, of course, the earlier use of a sovereignty thematic within the individual political body, but there had not been such on the international scene until there was a breakdown of the model that all countries made up some single political society. As states began to be recognized by each other as loci of power of final decisions, they began to think of each other as the sole agents on the international scene. (Thus the reference to international relations as a "state of nature" with the several states as the "persons" in such a state of nature was not incongruous.)

It follows that each state would be "above" any international law and could decide for itself if following some international agreement would be in its interests. The rubric here often was to distinguish between a "legal" matter and a "political" matter, which distinction is always up to the sovereign state to make.[9]

Besides noting the absence of international institutions or a basis for cooperation and the presence of certain practices, many such as Emmerich de Vattel and David Hume have argued that there is not the same need for agent states to be in a societal

9

arrangment as there is for individual persons to be citizens in a civil society.[10] For one reason, there can be a degree of tranquillity even without some institutionalized international society, thanks to the practices mentioned above. For another, there is no common culture shared by all states that would make the people involved want organizations to assist everyday living.

IV. The Relation of Personal and State Morality

Some have argued, as did Spinoza, that government leaders have moral obligations germane to their international decisions, but that the primary standard is to act well in the interest of the state, no matter how the selection of means to this state interest might conflict with other moral standards the leaders might have.[11] Treitschke agreed, and in reference to the conflict between one's moral obligations of office and one's private individual moral standards, wrote that the conflict was to be circumvented whenever possible, but that it was despicable for a statesman

> "to warm his hands with snug self-laudation at the smoking ruins of his fatherland, and comfort himself by saying 'I have never lied'; this is the monkish type of virtue."[12]

Bismarck held that one's personal morality put a sharp limit on the range of options one had as a government leader. But he understood this limit as a rein on that use of power toward which a leader has a natural proclivity: to use state power to act as an agent of international "justice," or as an agent of "God's spirit in history."

> Every great power which endeavors outside its own sphere of interests to bring influence and pressure to bear on other lands and to direct affairs, runs a risk in going beyond the sphere which God has allotted to it. It pursues a politics of power rather than the politics of interest, and makes a bid for prestige. We shall not do this.[13]

Most people accept that the duties of office both justify and require that government leaders recognize certain public values high in their decisions. Even those who do not accept special moral standards for state leaders acknowledge that these leaders may have to do actions that are unacceptable in other contexts.[14] But few people accept that this requires or justifies that government leaders do simply whatever may be expedient for the achievement of some public common value. Richard Wasserstrom acknowledges the analogy of the state leader to the parent, the lawyer, and the corporation president who morally ought to prefer their "own" to others. But he argues that this preference still does not always override all other moral obligations.[15] There still may be some things it is morally impermissible to do, because of limiting and competing obligations from moral standards proper to other dimensions in one's life. So the fact that there are different moral standards operative for public office holders need not deny that there are limits and real moral conflicts at points where the different standards overlap.

But it seems that this involves only limits on the choice of means, not of the stateman's goals. There is little evidence until recently that people sacrifice family or societal values for personal values. Most seem to decide that it is always moral to subordinate how one would act as an private individual for the sake of family or society. Abraham Lincoln replied as follows to Horace Greeley, who in an editorial had demanded that Lincoln commit himself to emancipation of the slaves:

> I would save the Union. I would save it the shortest way under the Constitution.... If there be those who would not save the Union unless they could at the same time save Slavery, I do not agree with them. If there be those who would not save the Union unless they could at the same time destroy Slavery, I do not agree with them. My paramount object in this struggle is to save the Union, and is not either to save or destroy Slavery. If I could save the Union without freeing any slave, I would do it; and if I could save it by freeing all the slaves, I would do it; and if I could do it by freeing some and leaving others alone, I would also do that. What I do about Slavery and the colored race, I do because I believe it helps save this Union; and what I forbear, I forbear because I do

11

not believe it would help to save the
Union. I shall do less whenever I shall
believe what I am doing hurts the cause,
and I shall do more whenever I shall
believe doing more will help the cause....
I have here stated my purpose according to
my view of official duty, and I intend no
modification of my oft-expressed personal
wish that all men, everywhere, could be
free.[16]

Even though the choice of a state policy or
action would be made in terms of that state's own
interest, the consensus has been that any negative
effects on the physical, social, or economic lives of
other nations (existential evils as a "second effect")
also are of ethical significance. This "double
effect" locates the problem of limits in the ethical
justification of the means taken by a state to advance
its own interests.

When some contemplated means is foreseen to have
both beneficial and harmful effects, the tradition has
held that it is always ethically proper to use the
means if the benefits are to the "more important"
value, even though the acting causes the negation of
the "less important" value. (The U.S. Supreme Court
in recent years has adopted a similar approach as it
employs various degrees of "scrutiny" to give
constitutional validity to state programs that negate
the rights of some citizens.) This assumes two things:
first, that the means selected are reasonable in the
sense that no equally effective means would cause
lesser bad effects on anyone; second, that it is
possible to rank values. The formal term that covers
these assumptions is "proportionality".

Three items are operative in such a
proportionality judgment: how important is the value
to be promoted; how important is the value to be
negated; and how necessary are the means taken to
promote the higher value.

The proportionality is always judged in the
situation. In any "double effect" conflict, it is
reasonable and justified to opt for the more important
value and negate that which, in the situation, is the
lesser. (These proportionality elements, when joined
with the reluctance in negating a value one still
respects, comprise the fundamental intelligibility of

12

the traditional procedural rule for a reasonable resolution of moral conflicts: the principle of the double effect.)

The evidence that proportionality is not an otiose guide comes from history. Those trying to act morally well as leaders have made decisions some of which, for a time at least, have achieved a consensus among other leaders. Ordinarily, these consensus positions have been referred to by set phrases, such as "acting against unjustified aggression," "acting for territorial integrity," and the like. These were shorthand ways of sending forth the message that, even though the state's international actions were causing physical evils for other states, nevertheless, the values that were being secured or advanced were more important in the thinking of all reasonable people.

So it is not true that many who hold a special political morality would "sanction unlimited violence as political means or national self-aggrandizement as a political end."[17] The hypocritical imperative has never permitted state leaders to acknowledge either of these publicly. This has been true even though the consensus has been that there is a special political morality for governmental leaders.

The ability to weigh proportionality in a conflict of values does not mean that the public common good values are on the same hierarchy of values as are those of private and individual values. Nevertheless, on broad issues, such as military defense in response to military attack, they may be compared. [Here is a place for the political enlightenment of the people. The more they are capable of reasonable political judgment (Jefferson's ideal goal of education), the more people can discern how to compare values in conflict.]

The analogy of a head of a family is not without application. Being responsible for the common good of the family means certain duties justify and require the family head put the good of the family above the good of other people outside the family. But few would say that this sanctions taking any means to achieve that good, or pursuing any family aggrandizement as an end for the family. The reason is that proper living with all fellow humans is part of the common good of that family. Similarly, living properly with other states and other peoples is part

13

of the public common good of any people.

V. General Attitudes on International Ethics

As we do the historical overview, we must keep in mind the dangers of doing it with certain general attitudes that predispose its results.[18] Two attitudes, the pacifist and what I term the "natural realist", deny that special moral categories apply to international affairs; two attitudes, the idealist and what I term the "moral realist", affirm that they do. Two attitudes, the pacifist and the idealist, aim directly at morally improving international affairs; two attitudes, the moral realist and the natural realist, do not.

These attitudes function as do theories in investigative sciences, that is, they control what counts as significant data and they guide how to interpret that data. Consequently, they can never prove or disprove their own basic axioms. But that is not their most troublesome effect, which is that those who hold them find it difficult to carry on fruitful discussions across attitudinal lines. The ethician must eschew as much as possible such predispositions.

A. The Pacifist

Because of its unique position of never having been used in societal decisions on international relations, we will take pacifism on its own in chapter six. Here we might mention two items. (a) The pacifist does not distinguish societal ethical standards from the standards of personal ethics, maintaining that conflicts between societies are to be resolved by the same practices that are morally permissible to individuals: reasonable dialogue, non-violent dissent, or the example of unmerited suffering. (b) One type of pacifist, the absolute pacifist, rejects any effort at an ethics for the use of force in human dealings. Thus, the absolute pacifist cannot produce guidelines for those who morally are obligated to make decisions about the international use of force.

B. The Idealist

To identify the attitudes of the Idealist, the Moral Realist, and the Natural Realist and their effects on thinking about international ethics, it will be profitable to indicate some characteristics of each and then join to each some critiques. This is not to refute one in favor of another, but rather to loosen our thinking so that we might better learn from the past and adapt it for today.

1) The idealist holds that improvement in international affairs is practicable. Change for the better can come through education, dialogue, the acknowledgement of shared values from a "common humanity," and the identification and elimination of oppressive structures. With improvement feasible, the idealist holds it as a moral imperative to take even risky steps toward achieving a political order more consonant with certain interpretations of "peace," "justice," and "selfless cooperation."

Woodrow Wilson, in a speech before Congress on January 8, 1918, proposed a "14-Point" plan for international relations. Among these points were the promise of an "open" world after the war, marked by "open covenants, openly arrived at" and a "general association of nations". He hoped that such items would inspire "political independence and territorial integrity" for all states, no matter whether great or small.

2) Starting from the concept of "common humanity," some idealists today identify the main international problem as one of suspicion and mistrust stemming simply from inadequate communication of attitudes. Consequently, they consider it proper to make appeals more to aspirations than to historical precedent, more to motives for actions to be taken than to consequences of how effective such actions have been or might be. President Jimmy Carter insisted that "in every person there is something fine and pure and noble....The greatest challenge we Americans confront is to demonstrate to the Soviet Union that our good will is as great as our strength, until, despite all obstacles, our two nations could achieve new attitudes and new trust."[19] To make this demonstration, Mr. Carter cancelled the B-1 bomber, the neutron bomb, and the plans for the MX mobile ICBM system, and he reduced the range of the cruise missle. The maxim for such idealistic measures might be "Sincerity justifies the means," which implies that it is more important that actions are means to express the sincerity of the agent's motives than it is that they are means to achieve realization in political

15

situations of the values indicated by the motives.

3) Most idealists hold that "justice" is the highest virtue in international relations, but its meaning varies with whether one accepts that governmental office holders have special duties to their own people. Those, such as Peter Singer, who deny such special duties, maintain that leaders are to act solely for the promotion of the greater(est) happiness of all affected by any act.[20] This would mean that members of one's own society are not more morally significant for the leaders' decisions than are members of any other society. For such an idealist, "justice", understood as "giving the legitimate interests of other states, as well as one's own, the weight due each" would be interpreted as implying an equality of weight in policy decisions.

Other idealists accept that the leaders of societies have special duties to their own state interests. Leaders, therfore, are to give serious, but never equal, weight to the interests of other states. For these idealists, "justice" is more precisely defined as "acting always for one's own state's interests but refraining from advancing one's own state interests by means that violate the basic interests of other states."

4) Some idealists reject the legitimacy of the institution of war. They consider war as a breakdown of international relations, not a rational condition at the extreme end of a spectrum. Since it seems self-evident that war is endemic in the present system which rests on the principles of self-help, independence, and sovereignty, they seek a practical dynamic which will change the system. This dynamic would include the end of state power politics by means of some world organization that has executive enforcement capabilities.

6) A few idealists advocate measures such as unilateral nuclear disarmament, or even cessation of production and sales of "conventional" weapons as a major step to advance the cause of peace. Such people are convinced that the causes of war and other international problems are all external to the human psyche. Therefore, all solutions can come by correcting external structures that habituate human thinking on the range of possible courses of action.

16

Let us see if by some brief comments we might uncover some nuances that are needed in these characteristics of the Idealist.

1) The assumption that progress toward the actualization of a rational and peaceful world is possible can find supporting evidence only in reference to relations between those states that have "market and private property economies, polities that are externally sovereign, citizens who possess juridical rights, and republican, representative governments."[21] There is little to support thinking that leaders of countries of other types, when speaking of eliminating war while keeping the status quo, engage in anything other than political advertisement due to the recognized importance of communication images.

Even if these other leaders do evince "good intentions" or are "sincerely meaning well," their statements seem to be significant only if we wish to estimate the private character of the individuals who happens to be the office holders. But these qualities are irrelevant for the virtue of leadership and of themselves can never ensure good action in contingent affairs.[22]

2) The idealist sometimes portrays the goal in ideal terms (for example: "a world of peace and justice"). These terms, as such, are formal and empty. [Hegel would say they have "intensity without content and are only for edification since they lack concreteness."[23]] That is, one cannot directly and deductively indicate specific steps to actualize the goal. Consequently, when one does specify steps, (a) there is the danger of arbitrarily identifying particular means as "the" ways to achieve the goal (which commits the fallacy of _ignorantio_ _elenchi_, e.g., "If we will only stop supplying arms to El Salvador, peace and justice will come to that country"); or (b) there is the danger that motives for the specific step are taken as a sufficing expression of moral sincerity independently of whether the step would eventuate in the desired consequences [e.g., President Carter's insistence that the Shah of Iran not use troops to control uprisings in 1978-79 as the way to show a commitment to human rights and political compromise[24]].

17

3) Some idealists assume certain factors to be self-evident causes of war. For example, to call a march against any military buildup "a march for peace" must assume that ceasing military buildup is a sufficient, or at least a necessary condition to gain peace. But since others point to other causal factors, the idealist without more argument fails to show that the assumed factors are the only factors or indeed are factors at all. There is also some historical evidence which indicates that there is no significant statistical correlation between arms races and the onset of war.[25]

Conversely, one might ask whether military budgets are causes or symptoms of mistrust. There is danger here of the non causa pro causa fallacy.

In addition, this approach seems to consider the causes of war to be external to the human psyche, and it ignores long-standing convictions that people, including leaders, also act from their character, their virtues and their vices, greed, hatred, ambition, pride, which no external changes can ever totally eradicate.

But most idealists, reluctantly, do not have these assumptions, and admit that, "as long as people remain weak, changeable, and even wicked as they often show themselves to be, defensive arms will, unfortunately, be necessary." [Paul VI, U.N. speech, just after he said, "No more war, war never again."] "As long as the danger of war persists and there is no international authority with the necessary competence and power, governments cannot be denied the right of lawful self-defense, once all peace efforts have failed."[26]

Carl von Clausewitz argued that war is occasioned by those groups who are too weak to defend themselves militarily. He wrote: "The aggressor is always peace-loving..., he would prefer to take over our country unopposed. To prevent him from doing so one must be willing to make war and be prepared for it."[27]

18

C. The Moral Realist

Before the analyses of the moral realist and the natural realist, we need to give some attention to the term Realpolitik. This term is often applied to both attitudes without any distinctions, which is understandable since in the original use of Realpolitik one can identify elements of both the attitudes.[28] Moreover, many authors today meld the two attitudes under the one title "realist." But I want to distinguish the moral realist from the natural realist. The importance of the distinction brought out below is that some realists acknowledge ethical standards applicable to the means used to carry out state duties, while other realists do not. I also want to distinguish the former group of realists from the idealists. The distinction here is that, for the moral realist, the controlling virtues are prudence and contributive justice for the office-holders.

1) The working assumption of the moral realist is that the evils in the international political order come not merely from failures in communication which provoke false suspicions, but also from forces endemic to human groups and individuals (e.g., opposing interests, pride, greed, envy, ambition for power, ambition for hegemony, etc.), and that such forces will remain operative for the foreseeable future. Moral realists such as Hans Morgenthau criticized the failures of the Western democracies in the late 1930's to understand what was at hand and unitedly to confront Hitler.[29]

2) From this assumption it follows that "perfect world" moral ideals cannot be actualized now, only approximated. The Principle of the Double Effect or the Principle of the Lesser Evil must be the moral measure for decisions in conflicts between states. Prudence is the virtue higher than Justice in international actions because of the values in the national Common Good for which decision makers are primarily responsible.

> The outsider thinks in terms of absolutes;
> for him right and wrong are defined in
> their conception. The political leader
> does not have this luxury. He rarely can
> reach his goal except in stages; any
> partial step is inherently morally
> imperfect and yet morality cannot be

19

approximated without it.[30]

Prudence may be defined here as "the moral virtue of acting excellently by taking into account the particular situation and the concrete data as one decides the most appropriate course of action when there are conflicts of values."[31] The prudent individual resolves such conflicts by an analysis of the real possibilities for achieving goals proportionate not only to all the risks but also to all the costs. The prudent moral realist would reject a resolution achieved through sheer expediency, that is, one wherein the goal of the action was considered independently of the cost in other values.[32]

3) In carrying out policy, the moral realist holds that force is needed to give time for human ideals to take root, develop, and continue.

> Moralists may find it a melancholy thought
> that peace can find no nobler foundation
> than mutual terror. But for my part, I
> shall be content if these foundations are
> solid, because they will give us the extra
> time and the new breathing space for the
> supreme effort which has to be made for a
> world settlement.[33]

The included task, according to the moral realist, is to limit the effects of the uneradicable power struggles and to mitigate the clash of interests. The means taken for this involve the planned and deliberate use of power politics.

4) Motives for actions are not as important as consequences in terms of the society's common good, since good motives alone often make the political situation worse. The moral realist appeals to historical precedents more than to ideal goals.

The maxim here is "The end justifies the means that can be justified." This implies that the ground for the moral evaluation of the means chosen is that they are means to achieve, with some degree of adequacy, the agent's values. But the maxim also implies that certain other steps that could be used involve costs that are not morally acceptable even though they would be expedient.

The major problem with the realist is the tendency to stress the distance between the practical imperatives and the abstract ideal. The realist often conceptualizes the disparity in ways that approach the "natural realist's position of "only expediency in means, ethics only in goals." Consequently the moral realist has to work to keep both means and goals within the ethical conscience.

A second problem is that any appeal to the principle that "force gives moral ideals time to take root" usually ignores that such a principle historically has been inconsistently followed through. Priority given to force does not necessarily mean morally ideal goals will follow. So the moral realist must always keep tentative and uneasy about compromises that use the double effect or lesser evil principles.

Finally, William James noted in "The Will to Believe" that some truths only become actualized because of a previous belief that they are possible to be achieved by our efforts. And Reinhold Niebuhr wrote that a truly just society "can be approximated only by those who do not regard it as impossible."[34] But to believe that the impossible in international relations can at least be approximated seems to be more than what is implied by "the art of the possible." If power to do the necessary and dreams to reach for the impossible cannot blend, the task is to have them at least co-exist in the statesman's purview.

D. The Natural Realist

1) The natural realist maintains that goals alone are matter for ethical standards in international relations. Consequently, expediency is the sole measure for those actions that are means to the goals. The argument here is that ethics has no place in international relations, for it is an area of constant competition wherein concerns for morality cannot obtain without danger to the societal common good. The maxim would be "The end justifies any means that are expedient."

2) Thomas Hobbes argued that the obligation to act morally is based on a reasonable expectation of reciprocity. Such an expectation of civility is only

assured when there is effective authority. Where this expectation of reciprocal observance of moral rules is missing, there is no obligation to act in such a way as to make oneself a prey to others. In the absence of civil order, there is only the anarchy of a state of nature. Hobbes saw this state of nature as a state of war, even if only potentially so. (He used the analogy of threatening weather.) In this state of war, "nothing can be unjust. Notions of right or wrong, justice or injustice have there no place. Where there is no common power (i.e., no effective common authority over all participants), there is no law; where there is no law, there is no injustice."[35]

3) Others have argued that leaders have obligations which are categorized solely as strategic or "prudential" in terms of national security. (Prudence here means "cautious foresight" or "circumspect consideration of needs arising from future contingencies.") Any inclusion of "moral" considerations is simply misplaced. Dean Acheson wrote:

[T]hose involved in the Cuban crisis of October, 1962, will remember the irrelevance of the supposed moral considerations brought out in the discussions. Judgment centered about the appraisal of dangers and risks, the weighing of the need for decisive and effective action against considerations of prudence; the need to do enough, against the consequences of doing too much. Moral talk did not bear on the problem. Nor did it bear upon the decision of those called upon to advise the President in 1949 whether and with what degree of urgency to press the attempt to produce a thermonuclear weapon. A respected colleague advised me that it would be better that our nation and people should perish rather than be party to a course so evil as producing that weapon. I told him that on the Day of Judgment his view might be confirmed and that he was free to go forth and preach the necessity for salvation. It was not, however, a view which I could entertain as a public servant."[36]

22

In many ways, the position of the natural realist is the easiest attitude to critique. The task is to do it without denying the truths contained in its arguments.

1) There are three serious weaknesses (suggested by Hedley Bull) in the argument that lack of international authority implies no ethical relations between nations.[37]

First, the modern international system does not entirely resemble the Hobbesian state of nature. Hobbes gave the state of nature three principal characteristics: (a) no industry, agriculture, navigation, trade, etc., can be carried on, because the individuals' strength and invention are absorbed in providing security; (b) there are no legal or moral rules; (c) there is a constant state of war, that is, "not in actual fighting, but in the known disposition thereto, so that there is no assurance to the contrary."

Clearly (a) does not fit the international situation. While the armed forces of each nation provide security against external attack as well as internal disorder, most citizens are engaged in the economics of the country. Clearly (b) does not pertain either, as appeals to right and wrong long have had a place in international relations. But this evidence by itself would beg the question. Perhaps (c) in many ways does fit. Sovereign states, even while at peace, display a disposition to go to war with one another, inasmuch as they prepare for war and treat war as one of the options open to them.

Second, the assertion rests on an analogy with what motivates individuals to act civilly with each other. Hobbes held that only fear of governmental power can produce order among individuals and private groups. To use this in analogy with the relations between states ignores many possible other motives for international stability, such as reciprocal interest.[38]

Third, the assertion presumes an analogy of results between an anarchical situation involving human individuals and one involving states. But states are not human individuals. So anarchy among them may be tolerable much more than it would be among individuals.[39] (a) The energies of states need not be so absorbed in the pursuit of security that life is solitary, poor, nasty, brutish, and short. (b) Until our day, states were not as vulnerable to violent attacks as individuals are since the means of defense could exist independently of the frailities of individuals therein. (c) Until our day, war could never be absolute in its results, or take the form of a single, instantaneous blow (Clausewitz). (d) All states are not equally vulnerable, which equality on the individual level renders anarchy so intolerable there.

2) Two currently studied phenomena evidence structural cooperation mixed in with competitive independence on the international stage. One is the rule-guided and norm-governed arrangements in the world economy which show themselves in the stable expectations emerging from the repeated economic transactions between the independent states.[40]

The other is the "hegemonic stability" situation, which manifests itself in various ways along a spectrum from benevolent to coercive.[41] In the pure benevolent situation, a single dominant state (the hegemon) brings about and bears the cost of certain international "collective goods," starting with international stability, that benefit a number of other independent states. In this situation, these benefits are free to the other states and so the hegemon's actions promote voluntary cooperation among the states.

In such a pure benevolent situation, the hegemon cannot get the other states to bear the costs of the collective goods, nor yet prevent them from sharing in them. Still it finds it in its own self-interest to bear all the costs in producing them. So in this situation the other states exploit the hegemon.

When the dominant actor effects such international collective goods but can somehow extract contributions from the other states to cover some of the costs, the hegemony moves along the spectrum to a mix of benevolence and coercion. If the other states, even though somehow charged, still receive net benefits, the hegemony is mixed yet stable.

In the pure coercive situation, the hegemon extracts contributions from the other states even though these others do not achieve net benefits. But this, too, can be stable if the hegemon can prevent withdrawl of the dissatisfied states from its international regime by making the costs of withdrawl higher than those of remaining. This makes the pure coercive hegemony analogous to imperialism or asymmetrical dependency. But not in this, nor in any other of the scenarios of hegemony, is there international anarchy.

NOTES

(1) Kenneth W. Thompson, Understanding World Politics (Notre Dame: Notre Dame University Press, 1975), 210-211.
(2) I am indebted here to James T. Johnson, "Historical Tradition and Moral Judgment: The Case of Just War Tradition," Jour. of Rel. 64 (1984), 299-317.
(3) White House Years: I (Boston: Little Brown, 1979), 54.
(4) Compare Michael Walzer, Just and Unjust Wars (New York: Basic Books, 1977), 39.
(5) See the discussion on "Probabilism" in Meaning and Reason in Ethics, revised edition (Washington: University Press of America, 1979), 117-119.
(6) The argument that those in public office have special moral standards that differ from those of a private individual has been strong in the ethical tradition. See, for example, Plato, Republic, IV; Aristotle, Politics III, ch. 4; Augustine, De Libero Arbitrio, I, 4 & 5, Epis. 47; Aquinas, Summa Theologiae II-II, 64,3 and ad 1; for Machiavelli, see Isaiah Berlin, "The Originality of Machiavelli," in Studies on Machiavelli, ed. Myron Gilmore (Firenze:Sansoni, 1972), 147-206.
For some contemporary investigations, see Arnold Wolfers, "Statesmanship and Moral Choice," in Discord--Collaboration (Baltimore: John Hopkins University Press, 1965); Stuart Hampshire, "Public and Private Morality," in Public and Private Morality, ed. S. Hampshire (Cambridge: Cambridge University Press, 1978), 23-54; Thomas Nagel, "Ruthlessness in Public Life," in S. Hampshire, Public and Private Morality, 75-91, esp. 76-77, reprinted in Nagel's Moral Questions (Cambridge: Cambridge University Press, 1979); Mark H. Moore, "Realms of Obligation and Virtue," in Joel L. Fleishman, Lance Liebman, and Mark H. Moore, Public Duties: The Moral Obligations of Government Officials (Cambridge: Harvard University Press,

1981), 3-31; Stanley Hoffmann, Duties Beyond Borders (Syracuse: Syracuse University Press, 1981), ch. 1; Marshall Cohen, "Moral Skepticism and International Relations," Philosophy and Public Affairs 13 (1984), cited from International Ethics, ed. by C.R. Beitz, M. Cohen, T. Scanlon, and A.J. Simmons (Princeton: Princeton University Press, 1985), 3-50.

On special responsibilities because of social relations, see Sir David Ross, The Right and the Good (Oxford: Clarendon Press, 1930), 21; Bernard Williams, Moral Luck (Cambridge: Cambridge University Press, 1981), 17-18; and Derek Parfit, Reasons and Persons (Oxford: Clarendon Press, 1984), 95. For a utilitarian opposition, see R.M. Hare Moral Thinking (Oxford: Clarendon Press, 1981), 138.

(7) See Werner Levi, Law and Politics in the International Society (Beverly Hills, Cal.: Sage, 1976), 52-53.

(8) Quoted in Arthur Schlesinger, Jr., "Foreign Policy and the American Character," Foreign Affairs 62 (1983), 2.

(9) See Werner Levi, 56.

(10) Vattel, The Law of Nations, tr. Charles G. Fenwick, The Classics of International Law (Wash., D.C.: The Carnegie Institute, 1916), Preliminaries, 16; David Hume, A Treatise of Human Nature, III, Part II, sect. xi (p. 569).

(11) Spinoza, Tractatus Theologico-Politicus in The Political Works of Spinoza, ed. A.G. Wernham (Oxford: Clarendon Press, 1958), 141.

(12) Heinrich von Treitschke, Politics, ed. by Hans Kohn (New York: Harcourt, Brace, and World, 1963), 57; see also 52-55. One of the most notable "moral realist" defenders (see chapter 2) of the independence and superiority of the state obligations for office-holders was Hans Morgenthau. See for example his In Defense of the National Interest (New York: Alfred A. Knopf, 1952), 242.

(13) Speech in the Reichstag, February 6, 1888; in Horst Kohl, ed., Die politischen Reden des Fursten Bismarck (14 vols.; Stuttgart: Cotta, 1892-1905), XII, 447. Cited from Helmut Thielicke, Theological Ethics, Vol. II, Politics (Grand Rapids: Eerdmans, 1969), 106.

(14) Marshall Cohen, "Moral Skepticism..," 8-9,10.

(15) "On the Morality of War: A Preliminary Inquiry," in War and Morality (Belmont, Calif: Wadsworth, 1970), 84.

(16) Lincoln to Greeley, August 22, 1862.

(17) Cohen, "Moral Skepticism..," 5.

(18) For some of the problems that come with such attitudes, and for a helpful analysis of the heuristic schemes of attitudes by Kenneth Waltz and Martin Wight, see John J. Weltman, "On the Interpretation of International Thought," Rev. of Politics 44 (1982), 27-41.
(19) Jimmy Carter, Why Not the Best (New York: Bantam, 1976), 147; A Government as Good as Its People (New York: Simon and Schubert, 1977), 120.
(20) "Obligations and the Understanding of International Relations," in The Reasons of State, ed. Michael Donelan (London: George Allen, 1978), 153-170. See also Derek Parfit, "Prudence, Morality, and the Prisoners' Dilemma," Proceedings of the British Academy 65 (1979), 556-564.

David Hume, considered a predecessor of utilitarian thinking, approved that a government leader should favor his own country in international competition.

"When the interests of one country interfere with those of another, we estimate the merits of a statesman by the good or ill, which results to his own country from his measures and councils, without regard to the prejudice which he brings on its enemies and rivals.... And as nature has implanted in every one a superior affection to his own country, we never expect any regard to distant nations, where a competition arises." An Enquiry Concerning the Principles of Morals, L.A. Selby-Bigge, ed. (Oxford: Clarendon, 1970), V, ii, #182n.
(21) See Michael W. Doyle, "Kant, Liberal Legacies, and Foreign Affairs," Phil. and Public Affairs, Part I: 12 (1983), 205-235; Part II: 12 (1983),323-353, at 212. But the correlations are not necessarily indicative of causes. See Bruce Russett and Harvey Starr, World Politics: the Menu for Choice, 2nd ed. (New York: W.H. Freeman, 1985), ch. 15.
(22) See Thomas Aquinas, Quaestio disputata de virtutibus in communi, 6.
(23) Phenomenology of Spirit, Preface, A.V. Miller, tr. (Oxford: Clarendon Press, 1977), 6.
(24) See Zbibniew Brzezinski, Power and Principle: Memoirs of the National Security Advisor, 1977-1981 (New York: Farrar, Straus, and Girous, 1983).
(25) See Lewis Richardson, Arms and Security (Pittsburgh: Boxwood Press, 1960), 740, cited in Seyom Brown, The Causes and Prevention of War (New York: St. Martin's Press), 108.
(26) Vatican II, Gaudium et Spes, #79. See John Paul II, "World Day of Peace Message, 1982," #12, Origins

11 (1982), 478. Quoted in U.S. Catholic Bishops Letter, The Challenge of Peace (Washington, D.C.: U.S. Catholic Conference, 1983), #78.
(27) On War, ed. and trans. by Michael Howard and Peter Paret (Princeton: Princeton University Press, 1976), Bk. VI, ch. 5.
(28) The original statement of the principles of Realpolitik appeared in A.L. von Rochau, Grundsatze der Realpolitik (1869). Important elements of the principles appear in W.M. Simon, Germany in the Age of Bismarck (New York: Barnes and Noble, 1968), 133-134.
(29) Hans Morgenthau, Scientific Man versus Power Politics (Chicago: University of Chicago Press, 1946).
(30) Henry Kissinger, White House Years: I, p. 55.
(31) See Raymond Aron, Peace and War (Garden City: Doubleday, 1966), 585.
(32) The "tactician," therefore, who holds that the leaders' decisions are measured only by expediency and not in any way by substantive values, is spuriously prudent. See Thomas Aquinas, Summa Theologiae II-II, 55, 3-5.
(33) Winston Churchill, Parliamentary Debates, Vol. 473, March 28, 1950, p. 198. Quoted in Kenneth W. Thompson, Winston Churchill's World View (Baton Rouge: LSU Press, 1983), 45.
(34) Moral Man and Immoral Society (New York: Scribners, 1932, 1960), 81.
(35) Leviathan I, c. 13. Samuel Pufendorf elaborated this in his Law of Nature and of Nations, Bk. II, ch. 2.
(36) "Ethics in International Relations Today," in The Puritan Ethic in U.S. Foreign Policy, ed. David Larson (Princeton: Van Nostrand, 1966), 136-137.
(37) See his The Anarchical Society (New York: Columbia, 1977), 46-51.
(38) There is much study and debate today concerning what are called "international regimes," which Robert O. Keohane describes as "sets of implicit or explicit principles, norms, rules, and decision-making procedures around which actor [the state] expectations converge in a variety of areas of international relations." "The Demand for International Regimes," International Organization 36 (Spring, 1982), 325. That entire issue of IO, ed. by Stephen D. Krasner, is on International Regimes. It includes an opposing analysis by "naturalist" Susan Strange, "Cave! Hic Dragones: a Critique of Regime Analysis," 479-496. See also (pro) Terry

Nardin, Law, Morality, and the Relations of States (Princeton: Princeton University Press, 1983), 55; and (con) Kenneth Waltz, Theory of International Relations (Reading: Addison-Wesley, 1979), cc. 5 & 6.

(39) See David Hume, Enquiry Concerning the Principles of Morals, IV, #165.

(40) See, for example, Charles Lipson, "International Cooperation in Economic and Security Affairs," World Politics 37 (1984), 1-23; Robert Axelrod, "The Emergence of Cooperation among Egoists," American Political Science Review 75 (1981), 306-318; Robert Keohane, After Hegemony: Cooperation and Discord in the World Political Economy (Princeton: Princeton University Press, 1984); and the special issues in the next note.

(41) This summary draws especially on Duncan Snidal, "The Limits of Hegemonic Stability Theory," International Organization 39 (1985), 579-614. For main points of the discussion, see also the special issue of International Organization 36 (Spring, 1982), International Regimes, ed. by Stephen Krasner, and the special issue of World Politics 38 (Oct., 1985), Cooperation Under Anarchy, ed. by Kenneth Oye.

CHAPTER TWO

EARLY THOUGHT ON INTERNATIONAL ETHICS

Not from the beginning have the gods
revealed all things to mortals, but by long
seeking humans find what is better.[1]

A. Before Cicero

The ancient Greeks held a distinction but close
connection between personal and political ethics. The
individual was primarily a member of society and so
the problem of living well as a person essentially
involved relations to the polis as a whole. Plato
described the analogies between personal and civic
virtues in his Republic. Aristotle wrote his Politics
as a continuation of his Ethics.

The cultural achievements of the Greek
city-states promoted the idea among their citizens
that there was a natural disunity and inequality that
characterized the members of the human race, and that
the Greeks were the supreme examples of what it meant
to be human. This was no casual civic myth, either.
The Athenians so identified with their city-state that
their devotion to its welfare inspired some of the
most courageous acts in military history.

Even in peaceful times, the Athenian considered
the foreigner as inferior and untrustworthy. Justice
was to be observed between citizens, but where the
city-state's interests were concerned in foreign
relations, expediency and utility were the norms.
This antagonism toward the foreigner was normal in
ancient times. The Hebrew Bible indicates that calls
for justice had as their content the care for the weak
who were members of the Covenant tribes. For example,
it was against justice to practice usury toward fellow
Israelites, but not toward foreigners.[Dt.
23.19-20(20-21)] And many texts have the Hebrew deity
calling for, or approving of indiscriminate violence
against those who were not of the Covenant.[e.g., Nm.
31]

The Greeks generally premised concern about
justice on proportionality. Since foreigners were
considered inferior, there usually (Plato is a notable
exception here) was little thought about moral

obligations with them. How could one have a code of behavior with those who lacked reason? And Athenian experience with the kind of war waged by the Persians reinforced this conviction.

Since there was considered little possibility of a reasonable communication with foreigners, the only way to settle disputes with them was by battle. And the only norm in such battle was what benefitted the city-state and its needs. All particular actions or general practices in battle were judged solely by how expedient they were toward military and thus civic success. This criterion later will be called the principle of raison d'etat.

Thucydides suggested a moral law applying to all nations. But he also reported, in reconstructed speeches of the Athenians, strong convictions that there are necessary laws of nature and of war that override ordinary considerations of moral limits on actions.[2] Two of these speeches might be taken to uncover some of the moral standards for interstate relations during the period of the Peloponnesian War. Again we employ the "hypocrisy requirement": even if the appeal made is hypocritical, the appropriateness of the appeal itself must be accepted by consensus, or else that particular appeal would not be made.

The Boeotians charged that the Athenians had broken the Panhellenic code by seizing a temple and using the sacred water therein. The Athenians responded:

> [T]hey had not done any injury to the temple, and would do it do it no more harm than they could help.... not having occupied it originally in any such design, but in defense against those who were the true aggressors.... Even though they had used the sacred waters in the temple, they did it only from necessity because of the situation they themselves did not provoke, having been forced to use it in defending themselves... [A]nything done under the pressure of war and danger might reasonably claim an excuse even with the god himself.[3]

The claim is that the army engaged in defense against unjust aggression does no moral injury even when it does existential harm. Three points are stressed: (a) the harming action is necessary in the defense; (b) the harming action is morally involuntary, and thus not an "injury" (an injustice), since the defense had no choice but to defend itself against unprovoked aggression; and (c) the necessity that compels covers even sacred things (i.e., things of value in themselves, and not merely utility values) which can be put in such necessity to profane (mere utility) use. There is here a presumed distinction between "physical harm" and "moral injury." If doing physical harm can be justified, it would thereby not be morally wrong. It is justified because it is done for defense, and only done as much as is necessary for that defense. Even if the facts would belie the appeals, that the Athenians make the appeals indicates that such ideal standards were somehow recognized by a consensus. This is a very early argument for military necessity transcending values that ordinarily would be inviolate.

Later, in the Melian dialogue, the Athenians argue in support of some aggression of their own, here citing another necessity: an overreaching (pleonexia) dynamic of political power itself.[4]

> We shall not trouble you with specious pretences...of how we are now attacking you because of wrong that you have done us.... since you know as well as we do that right, as the world goes, is only in question between equals in power, while the strong do what they can and the weak suffer what they must....
> Neither our pretensions nor our conduct being in any way contrary to what people believe of the gods or practice among themselves. Of the gods we believe, and of men we know, that by a necessary law of their nature they rule wherever they can. And it is not as if we were the first to make this law, or to act upon it when made. We found it existing before us, and shall leave it to exist forever after us. All we do is to make use of it, knowing that you and everybody else, having the same power as we have, would do the same as we do.[5]

The appeal here is not to a standard of "might makes right." That is too imprecise, since it would suggest that those with might may morally do whatever they want. Rather the appeal is to a necessity, the following of which is morally justified because it is a necessity. The morality is not in the performance of right action that befits relations between countries, since the Athenians argue that such a standard only pertains between equals. What is at stake is a matter of right action toward one's own country in a world of other countries. Both their beliefs and their experience teach them that all countries rule wherever they can. Consequently, if a country has the power to rule other countries, it becomes a matter of security to do so.

This necessity of the overreaching dynamic was a consequence of the interstate situation. If those who had power today did not take control of the scene, experience taught that two dangers could easily arise for the city-state. (1) Petty power squabbles could keep the entire situation insecure for many levels of interstate activity. (2) The major power vacuum would attract some external state power (such as Persia) to test the whole area for conquest.

There were some seeds for internationalism. The widespread myths that showed up, among other places, in the early chapters of the Hebrew book of Genesis portray all people as created by one deity. The common problems of all people are often emphasized by Homer. But these seeds were killed by events in the real world of foreign wars and invasions.

In Greek philosophical thought it was the group called the Cynics who made the first breakthrough. Their title was first applied to followers of a philosophy developed by Antisthenes and later Diogenes. Their main themes were that virtue was the only good and that it was to be found in simplicity, self-control, and individual dignity. After the time of Plato, and coincident with the spread of the Macedonian empire under Philip and Alexander, these individuals conceptualized the ideal of the wise person, the sophos, as the one who saw through the values of the "the many" and rejected them. Thereby, the wise one transcended ordinary laws, regulations, and conventions which did not express true wisdom.

The major corollary to such a cynical attitude was the concept of a universal single community of humans. This would be founded on wisdom with no one

33

apriori excluded from possible entry. All distinctions between peoples based on criteria other than wisdom would be invalid. To spread their message, they sent members out in twos, taking nothing with them on their mission but relying on receptive people to care for their daily material needs. This mission style spread into various countries with the expansion of Greek political control.

Events gave a boost to theory. With the spread of the Macedonian Empire under Alexander, Greek culture and everyday Greek language spread throughout the Mediterranean lands. People became able to deal more easily with people from other places. An era of inter-societal politics gained an empirical footing.

Epicurean thought made the next theoretical contribution, that of universal individualism. This denied appeals to patriotism and traditional political principles to validate actions. The state was viewed as merely an expedient for the needs of the individual, and all its laws were merely conventions. All human beings were fundamentally alike and equal as essentially independent moral "atoms."[6]

The Epicurean concept actually was a negation of any basis for unity in any kind of society. Each person was equal to each other person, but the equality was based on radical individualism. A further conceptual step was needed for any theory of trans-societal politics.

This step was taken by the Stoics. Founded by Zeno about the time of Alexander's empire, it gave a positive analysis of the new political reality. It expanded the Cynics' idea of a possible universal union of wise persons (which explicitly would include women as well as men).

The main Stoic idea was that "the good life consists in a life according to nature." Nature was looked on as a system of regularity, as something rationally ordered independently of human activity. The individual, as a rational being, could participate in and come to understand (in a discovery way, fundamentally passive) the very essence of reality. All persons are alike in (a) this nature of being capable of the use of reason in such discovering; (b) in their active reasoning; and (c) in their ability to deal by active reasoning with the discovered reasonableness of nature. No one was inferior naturally, but could become inferior by allowing oneself to be ruled by the passions rather than by reason.

This positive universality of the Stoics undercut the aristocentrism of the Greek city-states. The sphere of political thought was now trans-societal.

The spread of Stoic thought came with the next major Western political change: the rise of the Roman empire. For the first time, the known Western world would be under one political hegemony.

B. Cicero

The Roman statesman and orator Cicero was a Stoic whose influence upon subsequent Western thought can hardly be overestimated. It was Cicero who first elaborated a natural law theory of civil and inter-societal politics and within this set forth the original theory of a justified war.

For Cicero, the basis of society was the Stoic concept of a discoverable, universal natural order. This order included the state as an natural expression of the social character of human beings and trans-societal principles of justice as the matrix for society's rules. Such principles of justice became specified and directive as they were formulated in laws which were consonant with right reason (reason correlated with virtuous attitudes). These correctly formulated laws were therefore valid directives for citizens. Positive law in society was not merely conventional (as the Epicureans held), but based on the law of nature. Politics was the art of leading and organizing society by specifying applications of universal reason and justice.

> There is in fact a true law (namely, right reason) which is in accordance with nature, applies to all, and is unchangeable and eternal. By its commands this law summons all to the performance of their duties; by its prohibitions it restrains them from doing wrong.... To invalidate this law by human legislation is never morally correct, nor is it permissible ever to restrict its operation, and to annul it wholly is impossible.... It will not lay down one

35

rule at Rome and another at Athens, nor will it be one rule today and another tomorrow. But there will be one law, eternal and unchangeable, binding at all times upon all peoples.... The one who will not obey it will abandon his better self, and, in denying the true nature of a human, will thereby suffer the severest of penalties, though that one has escaped all the other consequences which people call punishment.[7]

It is important that we appreciate this appeal to a "natural law", since it will be an assumption in the quest for international ethics until after Grotius. The Stoics held that human beings are involved in the social fabric and in a common humanity prior to any volitional acts of their own, and that people experience these "existential" relations to be charged with unavoidable moral significance. This position asserts that people are involved in morality just because they are human beings, and that certain relations with those around them are morally significant because of what human beings are. All this need not imply that there are specific directives, prior to human decision, as to what actions are morally necessary. But it at least implies that there are goals for actions and borders for morally acceptable options both of which are to an extent involuntarily acquired, and which are the objectively valid contexts for all voluntary choices and actions.

Cicero underlined his position on a universally valid objective basis for moral judgment with the alternative that any relativizing would undermine moral character in all matters. People shared a common humanity and a common involvement in universal and permanent ethical principles.

Moreover, if nature decrees that an individual should want to help another individual, whoever it may be, simply because the other is a human being, it is necessary according to the same nature that there be a common set of interests for all. If this is so, we are all subject to the same law of nature and, consequently, we certainly are prohibited from injuring

36

(doing injustice to) the other. The first hypothesis is true, and so the last consequent is sound.... (T)hose who claim one moral rule is to be observed toward fellow citizens but deny such toward foreigners break up the common society of the human race and by that completely take away kindness, liberality, goodness, and justice. We must see that such people are impious even against the immortal gods, for by them the union between people constituted by the gods is overthrown, of which the strongest bond is the conviction that it is more against the law of nature for an individual to deprive another for one's own advantage than to suffer all harms, either to one's goods, one's body, or even to one's soul.[8]

The acceptance of a universal natural law would seem to eliminate the significance of societal boundaries for justice. For Cicero, however, being in a family and in society were natural. So when he offered a ranking of the duties that obtain under justice, he ranked them according to "mutual helpfulness," which varies by familial and societal relation.

Since the basis of proof is now open, it is not difficult in the matter of duties what ranking should be given. In human sociableness there is a ranking of duties, from which the precedence of one to another can be understood: we owe the first duties to the immortal gods (that is, to the universal justice of the natural law); then to our country; third to our parents; and so on, in lesser degrees, down the remaining duties.[9]

With "degree of sociableness" the controlling function, the duties are ranked according to the degrees of centrality of a relation to concrete human life in the world.

Cicero consequently was ambiguous on what has become a perennial problem for a citizen who accepts the universality of justice: how does one reconcile a conflict between the justice in duties towards one's own society (contributive justice) and the duties towards foreigners. (Utilitarians much later, and Epicureans earlier, would hold that "each counts as one and no one for more than one" in claims on duties.) While he admitted a special obligation to one's own above the obligation to foreigners, Cicero insisted that there is a justice standard that transcends the specific interests of one's own society.

His reasoning here was that since the universality of the natural law forms an objective hierarchy of values, it follows that the true interests of one's own society will be served only by acting on this hierarchy.

> There are some acts so foul, some so base, that no wise individual would do them even to save one's own country.... But it is unlikely that the time would come where it would be of the benefit of the republic for a virtuous individual to do such things.[10]

Which were these acts that were prohibited "even to preserve one's own country"? Cicero did not give a complete list, but his position seems to have been that the acts would become known by the consensus of the "good people" who were influenced by the natural law, since that law was in each individual. Even though the state is a natural law entity and very high on the list of those to whom moral duties are owed, it is not the supreme moral entity. The "gods" are. (That is why the declaration of war by the Roman Senate had to be approved by the priests, as noted below.) The duties to the gods would be an internal guide for good people by which to identify the limits of what could be done in conflicts between one's own state and other states.

With the Stoic idea of the natural law as his premise, Cicero denied any real conflict between the interests of a particular society and the interests of all societies. (Actually this can be quite ambiguous: one could assert that "what is good for the Soviet Union is good for all countries" as fulfilling Cicero's position. But that is not what he meant. He meant that there were certain moral duties that were supreme no matter what individual societies judged were in their own interests.) Thus the principles of reason of state or nation expediency could never be conclusive for a society if such principles went against certain values. Ordinarily, however, reasons of state or national expediency could themselves be the way to concretize the demands of natural law, since the state was itself a natural entity, and so those acts and those policies for its survival and vigor were in the natural order of reason.

Cicero thereby concluded that a society's true interests were in terms of preserving certain values or ideals since to commit certain acts in the name of societal self-interest would be so to violate the natural order of things as to precipitate destruction of the society itself.

C. Cicero and the Just War

For Cicero, justice was the natural standard for all levels of interpersonal relations. Justice involves "conserving human society, rendering to each one that one's due, and being faithful to agreements"[11], that is, both what is due naturally and what is due by agreement. Justice itself is established by nature, not by convention, since it comes from natural law known by reason. It is the proper ordering of all human relations. (Recall from above that Cicero did distinguish and rank different type of justice to correspond to the religious, the societal, the familial, and the intersocietal levels in the sense that they might vary in their obligational strengths.)

The basis of moral judgments in human politics was the unity of mankind, which implied a society that transcended state boundaries. Yet the state itself was a moral entity under natural law, resting on pietas and iustitia (loyalty and justice). It was prima facie moral to do those things necessary to preserve and enhance it. War was one of those things. But how could it be, since it seemed to oppose the unity of mankind. Cicero resolved the paradox by thinking through how justice in war could be both toward one's own country and toward all other countries.

War was a political act that in no way was neutral to morality, since war involves existential evil. Cicero tried to articulate how it might be that, in a context of universally applicable moral rules, war was not also a moral evil.

He formulated ideas of _ius_ _ad_ _bellum_ (justice in undertaking war) and _ius_ _in_ _bello_ (justice in carrying on war). [Roman society already had a procedure he may have had in mind. The _fetiales_, fetial priests, were consulted to judge the morality of the Roman Senate's going to war.[12]]

First the goal of war must itself always be moral and in accord with the unity of mankind under natural law. This, in intersocietal justice, would mean a "just peace."

> Therefore, war should be waged for this cause, that the state may live in peace without injury.... My conception of the peace to be sought is that it be without deceit.[13]

From this basis, Cicero outlined a doctrine of _ius_ _ad_ _bellum_ in terms of the conditions that would justify going to war. (a) War had to be the last resort of policy.[14] (b) The only moral reasons for war were to avert or to correct those interstate situations that would undermine the just peace: injuries being done or already done. (c) But proportionality must be observed on this _ad_ _bellum_ level.

> Also, there are certain duties to be observed toward those who have done you injustices. There are limits to vengeance and punishment, and I rather think it is sufficient if the one who did the injury repents, so that that one and others are afterwards slower to do injustice.[15]

The last two requirements for _ius_ _ad_ _bellum_ were (d) a formal attempt to settle the matter by stopping or correcting injuries against a just peace without war, and (e) a formal declaration of war.

> Fair rules for war are set down with religious overtones by the fetial law of the Roman people. From these we can understand that no war is just unless restitution first has been demanded or unless there has been a formal warning and declaration.[16]

On the *in bello* level, Cicero introduced elements of *in bello* discrimination.

> In destroying and plundering cities, it is very important not to be randomly cruel. Thus, whatever the confusion of the moment, the truly great individual will punish the guilty, protect the (innocent) many, and in any situation keep to the moral and just standards.[17]

These latter were requirements because the common humanity basis of natural law justice continued even during war.

Cicero was convinced that the natural law hierarchy of values had an existential foundation. Thus, unjust political action in intersocietal affairs would destroy one's own state by corrupting its moral values. And this would in turn lead to a state's physical destruction.

NOTES

(1) Xenophanes, fragment 18.
(2) *History of the Peloponnesian War*, III, 56.
(3) *History*, IV, 98.
(4) Jacqueline DeRomilly calls it a "law of imperialism." See *Thucydides and Athenian Imperialism* (Oxford: Blackwell, 1963), 336-337.
(5) Thucydides, *History*, V, 89, 105.
(6) See Epicurus, *Principle Doctrines*, #35-39.
(7) *De re publica*, modified from tr. by G.H. Sabine and S.B. Smith (Columbus: Ohio State, 1929), III, 22.
(8) *De officiis*, III, 27-28.
(9) *De officiis*, I, 160.
(10) *De officiis*, I, 159.
(11) *De officiis*, I, 15.
(12) *De officiis*, I, 36.
(13) *De officiis*, I, 35.
(14) *De officiis*, I, 34.
(15) *De officiis*, I, 33.
(16) *De officiis*, I, 36.
(17) *De officiis*, I, 82.

CHAPTER THREE

EARLY CHRISTIAN INFLUENCE

There are currently many inaccurate assertions made about the attitude of early Christians toward war. Recent scholarship has forced us to be much more cautious in situating their contributions to political ethics.

Christian thought prior to Augustine carried three rather distinct attitudes toward the state. The first, mainly in the earliest years of Christianity in the Roman Empire, evinced the Judaic dimension in most of the first Christians. The Jews resented and resisted the rule of the Romans over Palestine, but in general accomodated themselves to the reality of the political situation. Most Jewish Christians continued this attitude both because of their Jewishness and because of their conviction that the apocalyptic end of time was near. After the year 80, at least some Christians, because of a self-image of sectarian separatism, were passively anarchic.

The second attitude, following Paul, accepted the Empire's protection and civil order as a precondition for being able to spread the faith and live morally. Paul insisted that all political authority came from God and thus was to be obeyed. Thus Christians would simply blend into the life of the _polis_.

The third attitude came with the persecutions of Christians by the state (off and on between the first and the fourth centuries). From such, some were intensified in their sectarian separatism, but most seemed to return to civil cooperation as the persecutions abated.

In the New Testament itself there is no direct mention of the ethics of intersocietal politics. Yet there are indirect comments. Jesus showed that his kingdom did not challenge the Empire as such. His main critique was of Jewish religious ideas and institutions. The gospel of Matthew has a personal ethic of non-resistance as it rejects the use of private force to settle injustices. This, however, is not the same thing as a political pacifism.

The terms "war" and "soldier" occur only incidentally, by way of illustration or in a purely neutral recognition of the fact that they exist. When there are dialogues with military men, e.g., in Jesus' meeting with the Roman officer, the soldiers are never advised to give up their position.[1] To the soldiers who ask for counsel, John the Baptist simply said things that could be done within the context of the military life, namely, that they rob no one by violence and that they be content with their wages.

Every advocacy by Jesus of non-violence was relative to context. It was a valid option to be a Messiah of force. Jesus decided against it. That is why he got so angry with Peter. But he used force to expel the traders from the temple. Even the injunction (Mt 5.38-39) not to resist evil was in distinction to the lex talionis, that is, it was to exclude doing exactly equivalent violence in revenge for injury done. This had nothing to do with the use of force in defense or in helping others.[2]

None of the other passages which deal with the use of physical force, love of enemies, and patient endurance has anything to do with the ethics of war. They all deal with the question of using force to protect Jesus or his followers in spreading the kingdom. That remains on the level of personal ethic and never had a political level application.[3]

Scholars are somewhat divided today on the matter of early Christian participation in the Roman military. Certain pacifist writers have felt that the early Christians did not participate and therefore must have condemned war as against the Christian message. Thus they have charged that the just-war doctrine elaborated by Augustine was a betrayal of true Christianity.[4] But there is some reason to think that these writers have looked down the well of time to see reflections of their own attitudes.

It does seem the case that Christians did not serve as Roman soldiers until the second century. But the causes for such non-participation are more complicated than the idea that political pacifism is an essential constituent of Christianity.

There were three major causes. (a) First, at the start of Christianity, the Roman armies were not normally dependent upon conscription. Also, the Jews

43

were legally exempt and the Romans correctly considered first-century Christians as a Jewish sect. And after they were expelled from the Jewish community, the Christians took on as part of their new identity many elements of sectarian separatism from the affairs of society.[5]

(b) Second, some of the activities of the Roman military, such as the police function exemplified in the events surrounding John the Baptist, Jesus, Peter, Paul, the control of the Jewish people, and in the persecutions under Nero, Trajan, Hadrian and others made army service unattractive to Christians. And since once one was in the army, one could not select which duty to avoid, most Jewish Christians at first were reluctant to volunteer.

(c) Finally, the early Christians were unable to avoid the appearance that the Roman military involved both emperor worship and Mithras worship (usually as Sol Invictus) with attending liturgies. This problem seemed central to the rejection of military service, at least on the level of centurion, for Christians by Tertullian.[6]

For these reasons, much of early Christian rejection of the military took place independently of the ethics of intersocietal politics. The scattered references to military violence as such rarely touched on the ethical question itself. When the early fathers did comment on war, it was often in terms that praised peace and claimed that Christianity was fulfilling prophecies of universal peace. Eusebius, the early Church historian, commented that the prophecy of perpetual peace started to be fulfilled with the advent of Christianity but added that the Pax Romana was the specific instrument of this fulfillment.[7] In writing on the Christian "Thundering Legion" (about 173 A.C.E.), there is only mention of the loyalty of Christians to the empire and no criticism of Christians serving in the legion. [John Helgeland summarized recently: "A great deal of evidence supports Eusebius' position over against the kind of pacifist interpretation that has been dominant in recent North American scholarship."[8] He went on: "If anything, the evidence suggests that pacifism may not even have been known among Christian laymen."[9]]

44

Origen (185-254) had an interesting analysis. He held that Christians were not to fight but that the condition for them to thrive precisely is that the Roman legions were willing to fight.

> The existence of many kingdoms would have hindered the spread of Jesus' teaching .... How could this peaceful teaching, which prohibits a person from avenging oneself even against one's enemies, have gained sway if the whole world situation at the time of Jesus had not been made more peaceful.[10]

Origen was not simply neutral or tolerant about being within a politically organized society. He saw positive values for the Christian community from the existence and activities of the Empire. Yet he argued that Christians could not fight in the army because of Christ's prohibition against killing. "Jesus considered it contrary to his divinely inspired legislation to approve any kind of killing whatsoever."[11] Origen here extrapolated the prohibition against using violence in retaliation, which he took literally and absolutistically, to the societal level, which is beyond the New Testament text. He admitted that the Jewish people had no commandment of pacifism, but he argued that this was proper, since they were a political entity and a divine commandment of pacifism for them would have been irrational since it would have "consigned them to complete destruction" as a nation.[12] We might note two things here: (1) Origen saw pacifism as a voluntaristic commandment of Jesus, not as a rational moral principle; (2) Origen wrote at a time when many of the Christians viewed themselves as a separatist sect, and not as religious institution within society whose members owe contributive justice to the society.

The pagan Celsus saw the free rider aspect and charged that Christians were not only bad citizens but even traitors, accepting the benefits, but refusing to share the burdens. In reply, Origen sought to combine acceptance of the role of the state with the personal idealistic perfectionism he saw in Christianity, wherein Christians generally would support the practices of the state but refuse to participate in some matters.

To this we should reply that when the

45

occasion arises, we provide the emperors with divine assistance, as it were, by putting on the 'armor of God.'... The more pious a person is the more effectively does one assist the emperors, more so than the troops that go out and kill as many of the enemy as possible on the battleline. This would be our answer to those who are strangers to our faith and who ask us to take up arms and to kill people for the common good.... The Christians fight through their prayers to God on behalf of those doing battle in a just cause and on behalf of an emperor who is ruling justly in order that all opposition and hostility toward those who are acting rightly may be eliminated.[13]

Origen accepted the concept that there can be justified wars, and, afortiori, justified killing in those wars. And he accepted that Christians had a duty under justice to support the international activities of the state, since the use of power internationally was necessary to protect the common weal. Yet he argued that those who offer prayers, etc., actually assist the emperor more effectively than do the troops who physically fight.

One notes that this does not imply that the troops are not still needed. And it certainly does not imply that the Christian is against their use. Rather it is a claim that the Christian has a task in respect to the protection of the common weal that is other than, and more important than that of physically fighting. (Origen was certainly no anarchist as was the early Lactantius.)

Origen's position allowed Christians to claim they were not free riders even though they chose to keep their personal perfectionism. Those who felt that the Gospel required total non-violence for themselves could still enjoy the benefits of a society that was defended by military practices. Thus, his position did not propose any ethics of intersocietal relations.

Actually, such a position was not really thought through. If it was moral for non-Christians to use physical violence in war, Origen seems to say, that was not because they were acting in ignorance of some

46

universal moral prohibition, but because they did not belong to a particular faith. This makes one's morality relative to whether one belongs to a particular religious group. It must also assume that morality has a voluntaristic base. A "voluntarist" morality claims that the basis of any moral standard is the arbitrary will of one who commands, as superior to inferior. It is therefore only a matter of accepting or rejecting the command as one's moral standard. The standard does not have in itself any intrinsic intelligibility as a moral guide so that it could be studied for its universal appeal to reason. This implies two characteristics for the standard. One, it only applies to those who have accepted the relation to the superior. Two, it is not a standard that includes some intrinsically rational basis.

It also contained an intrinsic inconsistency. It implied that Christians would not violate Jesus' commandment against Christians killing in action even though their prayers admittedly included in intention the successful use of military force. But if an action is wrong for a Christian, the intention by a Christian that another do that action in one's mutual service must also be wrong.

There were a few who did condemn all killing. Lactantius, for one, started with a voluntaristic command ethic, but he, unlike Origen, had it apply to all, even to non-Christians. About 305 C.E., he wrote:

> For when God forbids killing, he is not only ordering us to avoid armed robbery, which is contrary even to public law, but he is forbidding what people regard as ethical. Thus, it is not right for a just man to serve in the army since justice itself is his form of service. Nor is it right for a just man to charge someone with a capital crime. It does not matter whether you kill someone with the sword or with a word since it is killing itself that is prohibited. And so there must be no exception to this command of God. Killing a human being whom God willed to be inviolable, is always wrong.[14]

This seems an assertion of rigorous Christian pacifism that is based on an absolutistic reading of only selected passages of the Scriptures. It absolutizes Ex. 20.13, the commandment against killing, and ignores passages such as Ex. 32.26-29, which recounts how Moses and the Levites killed some 3000 Israelites in one day but do not violate the commandment. And it ignores Deut 13.6-11, which interprets the commandment to say only "Thou shalt not kill a fellow Israelite as long as he is a faithful follower of Yahweh." And it ignores those commands of the deity to kill others in war (e.g., Nm 31).

Interestingly, Lactantius connected serving in the military with testifying in a capital trial. He seemed to call for rejection of participation in societal affairs since the society authorized killing in either activity. Later, Christian writers would argue that both activities are civic duties under justice.

Lactantius himself saw that his position would imply acceptance of the destruction of the security Christianity received in the empire, since the empire itself would be destroyed by external barbarians.[15] He offered as the only valid alternative that all people should renounce military virtues and then all wars would simply cease.

> But if the one God were worshipped, there would be no dissension or wars because people would recognize that they are sons of the one God and thus bound together by a holy and inviolable bond of divine kinship. There would be no intrigues since they would know what kind of punishments God, who is aware of hidden crimes and even a person's thoughts, had in store for those who took human life.[16]

He would have been nonplussed with the events in later centuries of the wars by Christian nations against each other which Grotius remarked were embarrassingly brutal.[17]

Moreover, Lactantius himself seemed to have had second thoughts on the military implications of Christianity. In later works he shifted to moral guidance also from the order in human nature, very close to a natural law ethic, and had words of praise for military activities. For example:

48

These things which God in his wisdom has
instilled in people are not evil in
themselves. They become so through
improper use but are by nature good because
they have been given to us for preserving
life. Just as courage is good if you are
fighting for your country but evil if you
are rebelling against it, so too, with the
emotions. If you use them for good ends,
they will be virtues; if for evil ends,
they will be called vices.[18]

By A.C.E. 170-180, the Twelfth Legion of Marcus
Aurelius, called the Legio Fulminata (Thundering
Legion) recruited and stationed in Melitene, included
a majority of Christians.[19] Later, with the
Constantinian establishment of Christianity as the
state religion, war as a state policy option became an
explicit question for Christian study.

A decade before Constantine effected total rule
of the Empire, the Synod of Arles decreed in its third
canon: Ut qui in pace arma proiicient
excommunicentur. Even thought the exact translation
in context is still debated, the general meaning is
that Christian soldiers were told that leaving the
army in peacetime brought the risk of
excommunication.[20] The historical context seems to
be that Constantine's army was fighting to protect
Christianity and merited full support and
participation.

About the middle of the fourth century,
Athanasius justified warfare and killing as long as
the situation and the intention were proper.

Also in other acts, which commonly take
place in the course of this life, we find
that certain distinctions must be made.
One is not supposed to kill, but killing
the enemy in battle is both moral and
praiseworthy.... Thus, at one particular
time, and under one set of circumstances,
an act is not permitted, but when the time
and conditions are right, it is both
allowed and condoned.[21]

Here again the moral evaluation of killing in war
turned on making the proper distinctions. Athanasius
followed the tradition of distinguishing between the

49

physical evil brought about by the action and the context in which the action is done which context can make it a morally good action. (That the act's morality also depended upon the proper intention of the agent was assumed, but not quite to the point here. The proper intention was a necessary, but not a sufficient condition to make the act of killing in war moral.)

Later in the same century (c. 391), Ambrose also praised, as morally justified, "that kind of courage which is involved in defending the empire against barbarians, or protecting the weak at home, or allies against plunderers."[22]

Ambrose accepted the hierarchy of duties toward God, country, family that Cicero had discovered in natural law.[23] And he also distinguished the morality of using physical force as a private person and using it in service of one's country.

> There is nothing that goes against nature as much as doing violence to another person for the sake of one's own advantage. Natural feeling argues that we ought to look out for everyone else, to lighten the other individual's burdens and to expend our efforts on his behalf. Anyone wins a glorious reputation for oneself if one strives for universal peace at personal risk. Everyone believes it is much more commendable to protect one's country from destruction than to protect oneself from danger and that exerting oneself for one's country is much superior to leading a peaceful life of leisure with all the pleasures it involves.[24]

Cicero had set down certain requirements for justified war in his work De officiis. Ambrose, writing on the duties of the clergy (De officiis ministrorum) gave the first major Christian contribution to the matter.

For Ambrose, as for Cicero, the controlling virtue in matters of war was justice. Courage in war would be a source of wickedness if the war was not itself just.[25]

50

The war might be just if it was done for a validating reason such as defense[26] or punishing wrongs done.[27] However, virtue in the course of the war required that the rules of battle be honored [28] and that the defeated enemy be spared.[29]

The pivotal idea for Ambrose upon which he was able in his reflections to appropriate the theme of personal non-resistance with virtue in war was the distinction of duties to oneself, which may be set aside for the sake of the Gospel[30] and duties to others, which may not.

> The glory that courage brings resides not only in the strength of one's body or one's arms, but in the courage of one's soul, and the essence of this courage is not expressed in doing injury but in preventing it. For anyone who does not prevent injury to a friend, if one can do so, is as much at fault as the one who causes it. For this reason holy Moses gave this early proof of his courage. For when he saw a Jew being injured by an Egyptian, he defended him by killing the Egyptian and hiding him in the sand.[31]

To prevent injury to oneself is a duty that can be overridden by an appeal to a spiritual motive of imitating Jesus. But the duty to prevent injury to another cannot be so overridden. Ambrose's argument was that this would make one as guilty as the one who does the physical injury, because omission would make one a "cooperating" cause of the effect. On this, Louis Swift comments:

> The significance of this statement for the development of Christian ideas on violence and war is difficult to exaggerate. What is denied to an individual in his own case is not only permitted but morally required of him when it comes to defending another against aggression. Moreover, the example cited by Ambrose makes it evident that he is not thinking of passive resistance alone. The responsibility for looking out for one's neighbor can require a person to use force on another's behalf even to the point of taking an aggressor's life.[32]

51

To get at the point of Ambrose's distinction, it might help to expand on why he rejected the use of physical force in personal self-defense. It was to this action that he applied the Gospel admonition against "taking up the sword."[33] The reason he gave was that the use of force in personal self-defense "weakened the virtue of charity." In Christian terms, charity is a theological virtue, that is, one that must be given by God, not one that is developed by human practice. However, it can be lost by human actions. To use force in self-defense would be to prefer one's own life at the expense of another's, and that would go against the divine gift.

When it came to the defense of another, Ambrose, in the quote above, cited the virtue of courage and defined it in terms of "preventing injury." For Ambrose, showing courage was one way to specify how to act out the theological virtue of charity. When only a matter of personal self-defense, charity required that one not resist by force, for that would show a preference for self over another. But in the defense of another, charity must choose between two other individuals. The choice is weighted in favor of using force against the aggressor because to choose otherwise would be to partake of the aggressor's evil action. This choice would not violate charity because it shows a hatred of the evil action without necessarily showing a lack of love for the evildoer.[34]

Nevertheless, it is not clear why preferring one's own life at the expense of another violates charity while preferring a third party's life at the expense of the attacker does not. The only premise that would save Ambrose's position would be that one owed more love to others than one owed to oneself. (We will look again at this distinction with Augustine and Aquinas.)

It is interesting that no one who has been both canonized a saint and named a doctor of the Catholic church has ever defended pacifism as a social ethic. Many saints and doctors, such as Augustine, Bernard, Thomas, and Bellarmine, have defended justified war and the duty of all citizens to participate.

NOTES

(1) Mt. 8:10. Elizabeth Anscombe makes a nice

analogy on this. Jesus commended the centurion for his faith after the centurion had compared his authority over his men to that of Jesus over individuals. To the Christian pacifist, such a commendation must be as if Jesus had commended a madam in a brothel for her faith after she had compared her authority over her charges to the authority of Jesus. See her "War and Murder," in War and Morality, ed. Richard Wasserstrom (Belmont: Wadsworth, 1970), 49.

(2) See Albert Nolan, Jesus Before Christianity (London: Darton, Longman and Todd, 1976), 110-111.
(3) See Helmut Thielicke, Theological Ethics (Grand Rapids: Eerdmans, 1979), II, 453-454.
(4) See, e.g., Paul Oestreicher, "But I Say unto You," in Unholy Warfare, D. Martin and P. Mullen, ed. (Oxford: Blackwell, 1983).
(5) See Louis J. Swift, The Early Fathers on War and Military Service (Wilmington: Michael Glazier, 1983), 30, and James T. Johnson, Just War Tradition and the Restraint of War (Princeton: Princeton University Press, 1981), xxvii.
(6) De corona militia, II.
(7) Praeparatio evangelica, 10b-11a.
(8) "Military Force and the Christian Conscience in the Early Church," in Catholic Theological Society of America Proceedings, 37 (1982), 178-181. This report has been expanded and published as John Helgeland, Robert J. Daly, and J. Patout Burns, Christians and the Military: The Early Experience (Philadelphia: Fortress, 1985).
(9) See also Helgeland's, "Christians and the Roman Army, A.D. 173-337," Church History 43 (1974), 149-161; and Swift, Early Fathers.., 68-71.
(10) Contra Celsum II, 30. Adapted from Swift tr.
(11) Contra Celsum III, 8.
(12) Contra Celsum VII, 26.
(13) Contra Celsum VIII, 73. Adapted from Swift tr. See also VIII, 82.
(14) Divinae Institutiones VI, 20, 15-17. Adapted from Swift tr.
(15) Divinae Institutiones VII, 20.
(16) Divinae Institutiones V, 8, 6. Adapted from Swift tr.
(17) De jure belli ac pacis, Prolegomena, #28.
(18) Epitome 56, 3-4; and see other citations in Swift, 65-67.
(19) Eusebius, Church History V,v,3ff; see also Swift, 37.
(20) See Swift, 90-92.

(21) Epistula ad Amunem Monachum, P.G. 26.1173, quoted in Swift, 95.
(22) De officiis ministrorum I, 27, 129; P.L. 16.62. Adapted from Swift, 98.
(23) De officiis ministrorum, I, 27, 127.
(24) De officiis ministrorum, III, 3, 23; P.L. 16.151. Adapted from Swift, 98.
(25) De officiis ministrorum, I, 35, 176.
(26) De officiis ministrorum, I, 27, 129.
(27) De officiis ministrorum, III, 19, 110, 116.
(28) De officiis ministrorum, I, 29, 139.
(29) De officiis ministrorum, III, 14, 87.
(30) De officiis ministrorum, III, 4, 27.
(31) De officiis ministrorum, I, 36, 179.
(32) Swift, 102.
(33) De officiis ministrorum, III, 2, 27.
(34) See Swift, 103.

CHAPTER FOUR

AUGUSTINE AND MIXED JUSTICE

A. The Two Cities

By the end of the fourth century people in the Empire began to fear destruction from outside. The Goths, the Huns, and the Vandals frightened the Christians and angered the pagans of the Empire. The Catholic bishop Augustine took on the task of explaining the fall of "civilization." The basic problem, he maintained, was that human intellectual and moral capabilities were severely limited because of sin, and therefore the classical ideas of human progress and the perfectability of human society were not realistic in this world.

As with the basic problem, so also the basic solution for the human situation was "in the heart," in each person's orientation of the will. Each person has one of two fundamental orientations: love of self or love of God. Concentration on self rather than on God was the foundational sin of pride. (Religions of Semitic origins, which came in cultures dependent on tribal loyalty and obedience to the laws of the tribal leader and the tribal divine founder, consistently saw pride as the greatest sin. The Greeks and Romans considered pride, if proportioned to one's accomplishments, to be proper.)

Blinded by their pride and thereby made ignorant of what truly is good, people, personally and collectively, desire what actually does them harm. Their lust has two social manifestations: the insatiable lust for material things (avarice: cupiditas) and the lust to have power over others (libido dominandi).

Even if such people strive and achieve good habits of character, their virtuous actions would be qualitatively different than those with divine love. One's basic love orients the foundational virtues of prudence, moderation, courage, and justice and therefore orients how the virtuous person will judge what is the morally good action in any situation. Consequently, it is questionable whether one can accept the virtues of the one group as at all genuine.[1]

Using this analysis of two loves, Augustine described two "cities," two types of social union, in the structure of human affairs: <u>Civitas</u> <u>Terrena</u> and <u>Civitas</u> <u>Dei</u>.[2] Those people who live almost completely with the love of themselves are united by their common interest in this temporal world and form the first city. Those who are united by their common love of God form the second.

Nevertheless, Augustine did not consider the political situation within the Roman Empire to consist in the mere conjunction of these two peoples. Rather he accepted the end of the sectarian separatism of Christians, not the least because Christianity had become the Empire's official religion. In addition, a basis for some sort of political union between those of the two cities was that both, at least for a time, have a stake in maintaining a condition of social peace. The two groups, therefore, could cooperate to obtain this goal.

> Thus the things necessary for this mortal life are used by both kinds of individuals and families alike, but each has its own peculiar and widely different aim in using them. The earthly city... seeks an earthly peace, and the end it proposes, in the well-ordered concord of civic obedience and rule, is the combination of men's wills to attain the things which are helpful to this life. The heavenly city, or rather the part of it which sojourns on earth... makes use of this peace only because it must, until this mortal condition which necessitates it shall pass away.... Consequently... it makes no scruple to obey the laws of the earthly city, whereby the things necessary for the maintenance of this mortal life are administered.[3]

Augustine took this theme of the intermingling of two cities in human life and made it the framework for his political theory. Cicero had held that the core of society is justice. Augustine held that, since true justice was available only with the heavenly love, then only <u>Civitas</u> <u>Dei</u>, and not any earthly city, can qualify as a political society.[4] But a standard that makes all actual societies unethical violates ethical methodology on how to specify what counts as satisfying an ethical ideal. So Augustine quickly modified and accepted that the reality in the earthly city, _Civitas Terrena_, shows that there is a lower level of the virtues, including justice.

> But if we discard this definition of a people, and assuming another say that a people is an assemblage of reasonable beings bound together by a common agreement as to the objects of their love, then, in order to discover the character of any people, we have only to observe what they love.... (I)f only it is an assemblage of reasonable beings..., and is bound together by an agreement as to the objects of love, it is reasonably called a people; and it will be a superior people in proportion as it is bound together by higher interests, inferior in proportion as it is bound together by lower.[5]

With no state acting according to the ideal of _Civitas Dei_, Augustine could have simply judged all to be immoral. But he recognized that this would be of no help for those trying to live morally within a political framework. Yet neither did he want to say simply that all were acting differently in their goals and purposes. That sort of relativity he could not accept either. So he combined the ideal, the acting differently, and the falling short into a graded standard. Justice must have gradations within itself according to whether one state approaches the ideal more than other states, or less. Societies are "more or less" just associations and are to be judged ethically in their policies according to the justice in their goals and purposes and the actions they take to effect them. The comparison is to be made not only with the ideal but also with other states.

This means that a state can be relatively ethical without fulfilling the transcending norm of perfect justice. To demand that a temporal state measure itself by the rules of the heavenly city would confuse the orders of the two cities.[6] Each society is to be judged according to the degree that which it considers its common good, as indicated by its public policy and united purposes, approaches perfection. There may still be injustices done, but a state may be better than most, or the best possible at the time. Justice in _Civitas Terrena_ is a comparative virtue. States are more or less just compared to each other in reference to the ideal. No state would be just in reference to the ideal alone.

Let us summarize a few important elements in his theory of realistic justice in human society. The morality of all persons was seen to involve both the personal and the civic dimension. The society could be ethically tested in terms of the objects it sought. And the ends of policy and the means were connected but separable. The use of power was one of these means to be judged by the kind of desire to use it and what it was used for.

Augustine knew that the members of Civitas Terrena would never have the pure love of God as their Common Good. Rather they would love and strive for the pleasures, successes, and honors of this world. Furthermore, even if an individual might to some extent overcome the self-love rooted in the heart, a society cannot do so. (Perhaps it may not ethically do so, but that is not his point here.) Consequently the societies of this world will be characterized by conflict. Augustine did not think this would ever change. In the real world there are no perfectly just societies in intersocietal relations, and there never will be. Some may be more just than others, but there are and always will be countries that seek more than ordinary power and position.

Politics, therefore, is imperfect but reasonable as it proceeds by decisions and practices that do the best possible within the human condition. This minimally involves self-preservation as a state. Self-preservation amidst intersocietal competition is a necessary goal if the state is to do anything else.

So in a real sense, the imperfection of the individual is writ large in the institutions of a society and in the intersocietal world. Given the unregenerate situation of conflict, imposition of a country's will upon other countries is a constant policy of each. The only ethically significant differences between countries along the spectrum of "more or less just" will be in terms of what their wills entail and how they are imposed.

With a mixture of good and evil desires in individuals and institutions of societies, conflict and warfare are the usual state of affairs. Accepting this, Augustine did not despair of moral limits and guidelines amidst such practices in this imperfect world.

To start with, the object of war is peace. "Peace is the end sought for by war. For every individual seeks peace by waging war, but no one seeks war by making peace."[7] This sounds nice, but it says nothing specific. For one needs to know what counts as peace before one can begin to judge war as a means to it.

Obviously for Augustine perfect peace is not of this world. He could never agree with advocates who claim that some absolute condition of peace will come if only 'x' action is done by certain countries. In Civitas Terrena no one will ever know perfect peace. But this does not mean there will be no peace. Just as there is perfect justice and imperfect justice, so there is perfect peace and imperfect peace. The best possible situation at any given time in this world characterized by imperfect justice is some degree of imperfect peace.

The peace achievable in Civitas Terrena is an order between peoples brought about when one side conquers in competition. Each country that wins imposes its peace in substitution for the one that antedated it. The common structure of peace in this world is consequently like that of justice in this world, one-sided, short-lived, and penultimate. We must always keep in mind when there is talk of peace and justice exactly whose peace and whose justice we mean. For Augustine, the only basis for ethical preference comes when there is a significant difference in the degree of penultimate justice in one nation in comparison with its competitor. (That there are gradations of imperfect peace is, of course, ethically important, especially in our time with the advent of totalitarian capabilities. See the section on pacifism with its comments on what counts today as peace.) "The peace of an unjust people is not worthy to be called peace in comparison with the peace of a just people."[8]

B. Augustine's Theory of Just War

Since perfect peace and justice were not to be found in this world, Augustine could have despaired of discerning any moral direction in intersocietal politics. Instead he insisted that, given the real world, the task was to discern and act upon the more just rather than the less just course. He called for truly Christian soldiers who would be "the salvation of the commonwealth."[9]

As he thought out the implications, Augustine developed his own ideas of bellum justum which would be influential through the Christian era in Europe. His benchmarks were peace, order, and justice.

> Peace between individual and individual is well-ordered concord. Domestic peace is the well-ordered concord between those of the family who rule and those who obey. Civil peace is a similar concord among the citizens. The peace of all things is the tranquillity of order.[10]

Peace in this world then was some degree of adequacy for all concerned as to the ordering of the individual, domestic, and civil affairs of their lives.

So then the question was about "order." "Order is the distribution which allots things equal and unequal, each to its own place."[11] This sounds very much like the classical definition of justice. Apparently the difference is that order indicates one's place in a scheme, justice the treatment due because of, among other items, one's place. The two really overlap in Augustine's thought. The main point seems to be the acceptance and action subsequent to the acceptance of being in an adequate relation with others. (As Christians no longer formed a separatist group in the society, Augustine's emphasis on social order is not surprising.)

On the intersocietal level, each country seeks to achieve the imposition of its view of the order of affairs. As indicated above, Augustine considered that the only morally significant difference between the order one country imposed and the order another country imposed would be if one country's version of peace were more just than another country's version. This was to be judged, first, by evaluating a country's stated goals and, second, by comparing its actual behavior to these goals. Obviously, to make such a comparison, some external objective standard of societal peace and justice must be available. Augustine had supplied such with his earlier analysis of the general human tendencies to pride, avarice, and domination.[12] The test would be how well a country disciplined its pride, avarice, and _libido dominandi_ as it produced what it proclaimed to be its goal of peace.

The discipline of these tendencies will show in when, how, and why a country engages in war. Augustine developed his elements of a just war theory as he identified guidelines to recognize such discipline.

The starting point was that wars only made moral sense in the context of those kinds of wrongdoings of others that threaten the peace in which a state is secure.[13]

Yet it must remain clear that security is a necessary condition, not an end in itself. Unless one keeps hold of this, one will justify any overriding of other values in the name of security. This would turn Augustine's position into that of the naturalist and would make discussion of the elements in a justified war irrelevant. Henry Kissinger, sounding like a good Augustinian, writes:

> Foreign policy must start with security. A nation's survival is at its first and ultimate responsibility; it cannot be compromised or put to risk.... At the same time, security is a means, not an end. The purpose of security is to safeguard the values of our free society.... Finally, our values link the American people and their government. In a democracy, the conduct of foreign policy is possible only with public support.[14]

Augustine's first guide to a justified war was the strict limitation on who could decide that a state should go to war. His answer was the governmental leader (the prince) of each country. His argument here was a reference to the hierarchical order in human society.[15] The requirement of proper authority underlines that war must be a means to a valid political purpose since only those whose societal duty is making societal policy can morally involve the state in war. This was also crucial for justification

61

of killing in war, since Augustine denied that a private individual can justly kill on one's own authority.[16]

Again, we should pause to examine the limitations on the killing of another in these early stages of the tradition.

Following Ambrose, Augustine rejected the use of physical force in personal self-defense, but his reasoning differed. He argued that to use physical force in personal self-defense expressed an "inordinate desire" for physical life, which was a Civitas Terrena good. Against the objection that killing in personal self-defense would be a "lesser evil," since it is more evil that an innocent should suffer rather than an unprovoked attacker, Augustine maintained that all the attacker could harm were physical goods, but that killing another human being to protect such goods of one's self expressed an inordinate attachment.[17] Since the soldier or the civil leader acted on behalf of others and the common good, for such to kill another did not express such a disorder.

Unfortunately, like Ambrose, Augustine failed to be consistent in this distinction. If physical human life is so low among goods that killing in personal self-defense expresses a disorder of goods, then that ranking must apply to each one's physical life: one's own, the attacker's, and the third party's. If there is a basis for the choice of the life of the third party over the life of the physical aggressor, why is there not a basis for a choice of one's own over the aggressor? To claim that personal self-defense is wrong because it expresses an inordinate desire begs the question, as it is not inordinate to prefer a higher to a lower good, even if both are of Civitas Terrena. Moreover, if any preference between goods of Civitas Terrena shows an inordinate desire, the defense of some third party must also fall, since what one defends is the physical life of that other. The explanation why it was morally permissible to kill other human beings at some times but not at others still was not clearly worked out.

Nevertheless, in terms of killing others in war, the duty of the individual citizen, even the Christian citizen, was to obey.[18] The morality of the war was a question only for the policy level, not the level of personal ethics.

Augustine's second guide to a justified war was the limitation on the causes that would justify a society going to war. Since the moral leader would avoid war with all its physical evils if at all reasonable to do so, it was only "the wrong-doing of the opposing party which compels the wise leader to wage just wars; and this wrong-doing, even though it gave rise to war, would still be a matter of grief to an individual."[19] War was the lesser of two existential evils, and by it the just ruler tried to prevent wrongdoers from dominating just people and suppressing their life and liberty.[20] Since the security of its peace is a fundamental value in the hierarchy of a state's policy goals, it could be at times that policies that would otherwise seem unjust or ignoble could have to be embraced.[21] (This seems an acknowledgement of the choice to enact an existential evil.) This does not mean that Augustine held that morality and state safety contradict. Rather the hierarchical value of state safety reasonably demands the temporary overriding of lesser values. (This is a possible instance of the Principle of the Double Effect.)

Augustine also acknowledged that there might be a second justifying cause for war: the restoration of a previous peaceful situation.

Wars are defined as just when their aim is to avenge injury, that is, when that people or state against whom war is to be undertaken has neglected either to redress the injuries done by its subjects, or to restore what they have wrongfully seized.[22]

Even with these two causes, Augustine insisted that at best the justice remained somehow imperfect. No temporal state in its practices or intentions could transcend the spectrum of comparative "more and less" just.

The third guideline concentrated on the right intention of the state in going to war. This was expressed as a negative exclusion of certain intentions.

The eagerness to inflict harm, the cruelty

63

in (disproportionate) revenge, the unsatisfied and insatiable spirit, the savagery in (indiscriminate) warring, the lust to dominate, and things like this---these are the things which are rightly censured in war.[23]

On the other hand, right intention entailed that the political context always controlled the war.[24] Since the war was a means to a subsequent peace, the state must base its actions on those political considerations which will make it possible for the defeated enemy to accept the eventual arrangements.

NOTES
(1) Civitas Dei, tr. M. Dods, G. Wilson, J.J. Smith (New York: Random House, 1950), XIX, 24-25.
(2) Civitas Dei, XIV, 28.
(3) Civitas Dei, XIX, 17.
(4) Civitas Dei, XIX, 21.
(5) Civitas Dei, XIX, 24.
(6) See Epistolae 153, 6,26, and Epis. 157, 39. See also Etienne Gilson, The Christian Philosophy of Saint Augustine (New York: Random House, 1960), 177.
(7) Civitas Dei, XIX, 12.
(8) Civitas Dei, XIX, 12.
(9) See Augustine's two letters to Boniface, Count of Africa, who fought the Vandals. Epistolae 189, 220.
(10) Civitas Dei, XIX, 13.
(11) Civitas Dei, XIX, 13.
(12) Civitas Dei, III, 14; XV, 6.
(13) Civitas Dei, XIX, 7 and 12.
(14) American Foreign Policy, 3rd ed. (New York: W.W. Norton, 1977), 204-205.
(15) Contra Faustum, 22, 74 and 75.
(16) Contra Faustum, 22, 70. See also, Epistolae 47, 48, and 138.
(17) De libero arbitrio I, 5, 11-13.
(18) See Volusianus' letter to Augustine and the objections it contains, Epistolae 136.
(19) Civitas Dei, XIX, 7.
(20) Civitas Dei, XIX, 7.
(21) Quaestionum in Heptateuchum, VI, 10.
(22) Quaestionum in Heptateuchum, VI, 10.
(23) Contra Faustum, 22, 74.
(24) See Epistolae, 188, 189.

CHAPTER FIVE

THE MEDIEVALS AND THE RISE OF NATIONALISM

A. Canon Lawyers and Scholastic Theologians

From the seventh to the tenth centuries, some societal practices were beginning to be troublesome. In particular, there was no consistent legal structure or authority in Western Europe. Each little feudal lord and bishop ruled by local power alone. And so the rules promulgated and enforced by each feudal lord and bishop were authoritative only for the time and place. Furthermore, the local lord had the power to select and install ("invest") his own bishop. And these lords engaged in military action against each other for purposes of their own, which usually came down to honor and power.

As for the bishops, they were independent among themselves and each issued his own decrees regulating church or civil matters under the lords. It was a practice, with no significance or consequence early on, for each bishop to send a copy of each decree to Rome where the copy was stored as in a library. During the feudal times, the bishop of Rome was similar to all other bishops. He was elected usually according to the wishes of certain powerful lords, and quite often did not last long, at times falling victim to forced exile or assassination.

One gets the picture of a rather chaotic military and legal scene. In response, two major cultural movements began in the tenth and eleventh centuries which eventuated in a legal system for Western Europe and in the relative independence of church and prince.

The first was the codification of church laws ("canon" law). Officials grew aware of the need for a uniform set of laws in church and other matters. Accordingly, they set about codifying the collection of decrees held in deposit at Rome. They used as a model the old Roman law of the Empire. And, to avoid endless battles about interpretation and appeal, they took from Roman law the concept of an office "above the law" which would be the final arbiter for both interpretation and appeal. This office was thus "sovereign."

The second movement was correlative. For over a hundred years, the various bishops of Rome struggled with the various feudal lords for the authority to appoint all local bishops. The eventual triumph by the bishop of Rome in this matter, known as the "Gregorian reform" and taking place from the late Eleventh through the early Fourteenth centuries, not only enhanced the concept of the sovereignty of the "pope," but also encouraged the concept of sovereignty as a way to bring order in the various Western European lands. Certain "princes" arose to carry on the "Investiture" battle with the pope. And these princes also turned to the instrument of law to order the lords and others within their own lands.

After the revolution known as the Gregorian reforms, the feudal system slowly deteriorated and the centralization of Christendom accelerated through the rise of the importance of the Roman papacy. Fundamental to this latter, Canon law became codified and formally taught to the lawyers of the Catholic church. The need for experts both in canon and in civil law led to the establishment of academic centers which became the first medieval universities.

One result of this cultural turmoil was that there was no significant development of the just war doctrine for several centuries after Augustine. Nearly all Christian thinkers accepted his theory on the justification of war and seldom gave much direct attention to the moral question itself.[1] These included Jerome, Cyprian, Isidore of Seville, Anself of Canterbury, Peter Abelard, Bernard of Clairvaux, John of Salisbury, Peter the Chanter, and Alexander of Hales. The first new thinking came from the canonists starting with Gratian (Decretum, c. 1140). Still Gratian's most frequently cited authority was Augustine, and his citings became a reference source for later writers.

Yet a major change had occurred in the worldview that set the interpretation of war. The canonists and school theologians looked upon intersocietal relations as taking place within a unified system, Christendom, which was structured by divine, natural, and human law. This marked a shift from Augustine's temporal society of people with mixed ultimate values. Here the unity in the hierarchy of values, with Christian religious values the highest, was assumed. Going to war was justified analogously to the justification of civil punishment. This meant a juridical model had been joined to a societal model within which to think about intersocietal politics.

As was proper in a juridical analysis, the main concern for the canonists was the matter of authority.[2] Heretofore, local bishops and local lords had seen their way to engage in military action on their own initiative for the sake of honor and power and prize. As a way to eliminate this bane in Western Europe, the Canon lawyers repeatedly insisted that it was required for a way that it be called by a "sovereign," either the pope or a prince. This gave a crucial distinction between bellum and duellum, and was the medieval assumption for the distinction between killing as a private individual, which was rather consistently forbidden except in immediate self-defense, and killing as a citizen, under the authority of the sovereign, either as public executioner or as military soldier.

It was through the emphasis on authority that the canonists focused discussion of the other ius ad bellum topics (cause, intention, hope of success, peace as the end, and due proportion). The main problem was "who among existing political leaders had the authority to initiate war?" At stake was the relation between public authority and justified killing. The model used was the ius fetiale of early Roman law, since the canonists in general conceived of Canon Law as a parallel in the Christian Empire to Roman Law in the Roman Empire.[3]

Culturally the issue was important because of the need to control duels between nobles. In order to restrain frequent resorts to violence by private persons, the canonists insisted that only public authority justly can initiate violence within a society. The private individual is to seek redress of wrongs from the public superior. The public authority can summon together the people against internal disturbances or external enemies. This authority extends to having "recourse to the sword." The canonists argued that it was the charge of the public authority to do what is necessary for the common weal, and that Scripture [Rm 13.4] supported the position.

It was consequently the duty for a citizen when ordered to do what was necessary for the societal good. This societal hierarchy made the physical evil involved in killing into a moral good if ordered by one whose officer was responsible for leading all to the securing of the common weal. Such a use of a ranking of values indicates that the canonists were using the principle for resolving moral conflicts that has come to be known as the principle of the double effect. They acknowledged the presumptive moral significance of the physical evil in killing as they condemned killing in duels. But the values of the public good to be secured or advanced were at times so important that, if actions necessary for this also involved the negation of the values in human physical life by capital punishment or killing in war, these negations were judged to be negations of "lesser values", as long as the negations were unavoidable.

In addition to concentration on _ius_ _ad_ _bellum_ matters, the canonists made a few efforts in what came to be called _ius_ _in_ _bello_ matters. The three most notable are the Truce of God, the Peace of God, and a ban on certain recently introduced weapons.

The intent of the Truce of God was to limit the days of warfare among Christians. (It did not apply when doing battle against infidels.) It was most apt during sieges, which were the more common tactic of the times rather than large battles. The intent of the Peace of God was to separate clergy, monks, and others in religious duties from the processes of war. _De_ _Treuga_ _et_ _Pace_ (under Gregory IX) lists eight classes of persons: clerics, monks, friars, other religious, pilgrims, travelers, merchants, and peasants cultivating the soil, along with their animals, goods, and lands. (All of the lists of the times eventually contributed to the development of noncombatant immunity arguments.)

The limitation on certain weapons again applied only to warfare among Christians. However, the relative inhumanity of the weapons was never the issue. Rather the weapons, such as the crossbow, were those most likely to be used by soldiers who were not of the nobility in attacks on the nobility.[4] That the nobility were themselves opposed to such weapons was not inconsequential. And the ban (on crossbows, Second Lateran Council, 1139) did not last. By 1250, Hosteiensis gave what had become the general canonical opinion, that all weapons were licit in a just war.[5]

68

Historically it was not the canonists who succeeded in initiating _ius in bello_ rules. General _ius in bello_ acceptance came principally from the chivalric code of the nobles, which limited both the extent of military violence to particular sorts of persons (= the rule of discrimination) and what might be done in combat with other knights and footmen (= the rule of proportionality in battle, which is not the same as proportionality in going to war). The basis for the rules was more class honor than concern for any particular group of noncombatants.[6] There is historical irony here, in that the code of _ius in duello_, attacked by canonists, became the basis for all subsequent codes of _ius in bello_, usually not central to canonist thought. The attempt to reduce incidence of war (_ius ad bellum_) by restricting the authority to the sovereign (pope or prince) was primarily to separate ethical war from unethical duels, wherein knights had the right or even the duty to defend private honor. This attempt was contradicted by the use of _duellum_ rules in the genesis of _ius in bello_ rules. Hence the medieval just war traditions hold a tension in their essential structure. The _ad bellum_ and the _in bello_ parts are not deduced one from the other.[7] How the two parts have related and how they should relate continue to be problems.

B.   Thomas Aquinas

Thomas Aquinas added nothing substantive to Augustine, and even acknowledged this. But he failed to acknowledge that his worldview was different. Where Augustine in his realism considered war as a inevitable part of the human political scene in _Civitas Terrena_, Thomas held that war is prima facie against natural law and Christian virtue. He puts his basic question on war this way, "Is it always a sin to wage war?"[8] Thomas had a worldview that the normal intersocietal situation will be one of peace.

Thomas wrote in the academic style of the medievalists, which was quite different from the humanistic style of Augustine. One consequence of this was that later writers found it easier to use the orderly listings in Aquinas than the rather scattered references to war in Augustine. This helped the legalistic approach gain in dominance for several hundred years.

Aquinas, however, overtly claimed to be following Augustine in his central position on the justification of war, and continued to do so in answering objections to war based on certain biblical passages. Let us look at the major objections he cited, his responses, and then at the body of his main article on the ethics of war.

In response to the challenge based on Matthew 26.52, "All that take up the sword...", Aquinas, after quoting Augustine[9], distinguished "to take the sword" merely as a private citizen (as in a duel), from "to take the sword" as a private citizen by authority of the sovereign (as a soldier) or a judge (as public executioner), or as a public person "through a zeal for justice and by the authority, so to speak, of God" (as the sovereign or judge himself would do). This "is not to take the sword, but to use it as commissioned by another, wherefore it does not deserve punishment.[10]

In response to the objection based on the principle of non-resistance to evil (Mt 5.39; Rm 12.19), Aquinas argued that such injunctions of Jesus and Paul apply only to non-resistance by a private individual when only oneself is involved. They do not apply when it is a matter of punishment, a matter of public order, or a matter of defending other persons.[11] Even more, Aquinas argued that the toleration of wrong done to others in the name of "do not resist evil" is either at least a moral fault or even an expression of moral viciousness.[12] Citing Ambrose's distinction between personal self-defense and killing in the defense of another, Aquinas explained that an individual acts laudibly if one gives up that which is one's own, but not if one gives up that which is another's.

Following the approach common since Ambrose, he insisted that defending one's country, defending one's family, or one's companions was a matter of justice and not a moral option.[13] It followed for him that, since it it virtuous to act to preserve the good of another person, it is more so to act to preserve the good of the society.[14] He justified killing in punishment or war as a preference for the common good over the individual good when the latter threatens the former.[15]

For Aquinas, the political public good was supreme among human goods.[16] It was the role of the ruler, the prince, to promote this common good marshaling whatever forces, including political power over life and death, needed to do so.[17] Because of this hierarchy of goods, the prince, or someone authorized by the prince, could ethically intend the death of a human being for the sake of the common good.[18]

To answer the question "How does public office make morally valid the direct killing of a human being," he quoted Augustine: "The natural order conducive to peace among mortals demands that the power to declare and counsel war should be in the hands of those who hold the supreme authority."[19] With that societal context what would be an morally evil act done as a private individual becomes a morally good act done as a public officer.

> The killing and beating of a man involve some deformity in their object. But if it is added to this that an evildoer is killed for the sake of justice, or that a delinquent is beaten for punishment, then the action is not a sin; rather it is virtuous.[20]

The premise for this position was that the public common weal is more important than the physical life of the individual. Because this premise is historically so important, it is proper for this work's methodology to go somewhat into the understanding's elements. To help in identifying its pertinent features, I will compare it with a competitive understanding of individuals and society.

Fundamental to the position that the common weal is more important than the physical life of the individual is a set of assumptions making up what might be called the "classic" concept of society. This concept, which goes back to the Greeks but, with its stress on the natural order, comes especially from Cicero, holds that one is in society as part of the natural moral order of things. There is a social good, a common weal, that is proper to life in society, and which is shared by, not distributed to, all those in society. Political life is ordered to this common good, which is other than simply a sum of all individually private goods.[21] The relation of

71

private goods and the common good, of individual moral standards and societal moral standards, is that of a hierarchy, correlative to the hierarcy of ends in human affairs.

This understanding competes with a second concept of society, which might be called the "utilitarian" concept, which holds that individuals are in society as the result of a voluntary agreement to cooperate with one another (a social contract). For this "utilitarian" concept, society and its necessary institutions are the result of the decisions of a group of individuals who, from a "state of nature" in which each individual was sovereign and independent of all moral relations with others, voluntarily moved into a society established as for their individual and private ends. The government of such a society is moral only when, given the alternatives, it acts to bring about the greatest sum possible of cumulative private happiness. With such an understanding of what society is all about, there is no "common good" that has content other than the private goods. Thus there is no common good whose values are enjoyed by all citizens but whose values are more important than private values whenever there is a conflict between them. As a consequence, there is in the "utilitarian" society nothing about the moral relationships of individuals that is prior to, and superior to their volitional actions. Therefore, the government here would have no moral authority that did not come from the decisions, and thus the moral standing, of individuals. If one accepts the usual premise that the individual has the moral authority to kill only in self-defense, that would mean the only moral authority the government has to order killing in wars would be when the wars were of self-defense.

However, the "classic" concept of society considers individuals to be in society as part of the natural order, somehow prior to their individual volitional actions. Consequently, political authority is not merely the result of delegation from the individual citizens who give up or put in trust some of their pre-societal rights or powers. Consonant with this is the premise that the societal authority has a moral reach other than that of individual citizens. The authority has the moral reach and responsibility to maintain whatever order is conducive to societal peace precisely because of its hierarchical office. It is from this office in the natural order that the government authorizes killing in war and thereby makes it so that such killing can be morally good. It is more reasonable in the classic society than in the utilitarian society for an authority to ask individuals to risk their lives for the good of society.

Nevertheless, there is no implication in the "classic" society that the individuals were merely subordinate parts. There was no consensus that the authority could call on citizens to risk their lives if the cause was not proportionately serious.

This position has important consequences for contributive justice. For those who consider being in society to be natural, analogous to being in a family, there can be duties that are not the result of voluntary decision. For Aquinas, such duties were those consequent upon one's place in various hierarchical relations. But such hierarchical elements are not essential to a theory of social naturalness.

The "state of nature" postulate used by the social contract theorists in the early modern period was part of their effort to support the claims to equality of everyone prior to actual life in society and thereby to undercut the claims that the social, political, and historical hierarchies of society were natural. But, for Aquinas, "being in the world with others" was more primordial than being an individual. As later will be held by Hume and Hegel, Aquinas would have considered a pre-societal individual an abstraction, since one only became an individual with distinctive human characteristics as one related over time with fellow members of one's family, one's social groups, and one's society. It then followed that there were different standards for morality for the individual, the family, and those with societal positions,[22] yet all these standards were in the Natural Law.

When he took up the objection that the Christian was under the divine precept not to resist evil, Aquinas answered that the Christian should keep the predisposition not to resist or to defend oneself as long as it was not one's duty in respect to the common good.[23]

War may thus be undertaken if it is for the common good of a particular society. To test if it is, Aquinas gave three conditions to be met.

First, of course, is the matter of proper authority. "For it is not the business of a private individual to declare war, because he can seek for redress of his rights from the tribunal of his superior. Moreover, it is not the business of a private individual to summon together the people, which has to be done in wartime."[24] We recognize here the canonists' concern with duels. "And as the care of the common weal is committed to those who are in authority, it is their business to watch over the common weal of the city." Here Aquinas joined the hierarchy of goals and the notion of moral duty of those who hold societal offices.

In addition, he used the analogy of caring for internal and external order. "And just as it is lawful for them to have recourse to the sword in defending that common weal against internal disturbances, when they punish evildoers... so too it is their duty to have recourse to the sword of war in defending the common weal against external enemies." Aquinas here accepted the civil punishment analogy for war that went back at least to Cicero. Just as civil punishment was viewed primarily as social retribution for internal crimes against society, so war was to be viewed as social retribution for externally based injuries to society.

Two main components operated for "war as retribution" if it was just. The first has the retribution itself as morally required. There has been an action by state B that was an offense against state A's social order. The offense was of such a kind that it requires state A to respond. That is, state B not only caused physical harm to state A's social order, but also did moral injury since the physical harm was done knowingly and wilfully and without justification. The leaders of state A, having a moral obligation to the social order, must either publicly forgive or retaliate, but they may not disregard the offense.

The second component requires proportionality in the retribution. This proportionality controls not only the maximum physical harm that may (but need not) be done in the retribution, but also the minimum that must be done to communicate to all audiences the seriousness of the provoking offense.

The second condition for a justified war is that of the just cause. Again, Aquinas cited Augustine.[25] "A just war can be described as one that avenges wrongs, when a nation or state has to be punished, for refusing to make amends for the wrongs inflicted by its subjects, or to restore what it has seized unjustly." One finds, or rather does not find, something most interesting here. The just cause is in response to the immorality of another society. But there is no mention here of a society's self-defense as a just cause. The care of the common weal has already been declared an essential of the authority's duties under the first condition. Apparently Aquinas found it redundant, if not a category mistake, to designate a country's self-defense as a justifying cause for war. Self-defense is precisely what each war itself is generically. The burden of the just cause condition is to identify those specific actions of an enemy that justify the response of war as part of the authority's defense of the common weal. This would imply that the later distinction between offensive and defensive war was not interesting to Aquinas.[26] A war undertaken to recover, restore, or punish could be done well after the evil was committed, and would be an "offensive" war, but not an "aggressive" one.

It is worthwhile here to note that, for the tradition up to the time of Aquinas, the condition of the proper authority was ethically distinct from the condition of the just cause. The stress on the authority requirement was that only the one in that office had the duty and therefore the moral power to call the state of war for the common weal. Even though such a call would involve the decision that there was sufficient cause, there was the theoretical possibility of a separate judgment by others on the moral sufficiency of the cause. By the time of Grotius, the decision by the authority to call a war can will have guidelines from the consensus on the kinds of situations that justify a war, but the decision is practically unquestionable by others within the society.

The third condition Aquinas had for a just war is right intention, which somehow involves the advancement of good or the avoidance of evil. Once

75

again he cited Augustine as he ruled out going to war for vengeance, the lust for power, and the like. This certainly for Aquinas was connected with the condition of the just cause. War was moral if it was a response to objective injustice. However, in the second condition there is stress on the immorality, that is, the subjective guilt, of the enemy.[27] But it would be impractical in reference to protecting the common weal to require a ruler to discern the subjective guilt of an enemy. What is required is that the enemy intentionally did an act that was an injustice, and thus is objectively guilty. The right intention in going to war minimally is to be to attack the injustice (objective wrong). And while he avoided using the term "punishment" in his own phrasing, he did insert the following from Augustine:

> Just wars are usually defined as those which avenge injuries, when a people or a nation is to be punished.[28]

One might also note that all three conditions are on the level of ius ad bellum as this develops in the tradition.

Aquinas had no ex professo treatment or ius in bello. He argued that no one ethically could lie or break a promise made to an enemy,[29] even though one might prudently conceal the truth (as in an ambush).[30] And he argued that under no circumstances could one kill an "innocent" person.[31] The only exception was when so ordered by the deity.[32] But he never applied this prohibition directly to war.[33] And he agreed with Aristotle that postwar enslavement of prisoners could be ethical.[34]

C. Early Nationalistic Developments

1. Vitoria

The unity of Christendom was based on the acceptance of a common religion, a common culture, a common Canon Law, and the Chivalric code of the upper class. (The unifying political authorities of the Pope and Emperor were seldom decisive in practice.) Such unity, as it was, gave some support to the treatment of intersocietal relations, including war, as if they were intrasocietal affairs. The first real turning from the medieval examination of justified war came with Francisco de Vitoria. Writing after the revolution started by Luther and the renaissance of classical politics epitomized by Machiavelli, Vitoria saw the need to shift from the assumption that the relation between countries was that of members of "one society." Thanks to the rivalry between the popes and the kings, what was emerging in Europe was a collection of independent and sovereign nation-states, and for the first time foreign policy had as its subject international relations.[35]

Each state was sovereign, that is, above all law and the final arbiter in its own affairs. Part of this sovereignty was the legal right of each prince to judge the justice of his nation going to war to achieve his nation's own purposes.[36]

Vitoria still presumed unities in cultural, economic interests as well as moral principles for the states, but he gave new direction to later thinking in two important ways. (a) By emphasis on the natural law as the ultimate justification for his application of the just war tradition to intercultural relations, he abandoned recourse to theological presuppositions. Consequently, he denied the grounds for any war of religion.[37] This strengthened the limitations on ius in bello, since wars of religion are those most likely to get out of hand. (b) He was more cautious than his predecessors that humans could always identify the just side in a war. He did not deny an objectively just side, only that we could always identify it.[38]

Vitoria accepted three justifying causes that were common in the tradition: defense, recovery of property, and punishment.[39] Defense signified repelling an attack or avoiding an injury or wrong, and it was based on the right of defense in natural law.

Punishment signified a public action to ensure that a wrong or injury already done to the state would not be allowed to remain without physical condemnation. The natural law basis was the right of public authority to punish offenders against the common good.

Recovery of property had as its basis the restoration of natural law property rights.

Both defense and punishment could be valid justification for taking action to assist allies in their troubles, and even to assist "innocent" people anywhere.

The causes being such, Vitoria nevertheless argued that ad bellum proportionality also had to be observed.[40] What is involved with war is so terrible on one's own country and on one's friends, no war can be just if it is more harmful to the state than it is good and advantageous, no matter what other reasons may stand for its justice.[41]

Vitoria's early thought on war focused on European wars between Christian nations and on wars between Christians and Moslems. Late in his life he turned some attention on the use of military force in Spanish conquests in the New World. During the years 1537-1539, he became convinced that many of the justifications for the actions of the conquistadores were invalid. In 1539, at Salamanca, he gave two major Relectiones (solemn lectures): De Indis (January) and De jure belli (June).

As he applied just war concepts to events in the new era of conquest, Vitoria made the first serious attempt to apply natural law theory across cultural and religious boundaries. If there is such a thing as natural law, thought Vitoria, it can serve as a basis for truly general relations between nations, regardless of culture or religion. He thereby put a real challenge to the ethical worth of the theory of natural law itself. With no consensus possible out of a shared culture or a shared religion, if there could be objective ethical standards at all, they would have to come out of shared human experiences. That meant, if consensus did not come about, the ethician should suspect that natural law ethics was somehow merely cultural or religious ethics. During the Middle Ages, natural law just war theories were never extended beyond the borders of Christendom.[42] Vitoria thought that natural law must express something fundamental about how persons anywhere actually think, or at least ought to think, about the regulation of physical violence.

This meant that, if just war restraints are to be anything more than expressions of the cultural values of Western European society, then the single society model, with its assumption of shared values and shared basic moral principles, could no longer suffice. But since there were states with truly diverse cultural values, the only possible ways to obtain interstate value agreement would be either a process of cultural hegemony, in which one culture imposed its values on another culture, or some sort of reciprocal and inductive generation of common values. If natural law appeals are a way to bridge divergent cultural traditions, and are to work in supplying a unifying set of concepts and terminology for ethical standards, then natural law must begin with the uncovering of lived commonality in judgments between peoples. This is the only methodology from which to gain a mutually acceptable ethic. Even if it is true that different cultures vary in accuracy in ethical discernment, the only workable approach is that all proceed as if each has valid contributions to a valid ethic that is still in the making.

Vitoria did not go that far. He held that the American natives had rights because of their humanity and their social and political organizations, and that they could know and live by the natural law by use of their reason alone. But he did not use the new knowledge of Indian customs to modify the European understanding of natural values. The Amerinds did not develop a consensus with the Spanish standards. The Spanish were manifestly at fault here, as their behavior was often seriously immoral. But Vitoria also considered that perhaps the Amerinds contributed to the failure. Natural law standards could be discovered by all, but these standards were only confusedly and incompletely available to the Amerindian minds, unaided as they were by the clarifications and assistance supplied by Christian religion.

Vitoria thus criticized the Amerind cultural values, which he judged were the result of "invincible ignorance." But his main purpose was not to convince the Indians to abide by the natural law in war. Rather his purpose was to extend restraints on the use of superior military power by the Spanish on the Indians.

In his justification for the conquests, Vitoria took a major theoretical step. He argued that all people belong to one universal society because of their natural abilities to socialize and communicate. Consequently, even though there are independent states, the people in the states have natural rights across boundaries, such as the rights to trade, to travel, to settle freely, to communicate with all others, and to be treated fairly by all governments.

Thus the Spanish had the right to travel into the New World as long as they did no harm, to trade with the Indians, to communicate with them. Therefore, if the Indians refused the Spanish any of these rights, and persisted in the refusal, the Spanish legitimately could conquer them through war, which was, however, to be carried out with moderation and only as much as absolutely necessary.[43]

2. Grotius

From the time of Vitoria on, social, political, and intellectual forces continued to work away at the hierarchical structures of authority, both within each society, and in the relations between states. The idea of a "state of nature" condition, for individuals before entry into society and for states prior to any internationally binding laws, began to take on prominence as a device to conceptualize the equality of each individual and each state. The Treaty of Westphalia (1648) marked an important stage in the conceptualization of a system of sovereign states, equal to one another, and independent of any external authority, especially that of Pope or Emperor. Early on, these states were often small and were classified as duchies, principalities, bishoprics, and the like.

The move was away from a 'one society' (Christendom) model, which had all under the authority of the prince-emperor who was responsible for all (including religious) order within the realm, and in which war between countries was analyzed analogously to criminal punishment within a politically organized society.

The move was going into a 'society of states' model, which had no overall authority (each state is sovereign), but yet had consensus on: a common humanity of all people, objective and universal ethical standards (a natural law as ius gentium), the rights of states, certain values, and some common purposes. War here could still be compared analogously to criminal punishment, but, without any overall authority, each sovereign could undertake the task of punishment, even if not the one injured.

The move would culminate by the late Eighteenth century in a 'system of states' model, in which there was a group of states without consensus on universal ethical standards, values, or common purposes, but which had some consensus on ways of proceeding in interstate affairs, and accepted the sovereign absoluteness of each state to decide its own affairs and to enter into agreements (a ius inter gentes).

Hugo Grotius lived and wrote during the first half of the Seventeenth century in Europe. And, as usual, he used the experience of war as the primary type of interstate politics. The influence of his work testified to the need for new thinking in the emerging international situation.

Grotius argued for a natural law basis for political ethics, but it was an inchoatively secularized natural law. He said that moral evaluation by natural law could take place "(e)tiamsi daremus... non esse Deum... aut non curari ab eo negotia humana...." ("even if we stipulate there is no God... or that human affairs are ignored by a Deity....")[44] Such a secularization formula avoided any divine voluntaristic approach to natural law as well as the limitations if natural law were based on some specific religion.[45] It also represented the culmination of the Renaissance rediscovery of the Stoic origins of a natural law ethic.

His problem was to support an ethics in the situation wherein each of the states considered itself sovereign, equal to others, and independent. He knew that it would be methodologically improper as well as without effect for a philosopher to create a set of substantive ethical standards and try to impose them on states. It was therefore quite understandable that Grotius sought to discover the standards the states required of each other in their relations. He then would explain and organize this by use of the natural law theory from the Stoics and Cicero.

Grotius based his natural law position on the assertion that people by nature are reasonable and social beings with a teleological dynamism to develop these natural characteristics. Following Vitoria and explicitly citing the Stoic theme of the natural sociableness of people, he wrote that there is in humans "an impelling desire for society, that is, for the social life... peaceful, and organized."[46] The maintenance of the social order, therefore, is a universal goal for human intelligence and the source of all that which is properly called law, including the moral law that obtains between states.

With the analogy of individuals who, out of a "state of nature," entered a political society and agreed that certain standards were reasonably connected to the goal of a peaceful society, Grotius explained that independent and sovereign states, even in a "state of nature," have agreed that certain standards were reasonably connected with the peaceful order that they by nature aimed at. These standards were the substantive ethics of international relations, and the basis for the international "laws" to which they might agree in pacts. Grotius listed as common matters of this natural law: abstention from the property of another, restoration, the obligation to fulfill promises, reparation, and retribution.[47]

This natural law is specified further in two ways: the aposteriori evidence gathered from the consensus of people on what ways of acting tend to the peaceful social life necessary for humans and their development; and the consent based pacts, both within states and between states, made for the advantage of human sociableness.[48]

In formulating his 'society of states' model, Grotius stressed the ethical consensus that independent and sovereign agents achieved. Using the distinction from chapter one, I understand him to mean a consensus on standards that were formally unchangeable but that have content developed from the judgments by state leaders who make such judgments in common situations and circumstances.[49] Grotius assumed that the princes, the ones in the best position to know the situation and with the best available advice, would on the whole make decisions that expressed the principles and values of the natural dynamism of sociableness. The ethicians could identify these principles and values only aposteriori.[50] The methodology was to discover the consensus that developed among the many princes, kings, bishop-rulers, doges, and so on, on matters such as: what were valid causes to go to war; under what restraints, and so forth.

Consensus would come as an inductive process. Individual princes would make decisions on, for example, what causes justify the state going to war or intervening in matters between other nations. The princes of other nations would see the decision and hear its rationale, and either concur or not. And they would, in similar circumstances, make their own decisions and use or modify the rationale of the first decision. Eventually, a second-level principle would be acknowledged as the moral standard, at least as far as the prima facie presumption, rebus sic stantibus.

Grotius thought that the principles and values that would be expressed in such developed standards would be expressions of the natural law since he envisoned, as did the Stoics, that this natural law was somehow in the minds and hearts and would show forth in decisions by people of good will if they based their decisions on reason and not on selfish interests.

Yet Grotius sided with Augustine instead of Aquinas on the usual international situation. In this world, peace between states is not to be expected because of the "many people of a bloodthirsty, rapacious, unjust, and nefarious disposition."[51] Since war is aimed at the preservation of life and things useful to life, both history and right reason prove its moral permissibility.[52]

War could be just, consequently, when it was the use of physical force to achieve or to re-establish the conditions for human social life between states. And the specific moral standards in war reflect those of natural law in society generally: they come from consensus or from consent based pacts.

Contrary to the popular view of the time that inter arma silent leges (during war the laws are mute), Grotius insisted that "between enemies written laws, that is, laws of particular states, are not in force, but ...unwritten laws are in force, that is, those which nature prescribes, or the agreement of nations has established."[53] In fact, it was such unwritten laws that Grotius insisted were essential to ius ad bellum and ius in bello. "(W)ar ought not to be undertaken except for the enforcement of rights; when once undertaken, it should be carried on only within the bounds of law and good faith."[54] He was aware of the violations of such an ethical principle in wars between Christian nations and the understandable reaction of some that a Christian must embrace a life of total non-violence to avoid such evils. He judged it important to establish the errors in both positions, "that people may not believe either that nothing is allowable, or that everything is."[55]

> In giving to our treatise the title 'The Law of War,' we mean first of all... to inquire whether any war can be just, and then, what is just in war. For 'law' in our use of the term here means nothing else than what is just... that being lawful which is not unjust. Now that is unjust which is in conflict with the nature of a society of beings endowed with reason.[56]

War is a means to enforce justice, and it is the duty of societal leaders to use it to protect members within the society,[57] and, analogous to the function of punishment within the state, the prince is to punish those in other states who do wrongs across state borders, even if their violations are to states and subjects other than the prince's own.[58] This again shows Grotius' use of the 'society of states' model and a natural law that obliges all as the basis for ethics.

Grotius added two cautions, earlier affirmed by Vitoria, that helped deemphasize the role of "just cause" in ius ad bellum. The first was that certainty as to the justice of one's side is, in the real world, always incomplete.[59] The second was that it could happen that both sides are subjectively convinced they are in the right.[60] Even though he himself insisted on a just cause, Grotius saw that those wars in which one or both sides was convinced it fought under a clearly just cause had much less restraint (e.g., wars of religion). As Grotius insisted that the laws of war were to be observed on both sides, irrespective of the justice of their causes, he established an attitude that significantly reduced the justification of limitless behavior during wars. From his time on until the twentieth century, the downplay of just cause helped in the growth of humanitarianism in ius in bello. It was only with the wars of the twentieth century that the emphasis on the just cause has again proved to be to the detriment of humanitarianism, which he called charity.

Because he recognized the new nation-states as the appropriate agents in international action, for <u>ad bellum</u> justice, Grotius accepted that the sovereigns possessed the sole authority to wage war.[61] The prince alone held the competence to judge the justice of going to war, in the sense that his decision was final. The earlier separation of authority and just cause into two ethical moments was changed by Grotius into but one moment. Nevertheless, to act morally, the prince must identify some necessitating cause and use physical force only as a last resort. The range of such causes would be from the current consensus of the various princes themselves, and were not liable to outside evaluation, but only outside explanation, such as by the theory of the natural dynamic to sociableness. [From that consensus, Grotius followed Vitoria for the usual kinds of causes: defense, recovery of property, and punishment.[62]] In addition, the cause had to be proportional to the damages and loss of life likely in the war.[63]

Grotius suggested a further important aspect coming from state sovereignty, with implications for <u>in bello</u> justice: the responsibility of the entire society for the public actions of the prince. He argued that the new type of society entailed that, as long as they were approved by the people, the public acts of the prince should be considered as if the entire population did them. He used this theme of responsibility to modify the set of those who became targetable during a war.

> The right of killing enemies in a public war and other violence against the person extends not only to these who actually bear arms, or are subjects to him that stirs up the war, but in addition to all persons who are in the enemy's territory.[64]

He gave as the reason for this that all those within the hostile territory could be dangerous, since they owed allegiance to that state. War against a state is war against all the subjects of that state.

This was, at least indirectly, a further downplay of the importance of the justice of the war's cause. For Aquinas, only one side could have a just cause; so only the soldiers of that side were morally justified in killing their opponents. The corollary of this was, of course, that the soldiers of the other side were all, at least "objectively", morally guilty. For Aquinas, only the morally guilty were proper targets in a just war. For Grotius, because of the emerging changes in the makeup of states, those who somehow showed consent for the war were responsible agents and thereby (at least in some way) proper targets during the war. Even if they were "subjectively innocent" of any moral wrong connected with their state's involvement in the war.

Yet Grotius rejected, as did Vitoria, the suggestion of "collective guilt" and separated this from whatever made someone a proper object for killing in war. Vitoria held that, even in an unjust cause, most soldiers fought in good faith.[65] Grotius argued similarly that the "body politic" is a kind of being that has important distinctions from the kind of being that an individual is. While in some matters it is appropriate to employ the concept of the people as a single body, this is not proper in the area of merit.[66] Merit, or desert, is something that belongs only to individuals. Guilt only attaches to those individuals who have knowingly and formally cooperated with unjust actions.[67] Many in a state take part in the war for more general reasons which in themselves can be noble, such as compliance with the decisions of valid superiors, the presumption of the goodness of the actions of one's own state, and so on.

The compatibility of "being responsible" and "being subjectively innocent" coupled with the downplay of "guilt" as a criterion for targeting in war would make one expect an erosion in the importance of "innocence" in the matter of _in bello_ discrimination. For Grotius, it did and it did not. He seemed to maintain a distinction between being "subjectively innocent" for the war itself, and being "innocent" of particular activities in the war. This distinction permitted him to set forth lists of "innocents" for _in bello_ discrimination.

One result of this development was the uncovering of a major unresolved conflict in the Just War tradition: the tension in the means-end relationship on the _in bello_ level. Both Vitoria and Grotius seemed to accept that the _ad bellum_ end did justify any necessary means in the war. Grotius wrote:

> In war the things which are necessary to attain the end in view are permissible.[68]

> We ought not to attempt anything which may prove the destruction of innocents, unless for some extraordinary reason and the safety of many.[69]

This was the first explicit position on the ethical relation between the ad bellum and the in bello levels. It suggested that the justice of and the proportional cause for the war itself guided the outside limits on the destruction in military activities (the in bello proportionality). It also connected military necessity with what comes to be called the "indirect killing of the innocents" (the cloudy boundaries between in bello proportionality and in bello discrimination of targets).

Leroy Walters suggests the controlling premise was in terms of a state's subjective conviction it had a just cause: "If one side has a just cause for war, then justice will only be promoted if that side is successful in winning the war; if the nonrighteous side wins, justice will be frustrated."[70] If this suggestion has merit, then Grotius did not downplay the importance of the just cause as much as he at times appeared to do.

As further indication of this ambiguity on the decisiveness of the just cause, in a section that seemed to indicate his acceptance of the implications of "mutually subjective justice, Grotius included in his major work five lengthy chapters on items that tempered or moderated what counted as proper in bello activities (temperamenta belli), usually in terms of proportionality.[71] Moreover, he complied with the tradition by giving a list of "innocents" who were to benefit from the principle of discrimination.

NOTES

(1) Leroy Walters, Five Classic Just-War Theories, unpublished dissertation, Yale, 1971, 37-45.
(2) See Frederich Russell, The Just War in the Middle Ages (Cambridge: Cambridge University Press, 1975), cc. 4 and 5; and Walters, Five Classic.., 101.
(3) See Walter Ullmann, Law and Politics in the Middle Ages, (Ithaca: Cornell, 1975).
(4) Walters, Five Classic.., 26-27.
(5) Lectura, Tome X, 5, 15, 1, pars 1-2.
(6) See James T. Johnson, Ideology, Reason, and the

Limitation of War (Princeton: Princeton University Press, 1975), ch. 1.
(7) James T. Johnson, _Ideology_.., 48-49.
(8) _Summa Theologiae_ II-II, 40, 1.
(9) _Contra Faustum_ xxii, 70.
(10) _Summa Theo._ II-II, 40, 1 ad 1.
(11) _Summa Theo._ II-II, 40, 1, ad 2; 188, 3 ad 1; see also, 60, 6 ad 2; 108, 1 ad 2; 108, 2.
(12) _Summa Theo._ II-II, 188, 3 ad 1.
(13) See his Commentary on St. Matthew, wherein he distinguishes non-resistance in private matters and in matters of one's social relations. Here he cites with approval Augustine's comment: "Courage in defending one's country against foreigners, or defending the weak of one's family, or one's companions from robbers, plainly is (a matter of) justice." _Super Evangelium S. Matthaei Lectura_ (Rome: Marietti, 1951), #542. (This lecture is on the Sermon on the Mount.)
(14) _In Decem Libros Ethicorum Aristotelis ad Nicomachum Expositio_ I, lect. 2, #30.
(15) _Summa Theo._ II-II, 64, 2.
(16) _Summa Theo._ II-II, 124, 5 ad 3.
(17) _Summa Theo._ II-II, 65, 2 ad 2; 67, 4.
(18) _Summa Theo._ II-II, 64, 7.
(19) _Summa Thco._ II-II, 40, 1, quoting _Contra Faustum_ xxii, 75.
(20) _Questiones Quodlib._ 9, q. 7, a. 15.
(21) _Summa Theo._ II-II, 58, 7.
(22) _In Decem Libros Eth._ I, lect. 1, #4.
(23) _Summa Theo._ II-II, 40, 1, ad 2.
(24) _Summa Theo._ II-II, 40, 1.
(25) _QQ. in Hept._, q. 10, super Jos.
(26) See Walters, _Five Classic_.., 117, 138-139.
(27) Walters thinks it is essential for Aquinas, but acknowledges the controversy. See _Five Classics_.., 111-114 and notes.
(28) _Ques. in Hept._ VI, 10; quoted in _Summa Theo._ II-II, 40, 1.
(29) _Summa Theo._ II-II, 40, 3.
(30) _Summa Theo._ II-II, 40, 3; 71, 3 ad 3.
(31) _Summa Theo._ II-II, 64, 6.
(32) _Summa Theo._ I-II, 94, 5 ad 2; 100, 8 ad 3; 105, 3 ad 4.
(33) See Walters, _Five Classic_.., 162, n. 300.
(34) _In libros Politicorum Aristotelis Expositio_ I, lect. iv.
(35) _De Indis et de jure belli relectiones_, edited by Ernest Nys, tr. by John Pawley Bate (Carnegie Institute, 1917), _De jure belli_, 7 (on "what is a

state").
(36) De jure belli, 6-8.
(37) De jure belli, 10.
(38) De Indis, III, 6; De jure belli, 32. See James
T. Johnson, Ideology.., 185-195.
(39) De jure belli, 1, 5, 15-19. See Walters,
313-315.
(40) De jure belli, 14.
(41) Relectio de potestate civili 13. See Suarez, De
Bello, s. iv, 8 and 10.
(42) See James T. Johnson, Just War Tradition and the
Restraint of War (Princeton: Princeton University
Press, 1981), 75.
(43) See Alberto R. Coll, "Law and Power in
International Relations: Francisco de Vitoria and
the Limitations of a Juristic Approach," in The
Western Heritage and American Values (Washington:
University Press of America, 1982), 24-27. For a
clearer statement on native rights by a contemporary
of Vitoria, see Alonso de la Vera Cruz, Defense of
the Indians: Their Rights, ed. by Ernest J.
Burrus, S.J., The Writings of Alonso de la Vera
Cruz:II (Rome: Jesuit Historical Institute, 1968).
(44)De jure belli ac pacis libri tres, tr. Francis W.
Kelsey, et al. (Oxford, 1925), Prolegomena, 11. See
Suarez, De Leg. II, ch. vi, s. 3.
(45) Even Grotius has a hint of voluntarism in respect
to killing and taking another's property. See De
jure belli ac pacis, I, 1, 10.
(46) De jure belli ac pacis, Proleg. 6.
(47) De jure belli ac pacis, Proleg. 8.
(48) De jure belli ac pacis, Proleg. 17.
(49) See De jure belli ac pacis I, ch. 1, sec. 7.
(50) See De jure belli ac pacis, I, 1, sec. 12,
wherein Grotius puts forth his epistemological
position and cites many authorities that his is sound
ethical methodology.
(51) De jure belli ac pacis, I, 2, 8.
(52) De jure belli ac pacis, I, 2, 1; I, 2, 2; I, 2,
3.
(53) De jure belli ac pacis, Proleg. 26.
(54) De jure belli ac pacis, Proleg. 25.
(55) De jure belli ac pacis, Proleg. 29; see I, 2
(entire chapter).
(56) De jure belli ac pacis I, ch. 1, sec. 3.
(57) De jure belli ac pacis, I, 2, 8 and 9.
(58) De jure belli ac pacis, II, 20, 8; II, 20, 40;
II, 20, 44; III, 14, 1. In a new extension, Grotius
accorded princes not guilty of the same crime the
right to punish crime committed anywhere in the

world. Also see Suarez, De belli, II, 1.
(59) De jure belli ac pacis, II, 23.
(60) Vitoria, De Indis, III, 6; De jure belli, 32, 48, and 59. Grotius, De jure belli ac pacis, II, 23, 13; III, 11.
(61) De jure belli ac pacis, I, 3, 4.
(62) De jure belli ac pacis, II, 1, 2 and 3 (defense); II, 20, 1 and 38-51 (punishment); II, 1, 2; II, 2, 1; and II, 20, 1 (recovery of property).
(63) De jure belli ac pacis, II, 24, whole chapter.
(64) De jure belli ac pacis, III, 4, 6; and see III, 4, 8.
(65) Vitoria, De jure belli, 48.
(66) Grotius, De jure belli ac pacis, III, 11, 16.
(67) De jure belli ac pacis, II, 21, 7 and 21; III, 11, 3 and 16. See Leroy Walters, Five Classic, 325-326.
(68) De jure belli ac pacis, III, 1, 2.
(69) De jure belli ac pacis, III, 11, 8. Grotius argued that the direct killing of the innocent did not turn a justified war based on a just cause into an unjustified war. See De jure belli ac pacis, III, 26, 6.
(70) Five Classic, 364. For Vitoria, see De jure belli, 37. Vitoria's main modifier was proportionality, see De jure belli, 33, 56, 58, 60.
(71) De jure belli ac pacis, III, cc. 11-16.

CHAPTER SIX

PHILOSOPHICAL ANALYSIS OF PACIFISM

This is an appropriate place to make an examination of the attitude designated most often today as Pacifism. It is appropriate because the early modern period was the first time in the North Atlantic community that pacifistic movements started drawing some reflection by those writing in the just war tradition. As was done in chapter one for the other three attitudes, I will indicate elements of the position and give a critique.[1]

I. Some elements of the position

On the personal level, the pacifist holds to the practical principle, "One should not resist evil by directly 'violent' means." By 'violent,' the pacifist indicates any action using physical force that attempts to get someone else to change their behavior. This principle need not entail denial that one has the right to defend oneself by such means, but at least it says that one does not have the obligation to do so, and, because of some "higher" value, one never should do so. Most pacifists, moreover, do not stay at the personal perfectionist level but extrapolate that a society to be moral must always refuse to resort to the violence of war. When the term "pacifist" is used today, it ordinarily refers to the advocacy of this societal ethical standard.

The specification of this "higher" value varies among different pacifists. For some the value comes (a) from a philosophical position, such as a soul-body dualism, wherein others can harm one's body, but only one's own actions can harm one's soul (e.g., Epictetus). More commonly the value comes from some religious interpretation, such as (b) the call "to turn to the other cheek" interpreted absolutely to mean a command never to use physical violence in response to any violence or oppression used against persons, or (c) the trust in God's providential care which works in history to overcome evil. Often connected with the trust in divine providence is the requirement of voluntary suffering for humans as they participate in this history.[2] Also in our day some base the principle on (d) "respect for human life itself," claiming that it is not possible to show respect for the dignity of humans if one resorts to physical violence.

The four (a), (b), (c), and (d) are values of a personal perfectionism. That is, for the realization of the "higher value," none of them require that any verifiable good for others comes as a result of living by the value, and so the good involved is not open to empirical validation. Thus they are distinct from (e) which sees the principle as being more effective in the long run in reducing the total amount of physical aggression against persons than will a practice of violent resistance. Albert Einstein, for many years a public supporter of various pacifist groups between this century's two world wars, wrote:

> After many years of soul-searching and disillusionment over the failure of the disarmament conferences, I have become convinced that the world can be delivered from the scourge of war only by self-sacrificing men who refuse any and all military service.[3]

Gandhi also called for pacifistic actions to bring about less reliance on physical force.

> If the worst happens, there are two ways open to nonviolence.... The underlying belief in either case is that even a Nero is not devoid of heart. The unexpected spectacle of endless rows upon rows of men and women simply dying rather than surrender to the will of an aggressor must ultimately melt him and his soldiery.[4]

Here the conversion of others as a means to reduce the use of military force puts the principle in a utilitarian framework and makes it empirically testable.

In addition to the extrapolation from the personal to the societal level, some are pacifists not from a principle apriori to war itself, but from an interpretation of international history. That is, reflecting on past wars, some hold that there is no such thing as "real victory" in war for civilized people who have no wish to conquer others (=no valid war of conquest). Thus, they take it as a sign of progress in civilized sensibilities to reject resistance by physical violence (=no valid war of defense).[5]

II. Some problems.

A. Religious

Since this is a philosophical work, it is not the place to do a critique of appeals to religious convictions about pacifism. However, since such appeals are so heavily used today, it would be in place to indicate some matters for further reflection.

There is a problem with the interpretation of Scripture passages (e.g., the Sermon on the Mount) that are cited as requiring a pacifist stance. This appears to involve a double standard when the "no revenge" command is extrapolated into a justification for not contributing to the defense of one's country, but the "judge not" command is not turned into a justification for not testifying in court or serving on juries. Why are some passages held to be literally applicable in contemporary times, but others held to be only symbolic? For example, "Let the dead bury their dead" is cited by some scriptural scholars to be just as radical as "turn to the other cheek," yet few pacifists call for foregoing burial ceremonies.[6] Double standards usually indicate that some hidden principle other than those expressed is operative.

Also it is still to be explained why no one who has been both canonized a saint and named a doctor of the Catholic church has ever interpreted the passages as an absolute prohibition of a society's use of war or even a claim that it is always virtuous not to resort to war, while on the other hand many saints and doctors, in ex professo analyses, have found the passages compatible with justified war.[7] Historically, pacifism has often been considered a serious error for Christians.[8]

Finally, it seems that the exhortation "Turn to the other cheek" is expanded by pacifists to say, "And tell the other person also to turn to the other cheek, for what is being harmed in him or her is not important enough to make me give up my adherence to this principle of non-violence." This extension of the principle of personal non-vengeance to non-defense of another is not in the text. It would seem more proper that such an extension, if it is to be an expression of social love, would have to come from the victims of personal and structural oppression, and not placed upon them from outside.[9] Placing a religious principle above human needs was often refuted by Jesus in the Gospels.

B. Philosophical

James Childress has argued that those who are pacifists and those who follow in the Just War tradition share a common assumption against the use of physical force.[10] If that is so, then we might identify the difference between the two groups in this way. The latter accepts the possibility that some social values may be more important and, therefore, require the reluctant negation of the assumption. (This reluctant negation has often been articulated in the formal terms of the Principle of the Double Effect.) The former group do not accept such a possibility and hold absolutely against the use of physical force. The following comments, with some exceptions, assume that pacifists can be fairly identified as holding such an absolute position.

1) There is a definitional begging the question in the pacifist's use of the term "violence."[11] It is always dubious to define a moral concept by the description of a physical action. "Violence" is a term used to designate morally wrong behavior (just as are the terms "murder" and "lying"). To define violence to be the same as the use of physical force assumes rather than proves that no use of physical force can be justified morally. To hold that any use of physical force against individuals is an instance of violence and to be avoided deprives us of the ability to make a moral distinction between acts of oppression and acts of resistance. It deprives us of the ability to make a moral distinction between the physical force used by the rapist and the physical force used by a woman trying to resist a rape.[12] To fail to make necessary moral distinctions is to debase language. To identify lying with telling an untruth, or murder with killing a human being, or violence with the use of physical force would be to rule out by definition and not by argument any possibility of a justifiable telling of an untruth, or a justifiable killing, or a justifiable use of physical force. Since many do not rule such justifications out, there is a begging of the question involved in those kinds of definitions.

94

2)It is not clear whether non-violence itself is claimed to be the highest human value, or, what is nearly the same, the necessary condition for, or an expression of, what is specified as the highest human value. If this claim is made, then it certainly is reasonable to assert that non-violence must always be actualized and never negated to obtain some other value in a situation of conflict of values. However, such a ranking must be established by argument, since it is not self-evident. It would imply the sacrifice of every other value if there were a conflict situation. This cannot simply be asserted or assumed. For that would be to commit the fallacy of the complex question, in which a particularly significant assumption is presented as having to be accepted without debate in a discussion.

3)If the non-violence is not the highest value or a necessary condition for, or an expression of, it, then one must specify exactly how it fits into the scheme of human values. And, to avoid the fallacy of "abandoning the discussion" against an advocate of an ethical use of violence, one must establish that never would the principle of the double effect involve the negation of the value of non-violence in order to act in a conflict of values for a higher value. For example, one must establish that any degree and any duration of human rights violation must be endured even though the oppressed apparently could use violence with the hope of improving the physical situation.

Gandhi defended his support of the Boer War, the Zulu Rebellion, and World War I by saying that life is governed by a multitude of forces and that one cannot determine the course of one's actions only by the general principle of non-violence.[13]

4) If the position turns on the absolute value of human life, there is a danger of self-contradiction. Either one must argue "Human life is so valuable I will not kill to defend it," or one must argue "Human life is so valuable I will kill to defend it." Both positions assume the absoluteness of human physical life and are self-contradictory, for they say "the value is so important it is necessary that one deny it in order to affirm it."

5) If one deliberately omits taking violent action in a situation, one is morally responsible for the effects of such an omission. (Recall Ambrose's distinction.) Non-violence must be chosen in the concrete, not in abstract purity. This is especially important in the omission of intervention for the aid of another.[14] If one does not intervene where one could, one is partly responsible for the violence taking place on the other. Any resultant and preventable injury is morally accountable and must be justified. This is perhaps even more serious if the injury is societal as it comes from violence in the social structures themselves and effects all those in society.[15] Prima facie, since others have a right to self-defense, if they need assistance to actualize that right, then others who can help have an obligation, not an option, to help in an effective way, as long as the cost is proportionate. For example, the sniper who shot Huberty in San Diego could have thereby done a virtuous act. Gandhi himself wrote:

> Even manslaughter may be necessary in certain cases. Suppose a man runs amuck and goes furiously about sword in hand, and killing anyone that comes in his way, and no one dares to capture him alive. Anyone who dispatches this lunatic will earn the gratitude of the community and be regarded as a benevolent man.[16]

As Ernesto Cardenal said, the principle of nonviolence must not be above persons. And, as we noted above, Aquinas wrote that appealing to the principle of non-resistance to evil when the evil is happening to another seems more a moral viciousness than a moral virtue.[17]

If one argues in a utilitarian manner that, in the long run, a non-violent standard will reduce physical aggressions, at least one must acknowledge that one is thereby using the present negation of another's right of assistance as a means to the future goal. And there is an obligation to watch the empirical results whether the goal comes at such a cost. For example, it is an empirical question whether the pullout of American forces and aid from Vietnam in 1972-74 advanced the values of human dignity and freedom in the area.

6) There are the theoretical problems with the extrapolation of non-resistance to the societal level as pacifism. The well-known "fallacy of composition" alerts us to the dangers in any unexamined assumption that what is proper activity for the individual considered in isolation is proper activity for the societal group (or even for the individual as part of the societal group). The context for the individual's activity comes from the societal support structures. An undermining of these support structures could occur if every individual acted without regard for them. And a long tradition insists that there are special duties and values, other than those for individual ethics, that call for response from individuals because they are members of the societal group or are office holders in the society.

Any pacifist has to "be in society." Pacifists who are serious, that is, who object to the public use of violence but who do not object to being citizens, accept certain common premises concerning the relation of the citizen to the social order. Here are some examples of problems that arise for the pacifist-citizen.

6a) There is the "free rider" problem. A "free rider" is a citizen who enjoys the actualized values of the common good (values such as domestic tranquillity, common defense, and the assurance of the benefits of freedom for ourselves and for our children), but who by some deliberate choice will not support the institutional means used at present to obtain and maintain these values. That this lack of contribution probably does not have significant effect in terms of a reduction of these values is the reason that society can tolerate such "conscientious" non-participation in individual cases. But on the side of the individual, there is the reception of (since one cannot avoid benefitting from) or even the acceptance of (if one wants and approvingly enjoys) such values for whose achievement the society is formed, combined with a refusal to contribute to their achievement. This seems prima facie a failure in contributive justice and must be specifically argued. (There today is testimony of many Vietnam c.o.'s of guilt that others were wounded or killed in their place.)

6b) Every citizen has a moral obligation to contribute to the common good of society. Thus, an "appeal to one's conscience" to establish a pacifist decision commits the fallacy of _ignorantio elenchi_, for contributive justice is also a matter of conscience.

There is a philosophical question concerning the content of the judgment referred to by the appeal to conscience. How does one validate the specific content? It seems that the answer depends upon one's concept of conscience itself.

One concept (an older one) is that conscience is the self-given command internal to the individual to do the good act and avoid the evil act as these are understood in the particular situation. This concept detects three moments in the individual's ethical experience: the understanding that a possible action is right or wrong; the command given by the self to the self to act ethically in respect to that possible action; and the action itself as done or not done. Conscience is the second moment here: the ordering "do this" or "don't do this." To respect the integrity of conscience would mean not to force the individual to act other than what the conscience ordered. However, it is quite proper to question about the first moment, since the specific content in the conscience command (what is ordered as to be done or not) is not considered self-validating. Another individual could rightfully question "how the conscience was formed."

It is a more recent concept of conscience that makes it improper to raise such a question. Here conscience is understood as an originating movement of the individual who, insofar as one is not corrupted by external society, is naturally good and able to judge intuitively that a possible action is right or wrong. This spontaneous ability is a capability located somewhere between the intellect and the will. For such a concept of conscience, it is conscience itself that supplies the content of the judgment, and no rational defense or explanation is necessary or possible. To respect the integrity of conscience here would mean to accept each person's conscience command as self-validating even in its content. This concept of what conscience is has not been in the Just War tradition.

6c) There is the societal example problem. A
citizen who refuses to cooperate in the institutional
practices and appeals for justification to
"conscience" and thereby is "civilly disobedient,"
does an action that, experience indicates, has an
unwanted but definite second effect. Given the
present attitudes of people as they are, and given the
news media as they are (where stories of
confrontations are more exciting than stories of
cooperation), the publicity about citizen refusal
correlates with a recent deterioration in the
acknowledgment that there ordinarily is a moral
obligation to cooperate in the rules of society. (In
the tradition of civil disobedience, there was
heretofore a requisite that those who were to use the
appeal to conscience to be civilly disobedient
previously had performed always in ways that conveyed
to other citizens that the individuals had habitual
respect for societal laws.) Those who become aware
that the refusals of others are defended by an appeal
to "strong feelings of conscience" correctly
understand this to imply that anyone who has a strong
subjective conviction may break the law to express it.
For many others, subjective feelings qualify as
conscientious consideration of their position. The
danger of these "second effects" as consequences of
civil disobedience was always in the attention of
Gandhi and M.L. King, but does not seem so in many
today.[18]

7) Even if one denied the validity of differences
between the personal and the societal levels in
conscience, religious ideals such as "love of one's
enemies" and "forgiveness of harms done" still must
combine with other concepts before one could conclude
that they imply pacifism. Here are points that must
be examined.

7a) There is a prima facie, morally important
distinction between "Since I love and forgive all who
do evil actions, these people are not my enemy," and
"These are people from that country who do evil
actions such as war and pillage against people of
other countries." If country A militarily attacks
country B, and rapes, kills, and pillages the people
of B, what are the people of country C to do? It
seems fair to say that the people of country C, who
could use military force with an arguable possibility
of reducing the evil physical actions being done by
country A, are morally responsible for whatever they

choose to do or not do. There is no possibility of escaping moral responsibility in this (that is the nub of the "dirty hands" problem in international ethics), and no serious pacifist tries to do so. So the pacifist must, it seems, establish either that there is some apriori sovereign value at stake in pacifism (pacifism as an absolute principle), or that more existential evil would come about if country C intervened militarily (pacifism as a utilitarian principle).

Some pacifists take the first option and support it by appeal to the religious ideals of "love of enemies" and "forgiveness of harms."[19]

Certainly, the ideals of "love of enemies" and "forgiveness of harms" would lead to this conclusion: "Country C cannot hate either country A or country B." But it is not clear what positive choice that conclusion requires or permits. Direct deduction is not possible from "love means there are no enemies" to the choice between pacifism and military intervention. Some additional concepts must be introduced, ones that will indicate that, in such an international situation, pacifism is the (only? better?) way to live out the ideals of "love" and "forgiveness."

7b) If our country has these religious ideals in its foreign policy, then no other people is our enemy. No matter what the other country does, we cannot hate the people, we cannot morally want to do harm to them, to seek revenge, to get even, or the like. (This was the essence of the "right intention" requisite in the medieval just war position.)

But it is not clear that, to express these, our country must never use military force if such seems necessary to stop the evil actions of country A militarily attacking the people of country B. One faces a situation wherein there is a conflict in love: what to do in love when some country we love makes unjustified physical attacks on another country we love. The appeal to "love" or to "forgiveness" does not help in the choice. There is no assurance that some of those we love may not do very evil and very unjust actions. To conclude as the pacifist does, one must be assuming some further unspecified concepts. (One of these apparently is the dichotomy between "love" and "justice," which must bear the burden of explaining how this dichotomy is valid against the tradition that holds that acting according to the rubrics of justice is one way one specifies how to act out the formal principle of love.)

7c) Finally, there is a traditional moral distinction between "the intention to use physical force to express hate, to seek revenge, to get even, and the like," and "the intention to use physical force to prevent continued harm to others by the evil actions of some." The intentions, and thus the actions themselves, are not ethically the same kind. Both involve the intention to inflict physical harm (physical evil if one prefers). But the distinction denies that both involve moral evil. So again, it is not obviously necessary to move from "love means we must never act with the intention of doing harm to those we consider enemies, because with love we have no enemies," directly to the conclusion that pacifism is the only way to live this out internationally. Something as yet unexamined is assumed that makes such a conclusion convincing.

8) In reference to pacifism as a utilitarian principle, there are two major problems.

8a) If pacifism is advocated as the better means to achieve peace (war being the alternative means in Western tradition), then it can only be evaluated as a effective means if one specifies what counts as the goal, what counts as peace. As Clausewitz noted, countries with aggressive intentions often claim to be "lovers of peace," but by that they have in mind a condition of non-resistance to their aggressive actions. Is peace to be the absence of organized and continuous physical violence or the willingness to engage in such? (Hobbes identified a tone or atmosphere of willingness to engage in such organized and continuous physical violence as that which moved a status from a condition of peace to one of war. He used the analogy of threatening weather.) But if by peace one means that condition wherein there is significant order in the human values and human relationships that we include under the names of liberty and justice, then the peace of some governments does not count as peace.[20] Many after Marx have held that violence against a people can become institutionalized in the way things are done (the "structures") so that the situation can never count as one of peace. The tradition from Cicero and Augustine on has consistently maintained that, in

101

certain situations, war may be a necessary means to some minimum condition of a peace with justice and liberty. If this is true, it would seem that pacifism would entail the abandonment of just peace for the sake of the principle of no use of physical force.

In addition, many agree with Augustine and hold that one must not define peace so idealistically that no situation in human experience ever has or quite possibly ever will qualify. Augustine argued that we must talk of a "more or less just peace." The goal of peace must be specified as to what counts as peace but in terms of a condition achievable in the real world.

8b) A similar difficulty obtains with specification of the means. One must not conceive of peace with justice and liberty in such a way so that no identifiable steps could be means to get there. One must also avoid what could be called the "pistol fallacy." This fallacy occurs when it is claimed that because certain rules or policies would be out of place in a world of perfect peace and justice, instead of enacting such rules or policies, we should "work for" the immediate realization of that perfect world. [Hegel and Marx would remind us that the completely rational world cannot be "shot from a pistol," that is, without the necessary preparatory stages.[21] There is also involved, perhaps, the fascination with eschatological visions, that is, visions that pertain to the definitive end of an epoch.]

For example, instead of writing a constitution with checks and balances against the abuse of power, we should make sure that tyrants never get into positions of power (even though no one is sure how to prevent this). Instead of introducing stronger civil rights legislation, we should teach people not to be bigoted (even though no one is sure how to do this). And as we want children to become fully mature as free individuals, we should throw aside practices that have been used for their behavior modification and socialization.

The fallacy is this: one only recommends action (x) that would completely eliminate some evil, while rejecting (y1, y2...) that aim at correcting or mitigating the effects of that evil while it still functions in the real world. Yet if the complete elimination of the evil is unlikely, at least for a while (and this would be arguable from both past experience and some common theory of human nature and political society), then the time, effort, and resources spent on (x) but denied of (y1, y2...) actually will bring about a MORE IMPERFECT world, that is, one that lacks even those remedial devices that could have been installed and improved in effectiveness toward the lesser goal. The Best is often the enemy of the Good.[22] [Max Weber argued that the refusal to accept the challenge to consider the probable consequences of a proposed policy in the world at it is at the time often meant that implimentation of the policy set the stage and helped effect results far other than the better world the sincerely well-intentioned proposer was sure would come.[23]] This is behind the tradition that it is a moral duty, not one of several legitimate alternatives, for leaders and citizens to prepare for, and engage in the military defense of the country.

9) Finally, pacifism claims there is no hope for discerning moral guidelines to the use of physical violence in national policy. This means that when adherents, in time of war, enter into war under an application of contributive justice, they will be morally weaponless to make any distinctions in what they do. The resultant problems have been noted by Elizabeth Anscombe, as part of her defense of the _in bello_ distinction between combatants and noncombatants, wrote:

> Now pacifism teaches people to make no distinction between the shedding of innocent blood and the shedding of any human blood. And in this way pacifism has corrupted enormous numbers of people who will not act according to its tenets. They become convinced that a number of things are wicked which are not; hence, seeing no way of avoiding 'wickedness,' they set no limits to it.... Pacifism and the respect for pacifism is not the only thing that has led to a universal forgetfulness of the law against killing the innocent; but it has had a great share in it.[24]

NOTES
(1) Some recent philosophical work includes: Jan Narveson, "Pacifism: A Philosophical Analysis," _Ethics_ 75(1965), 259-271; Tom Regan, "A Defense of

Pacifism," Canadian Journal of Philosophy 2 (1972),
73-86; James Childress, "Reinhold Niebuhr's Critique
of Pacifism," Review of Politics 36 (1974); Craig
Ihara, "In Defense of a Version of Pacifism," Ethics
88 (1978), 369-374; and Cheney Ryan, "Self-Defense,
Pacifism, and the Possibility of Killing," Ethics 93
(1983).
(2) For trust in divine providence, see John Howard
Yoder, The Politics of Jesus: Vicit Agnus Noster
(Grand Rapids: Eerdmans, 1972), 238. For the role
of voluntary suffering in this historical
development, see James Douglass, The Non-Violent
Cross: A Theology of Revolution and Peace (New York:
Macmillan, 1966), 191-214, 234-254.
(3) Letter to President Masaryk, April 13, 1931, in
Einstein on Peace, ed. by Otto Nathan and Heinz
Norden (New York: Avenel, 1960), 130.
(4) Non-Violent Resistance (Ahmedabad: Navejivan
Trust, n.d.), 386-387. Gandhi spelled out some
specific requirements in many other places. "I have
always held that social justice, even unto the least
and the lowliest, is impossible of attainment by
force. I have further believed that it is possible
by proper training of the lowliest by non-violent
means to secure redress of the wrongs suffered by
them. That means is non-violent non-cooperation....
But it must be realized that the reform cannot be
rushed. If it is to be brought about by non-violent
means it can only be done by education both of the
haves and the have-nots." Mohandas K. Gandhi,
Harijan, April 20, 1940, quoted in Political and
National Life and Affairs, ed. V.B. Khe, 2 vols.
(Ahmedabad: Navajivan Trust, 1962), I, 109-113.
   James Douglass maintains that the energy released
from non-violent love can bring about conversions
from evil to good. See Lightning East to West:
Jesus, Gandhi, and the Nuclear Age (New York:
Crossroad, 1983), 14-54.
(5) See Kenneth Thompson, Understanding World Politics
(Notre Dame: Notre Dame University Press, 1975),
130-131.
(6) Norman Perrin, The New Testament: An Introduction
(New York: Harcourt Brace Jovanovich, 1974),
296-297.
(7) See, for example, Thomas Aquinas, Summa Theologiae
II-II, 40, 1 ad 2, commenting on Mt. 5 and war.
Also see Augustine, Contra Faustum, ch. 22; Robert
Bellarmine, Disputationes de controversiis
Christianae fidei, De membris ecclesiae, Bk. III:
De Laicis, ch. 14. And see Elizabeth Anscombe, "War

and Murder," in Richard Wasserstrom, ed., War and Morality (Belmont: Wadsworth, 1970), esp. 46-50, and also the above chapter three on "Early Christian Influences."

(8) See, e.g., Robert Bellarmine, De Laicis, ch. 14; Francisco Suarez claimed that some pacifists followed the Ancient Manichaens or certain medieval and Renaissance heretics, De Triplici Virtute Theologica: Fide, Spe, et Caritate, De Caritate, Disp. XIII: De bello, I, 1-5. Two other Jesuit authors of the early modern time might be cited: Gregory of Valencia, Commentariorum Theologicorum, Tomus Tertius, XVI, De bello, punct. 1; Louis Molina, De justitia et jure, Disp. 40.

(9) See George Soares-Prabhu, "Jesus and Conflict," The Way 26 (1986), 14-23.

(10) James F. Childress, "Just War Criteria," in War or Peace: The Search for New Answers, ed. by Thomas A. Shannon (Maryknoll: Orbis, 1980), 42-50. James T. Johnson concurs, "One Keeping Faith: The Use of History for Religious Ethics," Journal of Religious Ethics 7 (1979), 113. See also Richard B. Miller, "Christian Pacifism and Just-War Tenets: How Do They Diverge," Theological Studies 47 (1986), 448-472.

(11) For the distinction between violence and force, see, for example, Robert Audi, "On the Meaning and Justification of Violence," and Ronald B. Miller, "Violence Force, and Coercion," both in Jerome A. Shaffer, Violence (New York: David Mckay, 1971); J. Glenn Gray, "On Understanding Violence Philosophically," in On Understanding Violence Philosophically and Other Essays (New York: Harper Torchbook, 1970), 12-15.

(12) See The South African Religious Leaders' statement, "The Kairos Document," Origins (NC Documentary Service) 15 (Jan. 23, 1986), 522-532, at 528.

(13) Selections from Gandhi, ed. by Nirmal Kumar Bose (Ahmedabad: Navajivan Trust, 1948), pp. 167-168, 175-176. Quoted in All Men are Brothers, edited by Krishna Kripalani (Ahmedabad: Navajivan Trust, 1960), 47.

(14) See the proviso on approval of adopting any nonviolence stance in "Gaudium et Spes," Vatican Council II, #78.

(15) See John Harris, "The Marxist Conception of Violence," Philosophy and Public Affairs 3 (1974), 192-220.

(16) Young India, November, 1926; quoted in Raghavan Iyer, The Moral and Political Thought of Mahatma

Gandhi (New York: Oxford University Press, 1973), 207.

(17) Summa Theologiae II-II, 188, 3 ad 1.

(18) "A Satyagrahi obeys the laws of society intelligently and of his own free will, because he considers it to be his sacred duty to do so. It is only when a person has thus obeyed the laws of society scrupulously that he is in a position to judge as to which particular rules are good and just and which unjust and inequitous. Only then does the right accrue to him of the civil disobedience of certain laws in well-defined circumstances." Mohandas K. Gandhi, An Autobiography: The Story of My Experiments with Truth, tr. Mahaden Desai, 2nd ed. (Ahmedabad: Navajivan Trust, 1940), 470. See also, Collected Works of Mahatma Gandhi (Delhi: Govt. of India, The Publications Division, 1958--), XV, 436-437.

(19) For a liberation theologian's rejection of making a religious principle such as "forgiveness of enemies" into a rule of social life, which would imply a "forgetting" of the conflicts between groups on the society and international level, see Juan Luis Segundo, Theology and the Church (Minneapolis: Winston, 1985), 60-61. Compare Gandhi's position which emphasized the "manliness" of forgiveness, but that abstinence from the use of physical force is forgiveness only when there is the capacity to punish. See, e.g., Young India, August 11, 1920.

(20) See "Gaudium et Spes," Vatican Council II, #78. Also see U.S. Bishops' Letter, "The Challenge of Peace," ## 68, 69, 78.

(21) Phenomenology of Spirit, tr. by A.V. Miller (Oxford: Clarendon Press, 1977), Preface, 16.

(22) See David Hume, Enquiry Concerning the Principles of Morals, Sect. III, Part II, 154.

(23) "Politics as a Vocation," in From Max Weber, ed. H. H. Gerth and C. Wright Mills (New York: Oxford, 1958), 77-128.

(24) "War and Murder," 49-50.

CHAPTER SEVEN

MODERN POSITIVISM AND CLAUSEWITZ

> War is the state of affairs which deals in
> earnest with the vanity of temporal goods
> and concerns--- a vanity at other times a
> common theme of edifying sermonizing....
> War has the higher significance that by its
> agency... the ethical health of peoples is
> preserved in their indifference to the
> stabilization of finite institutions; just
> as the blowing of the winds preserves the
> sea from the foulness which would be the
> result of a prolonged calm, so also
> corruption in nations would be the product
> of prolonged, let alone 'perpetual'
> peace.[1]

A. Vattel

After the nation states became fully established
in Europe, no new doctrine identifying an objective
basis for an ethics of international relations
successfully secured universal acceptance. Instead
the eighteenth and nineteenth centuries were periods
of a shift in international theories from a natural
law to a positivist assumption on international law
which held that the only operative rules for
independent and sovereign states were those to which
they had somehow committed themselves. International
law gradually became the institution of law between
sovereigns who would not suffer a judge above them but
who could not carry on without a regularization of
their interrelated affairs. Diplomacy became the set
of those practices which express the determination of
the sovereign states to have the appropriate means to
settle their ordinary international relations. Raison
d'etat became accepted as a principle of international
right. This did not exclude publicists (as theorists
began to be called) from investigation of matters of
justice in international policy. But it did change
much of how they approached the questions.

One of the most popular and influential works in
the eighteenth century was Emmerich de Vattel's Law of
Nations.(1758) "The popularity of the work in its time
reflected and contributed to the maintenance of a set
of ideas about the nature of right relationships
between sovereigns and subjects and among sovereigns,

which in turn sustained a society of states in Europe."[2] The set of ideas quickly became items for consensus.

Vattel still appealed for objectivity and universality to a theory of natural law. But he emphasized that natural law applies primarily to individuals. When it pertains to other agents, such as states, "it must be applied in a manner suited to the nature of each subject."[3] This different yet analogous application became one phase of Vattel's ethical explanation of how an objective and universal natural law applied to international affairs wherein the units of action were states.

The other phase was his acceptance of the newer interpretation of why individuals themselves were in a society, since this was the interpretation of that to which the relations of states was analogous.

Vattel held that people are in society by voluntary contract rather than by birth. People choose to enter society because they have need of one another and have the ability to communicate with each other. Thus, by nature, the general law of such human society is that "each individual should do for the others every thing which their necessities require, and which one can perform without neglecting the duty one owes to oneself."[4] The social contract occurs as people subject themselves to the authority of the entire body in everything that relates to the common welfare, and entrust the exercise of that authority to some sovereign.[5] This is a Lockean model of the social contract theory with an addition of a utilitarian concept of what counts as the common welfare, that is, with the contracted union as simply a means to obtain and secure the private goods of the individuals who are conceived of as complete individuals prior to living in a family, private organizations, or society. Obligations come to the individuals from their voluntary entrance into the social contract and involve their agreement to act for the common good of that society.

All this implied two major changes in political ethics: political authority could validate only whatever power could be understood as coming from individuals; and citizens could not reasonably be required to sacrifice their private goods for the common good of the many.

108

In many ways, nations also are in a state of nature and yet need one another to do certain things and not do other things for the private good of each. Consequently, Vattel found an analogy with the social contract in international relations. But of course there is no basic contract, only actual agreements between individual states. Nevertheless, he argued that there is a natural society of states (not of all individuals), again based on mutual need and the power of communication. So the natural law requires that states, considered as independent agents living together in nature, have a duty to act for the common good (still taken in the utilitarian sense of "the sum of the several diverse individual interests").[6] By this natural law, each state is bound to act for the common good of the society of states, yet never so as to violate its own individual good.[7]

To apply it to nations, Vattel divided natural law into two components. First is the necessary law of nations which consists of inferences from the natural law which nations are absolutely bound to preserve.[8] Second is the voluntary law of nations, whose maxims are devoted to the safety and advantages of the universal society of mankind, and which must be consulted by a nation when there is a question of examining what it may demand of other states.[9] The basis for the voluntary law of nations is the freedom, independence, and equality that each nation enjoys from the natural law.[10]

Three ideas are at the basis of all content in the necessary law of nations: the nature of a state, its primary obligations, and its dynamism. As mentioned above, Vattel's model for the nature of a state was the Lockean social contract combined with the utilitarian common good. It then follows that the primary obligations of a state, in both its leaders and its citizens, will be the preservation and advancement of itself.[11] Whatever else, it is rational for a state to do whatever is necessary for these ends. Consequently, it is in the dynamism of a state to increase its power, its ability to effect its preservation and advancement. But here is the cause of competition and conflict even between ethical states.

On the one hand, a state that increases its power by all the arts of good government does not more than what is commendable...

109

on the other hand, it is but too well
known, from sad and uniform experience,
that predominating powers seldom fail to
molest their neighbors, to oppress them,
and even totally subjugate them, whenever
an opportunity occurs, and they can do it
with impunity.[12]

Vattel's views on the natural law requirement
that states preserve and perfect themselves also
determined the application of the necessary law of
nations to treaties. On the one hand, the keeping
treaties is the foundation of international
stability.[13] On the other hand, treaties which are
pernicious, that is, with such effects that would lead
to the diminishing of the state, are invalid.[14] In
respect to going to war, peace treaties are binding,
but they do not force a state to submit to injuries
and wrongs of every kind rather than procure justice
by force of arms.[15]

The obligations which come as a result of the
society of all nations are subordinate, in the
necessary law of nations, to the obligations of the
individual state to preserve and advance itself. That
is, unlike the individual, who might morally sacrifice
oneself for others, the state is obliged not to make
such a sacrifice. Thus, the obligations between
states in the necessary law of nations become a kind
of minimal samaritanism.

One state owes to another state whatever it
owes to itself, so far as that other stands
in real need of its assistance, and the
former can grant it without neglecting the
duties it owes to itself. Such is the
eternal and immutable law of nature.[16]

The voluntary law of nations, according to
Vattel, supplements the necessary law principles. It
treats the demands that a state could rightly make of
another state. Within a state, the sovereign power
rightly may give orders and punish violations. But
internationally, all states are equal.[17] Since civic
association is not equally necessary between states as
between individuals, there is no sovereign power
internationally.[18] So obligations based on rights
of nations are imperfect. That is, state A can
request that state B comply with its obligations, but
state B has the ethical right to decide for itself

110

whether the situation permits it to fulfil those obligations without violating its primary obligations to its own preservation and advancement.[19]

Besides the duties of preservation, advancement and mutual aid, there is another duty Vattel found for states, the diminution and mitigation of wars. But immediately he ran into problems because of his earlier assumptions. So he made a very practical judgment. Because each side in a war will claim that it has a just cause for war in terms of a basic right to be maintained[20], reason says that the necessary law of nations cannot prudentially be used to regulate war. Rather, only the voluntary law of nations will apply.

The first rule of the voluntary natural law with respect to war is "that regular war, as to its effects, is to be accounted just on both sides."[21] He agreed with Vitoria and Grotius that there should be a working position of "mutual ostensive justice" due to a skepticism about the ability to discern who is objectively in the right.[22]

The second rule is "Whatever is permitted to the one in virtue of the state of war, is also permitted to the other."[23] This rule not only followed from the first, but it had the same effect as that intended by Vitoria and Grotius; namely, that a state, which believed it had justice on its side, nevertheless would restrict the amount of physical force it did during the war because it knew that the other side, also regarding its own cause as just, would not hesitate to meet like with like. This would be especially significant in that neither side would receive pressures or hostility from non-belligerent states on account of any "injustice" in such response.

The third rule is "that this voluntary law of nations, which is admitted only through necessity, and with a view to avoid greater evils, does not, to him who takes up arms in an unjust cause, give any real right that is capable of justifying his conduct and acquitting his conscience, but merely entitles him to the benefit of the external effect of the law, and to impunity among mankind."[24] Under the necessity of choosing the lesser evil, the third rule grants impunity to all sides. The point here is that fear of punishment might lead one side to prolong a war irrationally.

The cause for a justified offensive or defensive war is that there is a right to be supported and the only way it can be done is by force.[25] Vattel did not think that war actually decides controversies, since victory ordinarily is on the side of strength and skill, not justice.[26] Only the injured party has the right to go to war against independent states. One state cannot assume the right to punish another for "faults that do not concern them."[27] Yet Vattel knew that predominant states usually make trouble for their neighbors, especially when they can do so with impunity.[28] So how long must a state wait as the storm gathers? Prudence, or sound statesmanship, says that one not wait until the time when one is no longer able to defend oneself.[29] When there is a reasonable presumption of intended aggression, preventive war is justifiable. And to reduce the chance of war, states should have confederations to preserve a balance of power.[30]

Vattel's work was very influential since it expressed the moral convictions and tensions in Eighteenth century European political leaders: sovereignty, a non-religious yet transnational objective moral order that was both compatible with and yet above raison d'etat, and property. Simple conquest, without reference to justice, is sufficient to provide title.[31] This rule would serve to diminish the number of international disputes.

B. Martens

In his major work (of 1788), George Friedrich von Martens moved international thinking further along positivistic lines.[32] He acknowledged that there is a natural law of nations, but he insisted that, just as positive law was needed within a society to avoid lack of specific content for natural law ideals, so specific guidelines were needed for international relations.[33] Nations have responded to this need by entering specific treaties, or by silently accepting and acting upon certain conventions and customs which form the general positive law of nations.[34] Martens' work collected and systematized such treaties, conventions, and customs dating back to the Romans, and identified this law of nations with European state practice.[35]

This approach reached its peak in the Nineteenth century and basically was a European conception. It included the notion that all states were formal equals, but also that some states were "great powers" with special rights and duties.[36]

The basis for substantive rights and obligations between states was solely "the mutual will of the nations concerned."[37] Consequently the specifics of international law were subordinate to the sovereign judgment of those involved.

> (I)f the accomplishment be physically impossible, either from the nature of the promise, or from the circumstances, or if the accomplishment interferes with the interests of a third, or tends to ruin the nation which has promised, the covenant becomes void, or, at least, ceases to be obligatory.[38]

Martens thus eliminated the tension between any standard from natural law and a standard from national sovereignty. There is no norm unless that norm is given status by the wills of the individual states. And a state is acting reasonably if it accepts only those norms whose consequences serve the self-interest of the state. The international order, therefore, is one of power and state interest.

In a simplistic sense, then, war is the ultima ratio of international politics. A state always has legitimate recourse to military force to defend or enforce its self-interest. War is thus expected and proper for the pure positivist theory of international relations. There was no argument about ius ad bellum except whether going to war really would serve the interests of the state.

As for ius in bello matters, Martens held that a sovereign would be wise to use the least amount of force necessary, since this would serve well in later international dealings. But, if necessary, there need be no limit on the use of military force even against civilian life and property.[39] Circumstances alone will guide the reasonable judgment on the proper courses of action. "War gives a nation an unlimited right of exercising physical force, against the enemy."[40] If international custom or treaties indicate limits, these can be overreached if

113

necessary.

In the pure positivist theory, war is potentially total.

C. Carl von Clausewitz

With the exception of a brief phrase to the effect that the only moral use of physical force is in action by the state and by the law,[41] Carl von Clausewitz (1780-1831) did his major study, On War, without deliberate attention to ethics. Rather, he concentrated on a concrete examination of war and the requisites for it to be a reasonable endeavor by states. In the course of his work, he made several generalizations that have been most influential in later thinking. These generalizations and their subsequent influence have undeniable significance for those who work toward an ethical study of war. They have even more significance for those who have as their methodology in such a study that we discover substantive ethical principles by induction from the decisions of those trying to act well in actual situations. It is therefore not surprising that it is important for the ethician of war to study Clausewitz. What is surprising, perhaps, is that his generalizations made contact with many elements in the Just War tradition of the ethics of war.

Clausewitz began On War with a severe but abstract definition: "War is thus an act of force to compel our enemy to do our will."[42] The political objective (Zweck) of war is to impose one's will on the enemy. To accomplish that, one uses as the means the maximum available military force with the military aim (Zeil) of rendering the enemy powerless ("disarmed," overthrown), a condition in which continuing would be worse than submitting.

In an ironic turn of history, Clausewitz employed the analogy of a duel, suggesting one look on war as but a duel on a larger scale. The model of the duel has the antagonism of wills expressed through physical force. Similarly, the dynamics of war arises from the reciprocal activities of two opposed and forcefully intentioned wills.

Which example of a duel Clausewitz used was also significant. He did not, as he could have, select something like fencing, but chose rather a wrestling match.[43] In the match, each opponent intends to impose its will on the other, and so they escalate efforts to the maximum. Each can gain security only in complete "throwing over" of the other, and so each strives for a final triumph.

In the wrestling match, each person has the goal of forcing submission of the other. Each is assumed by the other to be rational. This means there will be a dynamics in the match which will cause each to play without limitation. As one side uses force, the other side must respond in kind or suffer setbacks in its intention. But the response will pose a threat in kind to the first. Likewise, each side aims at disarming the other to render it powerless, which implies a dynamic to maximum disarming. Finally, there is a parallel dynamic to a maximum exertion of strength. This exertion targets the total means at the enemy's disposal, both physical means and the enemy's will to fight. The first is quantifiable, the second can only be gauged by a study of the enemy's motives and character.

Likewise, war, in its essential intelligibility, is always "absolute," that is, carried on without modification or inhibition. Even though the subjective feelings of hostility present at the beginning of a war may fluctuate, the intelligible structure of what war is makes any limitation prior to achievement of its military objective, the total overthrowing, irrational. In abstraction from other considerations, one is never certain to what lengths the will of the opponent will carry its own intention to compel us to submit.

The point Clausewitz made was this: Absolute War is simply fighting "all out." The opening sentence of Book II, chapter one is: <u>Krieg</u> <u>in</u> <u>seiner</u> <u>eigentlichen</u> <u>Bedeutung</u> <u>ist</u> <u>Kampf</u>. Peter Paret comments:

> True war was absolute violence because organized mass violence was the only feature that distinguished war from all other human activities.[44]

After the analysis that war in its intelligible dynamic is always absolute and unlimited, Clausewitz turned to the fact that, in the concrete world of practice, war is always conditioned and always limited. (It is well to note that "absolute" is not

115

the same as "total", even though Clausewitz wrote at the time war was becoming "total" in the concrete.) How could modification of military hostilities in war ever be rational?

Real war never loses its primordial physical vehemence, but it is never absolute because it is never abstract. War would be absolute in the concrete only if three conditions were true: that war could be a wholly isolated act, occuring suddenly and not produced by previous events in the political world; that war could consist in a single decisive act or set of simultaneous acts; and that the decision achieved would be complete and final, uninfluenced by any estimate of the subsequent political situation.

But these conditions have never yet been true. The opposed intentions in war are those of states, and these states exist with populations, resources, territory, allies, and history. It is out of such sets of concrete relations that each state in going to war has its causes and purposes.

First of all, war is never an isolated event. It comes out of the political situation, and the two gauge each other, with consequent moderation of the military dynamics. It is the political intention that controls the amount of physical force expressed in the military efforts.[45] [This relation between the use of military force at all and the overall political context parallels the moral relation between ad bellum cause and ad bellum proportionality.]

Second, up to now war cannot consist of a single decisive act or set of simultaneous acts, but rather needs several successive acts, each of which provides a setting for later ones. Involved here, thought Clausewitz, was the impossibility of employing at one stroke all a state's resources: its forces, its physical features and population, and its allies. Because of the difficulties endemic in every large scale physical enterprise, war in practice can never be absolute. [This is an objective reason for the other side to moderate its own efforts, and is one existential basis for in bello proportionality.]

Thirdly, in war, the results are never final. Even defeat can be made transitory by later political conditions. This also would moderate military efforts in war. Since the general political intention when the state went to war is the compelling of the enemy to do the state's will, then if no war's results are final, part of that political intention must be the quality of the peace that eventuates. [This point contacts the ad bellum right intention, which involves fighting so that the eventual peace will be tolerable even for the defeated enemy.]

All this is true not only of one's own state, but also of the enemy state. Consequently, how much effort to expend in the war becomes a matter of practical judgment, not theory. The judgment is based on the conditions in the actual situation and on what Clausewitz liked to describe as the "laws of probability." One has to study the enemy's character, institutions, and state of affairs, and estimate the enemy's likely intention and likely course of action.[46]

Since it is not reasonable to let war in the concrete become absolute, the political objective returns to consideration. We can identify in this "return" several points of contact with the Just War tradition. As the tradition has the ad bellum cause the essential guide to the leader who decides whether to go to war, so here, "the political object, which was the original motive (for war), must become an essential factor in the equation."[47] This political objective will determine the military objective and set limits to the effort spent. This is an important contact to what the tradition has seen as the relation between the ad bellum cause and the ad bellum proportionality. As we will see him develop a little later, Clausewitz held that the political objective need not always require the complete military overthrow of the enemy, and so there may be differing limits in differing wars as to what are reasonable military strategic objectives.

But this cannot be decided in the abstract, since different enemies react differently according to their character, institutions, and situation. [This is a contact with the connection between the ad bellum proportionality element and in bello proportionality on the military strategic as well as the military tactical level.] Exactly how to put the enemy in a situation where it will find it reasonable to do the state's will would vary with the enemy's tenacity, their type of political society, their economic relations in the world, and so on. The actual effort, consequently, may seem disproportionate to the casual bystander, or some later historian. (Perhaps an example of this point is the contemporary debate on Truman's decision to use the atomic bomb in World War II.)

More divergence from Absolute War develops because in actual war there are "interruptions" in the fighting.[48] This does not make sense in pure theory, since the desire for an interruption on one side would indicate it was an excellent time for the other side to strike. Also a condition of absolute balance wherein both sides would desire an interruption would suggest that one who went on the attack would have advantage. But in actual situations, Clausewitz argued, there would be three causes for interruptions in fighting.

The first is that attack is not the only way fighting occurs. Defense is also a mode of fighting, and it is often superior in its power to disarm the enemy. (Commanders talk of needing a 3 to 1 ratio for probability of success in attack.) This military fact mitigates the impulse to attack.

The second cause for interruption is the commander's imperfect knowledge of the situation, especially knowledge of the enemy's strength. (Those generals who are adept at discerning the enemy's actual strength from the generally dubious intelligence gathered often become singularly famous.)

The third cause would be the indecisiveness (an inertia of the will) that grows out of the weakness of the original motive for the war and even more out of ordinary human fear because of the danger and the responsibility involved.

In addition to the military handicaps and the situational difficulties, Clausewitz insisted that another factor be included in any analysis of war: the factor of "chance." War was in the actual world always a gamble.

> No other human activity is so continuously and universally bound up with chance. And through the element of chance, guesswork and luck come to play a great part in war.[49]

118

In some ways, it most closely resembles a game of cards.[50]

The element of chance amidst the violence of war gives room for a commander's courage, boldness, even foolhardiness. Yet however much it may be like a game of cards, it is no pastime with superficial delight in daring and winning.[51] War is a most serious means to a most serious end. For it involves the entire country.

> When whole communities go to war... the reason always lies in some political situation, and the occasion is always due to some political object. War therefore is an act of policy.[52]

Having identified the dynamic characteristics of Absolute War and the existential causes why it is reasonable that Absolute War does not take place in the concrete, Clausewitz put forth his interpretation, for which he is most known, of how war fits into the social scene.

> It is clear, consequently, that war is not a mere act of policy but a true political instrument, a continuation of political activity by other means.[53]

The Just War tradition had up to this time emphasized that war had to be called by the proper authority since only that office had the duty and the power to call all the people into concerted activity for the common good. Here Clausewitz emphasized that war is a political activity on a continuum with other political activities, and therefore it is only reasonable to go to war if it is a political decision to do so. (It is worth recalling here that his only explicit reference to morality in On War was that the use of physical force could be moral only if it was state action.)

War, if it is reasonably undertaken, is a "political activity by other means." The phrase "other means" refers to the fact that the means are the activities of military force. The sense of the term "other" seems to be: not ordinary, but within the spectrum of phenomena that properly belong to the category of actions called "political".

Nevertheless, it is precisely here that his earlier analysis of Absolute War returns to contribute substantially to the principle that war is a political activity. In the abstract, war has a dynamic toward unlimited escalation. That is why, when the organized mass use of military force is subordinated to politics, it is a "peculiar" means. It is the "peculiar nature" of this "other" means that brings a two-way tension between the political leader and the military commander. The uncovering of this tension is one of Clausewitz's major contributions and has, perhaps more than any other, insistent implications for those of us who think that ethical principles on war come by induction.

> What remains peculiar to war is simply the peculiar nature of its means. War in general, and the commander in any specific instance, is entitled to require that the trend and designs of policy shall not be inconsistent with these means. That, of course, is no small demand; but however much it may affect political aims in a given case, it will never do more than modify them. The political object is the goal, war is the means of reaching it, and means can never be considered in isolation from their purpose.[54]

The political leader would be irrational to use war for policy aims that would be inconsistent with the inner dynamic of war. And that inner dynamic is always expressed in the actual combat activities of the particular war, and not in some some ideal war planned out fully by some "cabinet." Each age calls forth its own special military strategy, yet this is more from the situation and the actual social relations than it is from any new weaponry. The political ends must be articulated accordingly.[55]

But, conversely, the military commander must keep in mind that the war is only a means to a political object beyond it. [Again, this contacts the themes of ad bellum cause, proportionality, and right intention.] For example, President Truman and General MacArthur could not resolve the tension in the matter of the bombing of the Yalu river bridges. (In many ways, the disharmony between the political and the military positions for the U.S. in the Korean War is a laboratory model of Clausewitz's point here.)

120

This two-way tension varies with the different natures of different wars. If there is a clear goal and strong motives, the more congruent are the dynamic of the war and the interest of the military commander with the political goals. But problems increase when the motives are weak and the political goal ambiguous (as for, e.g., the U.S. in the Vietnam War).

Consequently, any adequate understanding of actual war must take account of what Clausewitz called "the remarkable trinity."

> War is more than a true chameleon that slightly adapts its characteristics to the given case. As a total phenomenon its dominant tendencies always make war a remarkable trinity--- composed of primordial violence, hatred, and enmity, which are to be regarded as a blind natural force; of the play of chance and probability within which the creative spirit is free to roam; and of its element of subordination as an instrument of policy, which makes it subject to reason alone.[56]

The blind natural forces come from an innate impulse in people. From the factors of chance and probability, there is room for the creative ingenuity and expression of moral character by the military commanders, especially in terms of courage, taking risks, and being bold. Finally there is the subordination of this to the reasoning of the statesman in matter of policy. These three have the actual war suspended in their midst "like an object suspended between three magnets."[57]

Clausewitz's main contribution to overall thinking on war has been this concept: war is always an instrument of policy, and so the first thing to decide is what kind of war it is. This is the judgment that must be made and must be communicated to the rest of the government, to the military, and to the people. (For a laboratory model here, one may cite the U.S. political failures in the Vietnam War.)

Because war is a peculiar means of political policy, the precision of definition of that policy is vital if the war is to be successful. The political goal of "peace" is much too formal and amorphous to

121

help in deciding military objectives (in the matter of overall strategy). Some wars may be nearly absolute in their aim, and so the military objectives proceed untrammeled: to destroy the enemy forces, to occupy the enemy country to prevent rearming, and to break the will of the people, the government, and their allies. Often, however, "peace," in the Clausewitzian sense of "compelling the enemy to do one's will," can be, or even must be achieved without all of these. For example, if the states are unequal in military potential, the idea of defeating the enemy militarily must be interpreted by the weaker side in terms other than destroying their forces and occupying their territory. (This is essential to revolutionary war thinking.) Likewise, if the motivation for war on one side is less than on the others, it is possible that that side may find the war involves unacceptable costs [which implies that the two sides have different estimates of ad bellum proportionality], especially as gaining a clear victory becomes less probable.

Since Clausewitz insisted that the policy of war was determined by the intellect and not by senseless passion, "many roads lead to success, and they do not all involve the opponent's outright defeat."[58] There are many shortcuts to the goal, such as "passive attrition," which is the awaiting and avoiding enemy attacks in order to wear down the enemy's energies. [There are consequently variances of in bello proportionality concurrent with variances in military and political objectives.] Most of the shortcuts are effective in conjunction with the personal characters of the enemy's military and governmental leaders, but may also be effective in conjunction with the characters of the people of the enemy country. But all ways to peace, along the spectrum from all-out assaults to passive attrition, have one element in common: the overcoming of the enemy's will to fight.

Thus government officials will select different specific political objectives and oversee different general strategy (general military objectives and procedures) in terms of how they specify the political objectives. In turn, military commanders will select specific strategies and specific military targets and procedures (tactics) in coordination with the general strategy. [Here there seems some crossover between ad bellum intention of "peace" and in bello proportionality.] The military activity is always aimed at fighting at the right place at the right time. But this includes a correct appreciation of the other leader, boldness, energy, and imagination, and so cannot be completely determined "scientifically."[59]

All military fighting is but a means; in fact it is a means twice over. It is a means to accomplish the strategic military objective, and a means to accomplish the political objective. Consequently, the means in war, the "combat," as a "trial of strength," need not be a trial by physical forces only. The moral forces of the enemy are even more significant, and this refers both to the will of those responsible for carrying on the war and to the "heart and sentiments" of the people.[60] (In the Tet offensive in the Vietnam War, the North Vietnamese and Viet-Cong suffered militarily more than did the U.S. forces, but they won in terms of the publicity image received by the U.S. public.) In today's states, as we will comment on later, those responsible can often include, in varying degrees, all citizens.

Clausewitz wrote at the time in the North Atlantic area when war was becoming "total."[61] Total war may be described as that armed conflict between states wherein all the adult citizens and all pervasive institutions are mobilized for the effort. By urging that leaders attend to war as "a continuation of politics by other means," Clausewitz indirectly acknowledged that, in some sense, war was "total" from now on. But his insistence that war was never "Absolute" in the concrete contributed to all the major elements in the tradition of ethics in war, even though the ethical questions were not his main interest. Rather his emphasis was on how going to war or how the limitations on the military force in war were reasonable because they were instruments of political policy.

At many points he made a case for the military and political reasonableness of guidelines for war that have direct crossover application to the Just War tradition. Two things emerge. The ethical themes prior to his time gain some confirmation for their real world usefulness. Also, since Clausewitz has been so influential for twentieth century political and military thinking, there is a basis for arguing that the Just War tradition is still useful, even amidst the political and military changes that have occurred.

NOTES

(1) G.W.F. Hegel, Philosophy of Right, tr. T.M. Knox (London: Oxford, 1967), 324R.
(2) Peter F. Butler, "Legitimacy in a States System: Vattel's Law of Nations," in The Reasons of State, ed. Michael Donelan (London: George Allen, 1978), 45.
(3) The Law of Nations, or The Principles of the Law of Nature Applied to the Conduct and Affairs of Nations and Sovereigns, tr. Joseph Chitty (Johnson, 1863), Prelims, 6, 11.
(4) Law of Nations, Prelims, 10.
(5) Law of Nations, I, i, 1-3.
(6) Law of Nations, Prelims, 12.
(7) Law of Nations, Prelims, 14.
(8) Law of Nations, Prelims, 7.
(9) Law of Nations, Prelims, 28.
(10) Law of Nations, Prelims, 21.
(11) Law of Nations, I, ii, 15 and 16.
(12) Law of Nations, III, iii, 42.
(13) Law of Nations, II, xv, 219-221.
(14) Law of Nations, II, xii, 160.
(15) Law of Nations, IV, iv, 40.
(16) Law of Nations, II, i, 3.
(17) Law of Nations, Prelims, 18.
(18) Law of Nations, Prelims, 16.
(19) Law of Nations, II, i, 2, 8-9.
(20) Law of Nations, Prelims, 21.
(21) Law of Nations, III, xii, 190.
(22) Law of Nations, III, iii, 39-40.
(23) Law of Nations, III, xii, 191.
(24) Law of Nations, III, xii, 192.
(25) Law of Nations, III, iii, 26, 37.
(26) Law of Nations, III, iii, 38.
(27) Law of Nations, III, iii, 41.
(28) Law of Nations, III, iii, 42.
(29) Law of Nations, III, iii, 44.
(30) Law of Nations, III, iii, 49.
(31) Law of Nations, III, xiii, 195-196.
(32) A Compendium of the Law of Nations Founded on Treaties and Customs of the Modern Nations of Europe, 1788.
(33) Compendium, Intro, 1 and 2.
(34) Compendium, Intro, 4.
(35) Terry Nardin, Law, Morality, and the Relations of States (Princeton: Princeton University Press, 1983), p. 64.
(36) See Hedley Bull, The Anarchical Society (New York: Columbia University Press, 1977), p. 202.
(37) Martens, Compendium, II, ch. 1, 1.

124

(38) Compendium, II, ch. 1, 2.
(39) Compendium, VIII, ch. 1, 1 and 3.
(40) Compendium, VIII, ch. 3, 1.
(41) Carl von Clausewitz, On War, ed. and trans, by Michael Howard and Peter Paret (Princeton: Princeton University Press, 1976), I, 1, 2. Excellect recent secondary books on Clausewitz include Peter Paret, Clausewitz and the State (New York: Oxford, 1976), and Raymond Aron, Clausewitz: Philosopher of War, trans. by Christine Booker and Norman Stone (Englewood Cliffs, N.J.: Prentice-Hall, 1985).
(42) On War, I, 1, 2.
(43) See last part of On War, III, c. 16, on "fencing" and the former ideal of finesse in "cabinet-wars." Yet contrast this with VI, c. 30.
(44) See Paret, Clausewitz and the State, 368.
(45) On War, I, 1, 6.
(46) On War, I, 1, 10.
(47) On War, I, 1, 11.
(48) On this see On War, III, 16, and Paret Clausewitz and the State, 366-367.
(49) On War, I, 1, 20.
(50) On War, I, 1, 21.
(51) On War, I, 1, 23.
(52) On War, I, 1, 23.
(53) On War, I, 1, 24.
(54) On War, I, 1, 24.
(55) In VI, c. 30, Clausewitz noted that the change in modes from cabinet wars to total war was due more to new situations and social relations than to new inventions. Thus total war itself need not remain forever the style of war. That the strategies of war must change is a point in which he consciously agreed with Machiavelli. See Paret, Clausewitz and the State, 170, and Aron, Clausewitz: Philosopher of War, 198.
(56) On War, I, 1, 28. See also, Paret, Clausewitz and the State, 368-370, and Aron, Clausewitz: Philosopher of War, 66-67, 118-119.
(57) On War, I, 1, 28.
(58) On War, I, 2 (Paret tr., 119). See Paret, Clausewitz and the State, 369.
(59) On War, III, cc. 3-6,8.
(60) On War, III, c. 17.
(61) On War, I, 1, 23.

CHAPTER EIGHT

U.S. POSITIVISM AND MILITARY NECESSITY

A. Positivistic Thought in the United States

In the penultimate sentence of the Declaration of Independence, Thomas Jefferson wrote:

> We... declare that these United Colonies... as free and independent states... have the full power to levy war, conclude peace, contract alliances... and to do all other acts and things which independent states may of right do.

And, thirteen years later, the Constitution of the United States was written wherein Congress was given the power:

> To define and punish Piracies and Felonies committed on the high Seas, and offenses against the Law of Nations; To declare War, grant Letters of Marque and Reprisal, and make Rules concerning Captures on Land and Water; To raise and support Armies... To provide and maintain a Navy... To make Rules for the Government and Regulation of the land and naval Forces; To provide for calling forth the Militia to execute the Laws of the Union, suppress Insurrections and repel invasions; To provide for organizing, arming, and disciplining the Militia. [Article I, section 8]

The Constitution claims that Congress decides when to go to war, and how to fight the war. This is a claim to sovereignty even over international treaties and customs, even though the Constitution also says that approved treaties become part of the law of the land.

Since Congress is representative of the people, the United States accepts in theory the positivistic position that war is the use of military force between peoples. Hostile actions against entire populations makes sense in this model.

126

In practice, the United States has acted with shifting emphasis on natural law and positivistic principles in interpreting international policy. Perhaps the clearest evidence of its positivistic side is the claim that the will of the legislature and not some natural law ius ad bellum determines when to go to war and defines and punishes offenses against the Law of Nations. Ius in bello considerations are subordinated to the right of Congress to make rules for the Government and Regulation of the land and naval Forces. In practice, the authority to make such rules for warfare were delegated to military leaders.

The first major American statement of such rules was "Instructions for the Government of Armies of the United States in the Field," prepared by Francis Lieber, a professor at Columbia University, at the request of President Lincoln, and revised by a board of U.S. Army offiers. These came during the Civil War and were issued as General Order No. 100 of the Secretary of War on 24 April, 1863. Its background was as follows.

Early in the war, the Army of the North employed the strategy of Jomini, which was dominant then at West Point. The principle was to seize and control strategic points. Fighting was done to capture such points, to deny to the enemy those places from which to fight advantageously. Killing enemy soldiers was only involved in this strategy as necessary to accomplish such control. The tactics were those necessary to concentrate more pressure on a given spot than the enemy would be able to resist if things came to a fight. This pressure forced the enemy commander, if he acted rationally, to retreat or surrender. It was basically a war of position. Henry Wager Halleck was the general-in-chief of the North and was convinced of the soundness of such strategy.

After many reversals, Lincoln put General U.S. Grant in charge of the Northern Armies. Grant, starting at Shiloh, employed the strategy advocated by Clausewitz which was to aim directly at the destruction of the enemy's forces. He aimed at beating the enemy in pitched battle. The Civil War became a war of positive attrition. Such head-on fighting as this involved was the strategy of the United States Army until Douglas MacArthur. (A strategy of negative attrition, also from Clausewitz, would involve avoiding head-on battles in the effort to exhaust the men, materiel, and morale of the enemy.)

It is worthy of note that neither the Jominian nor the Clausewitzian strategies is particularly sensitive to non-combatants in the area. And while in his work Lieber stated that there are limits to the hostile acts toward the enemies, he also stated that all citizens of hostile states are to be considered enemies, even though some are noncombatant.

Any limitation on killing of the enemies is due to the consideration of the political end of the war (and so of the rationale of the war itself), which, in turn, justifies only the killing, but all the killing, that is necessary to achieve it.

> Modern wars are not internecine wars, in which the killing of the enemy is the object. The destruction of the enemy in modern war, and, indeed, modern war itself, are means to obtain that object of the belligerent which lies beyond the war.[1]

As Clausewitz insisted, the limits within war are dependent upon the political object of the war.

In an early work, Lieber had argued that war shifts standards of morality but does not eliminate them. There is a moral difference between various usages of military force that happen during a war.

> War does not rest on the contest of argument or reason; but it by no means absolves us from all obligation toward the enemy, on various grounds. They result in part from the object of war, in part from the fact, that the belligerents are human beings; that the declaration of war is, among civilized nations, always made upon the tacit obligations of certain usages and obligations, and partly because wars take place between masses who fight for others, not for themselves only.
> I have not the right to injure my enemy privately, that is, without reference to the general object of the war, or the general object of the battle. We do not injure in war in order to injure, but to obtain the object of war. All cruelty,

that is, unnecessary infliction of suffering, therefore, remains cruelty as among private individuals. All suffering inflicted upon persons who do not impede my way, for instance surgeons or inoffensive persons, if it can possibly be avoided, is criminal; all turning the war to private ends..., all use of arms, or the power which I enjoy as a soldier, for private purposes, as, for instance, the satisfaction of lust; all unnecessary destruction of private property is criminal; all avoidable destruction of works of art or science, in particular, and all unnecessary destruction of any kind is criminal.... So soon as an enemy is rendered harmless by wounds or captivity, he is no longer an enemy.... I ought not only to abstain from injuring the harmless, but I ought to protect them against the unlawful attack of others, simply because this becomes a perfectly private case.[2]

One finds here a continuation of the tradition distinguising violence done as a private individual and violence done as an agent of a social institution. But combined with Lieber's positivistic assumption ["can inflict any necessary (to the object of the war) suffering"], the distinction has important ramifications for duties toward noncombatants. Any restraints against attacking noncombatants could slacken if the aims of war are broadly defined, since all in the enemy land have some public dimension to their lives.

The nearest thing to a general statement of official policy on noncombatants is a letter by General Halleck to General Rosecrans distinguishing three classes of "civilians" in the secession states: those who were loyal to the Union, those who were not loyal but who did not act hostile to the Union, and those who, even though they did not bear arms, still did actions (e.g., spying) hostile to the Union.[3] Halleck's position was different than Lieber's. A month before General Order #100, he made a list, similar to lists in the late Middle Ages, of noncombatants. He listed three reasons to respect such a list at all times. (a) The limits of retributive justice forbid harming non-resistant enemies. (b) Such respect is self-evidently demanded

129

to civilized persons. (c) The hope that the enemy will treat one's own noncombatants reciprocally.[4]

Both Halleck and Lieber held that war itself should be as intense as possible for two reasons. An intense war likely would be short, thus saving lives in the long run. And the fear of an intense war would be a deterrent against entering many frivolous wars.

General Order No. 100 itself was instigated by a request from Halleck to Lieber who requested a paper outlining the moral limits of tactics by guerrilla bands ("irregulars"). Lieber answered along the following lines.

Guerrillas should be under military discipline and operate in direct aid of, and so submit to the authority of, a regular army. The reasoning here was that, if one assimilates guerrillas to the public form of war, they could be ordered to refrain from acting in a criminal manner. But then one should spell out precisely what is allowed to regular soldiers in wartime. Hence Lieber suggested what became General Order No. 100. There was a need for such a general directive since, by the middle of the Civil War, it became obvious that leaders had to spell out the external moral and legal controls that would restrain a war when that war was fought by large popular armies that had come together in the service of goals so high they seemed to justify anything.[5]

The heart of General Order No. 100 is the positivistic treatment of "military necessity."

> Military necessity, as understood by modern civilized nations, consists in the necessity of those measures which are indispensible for securing the ends of war, and which are lawful according to the modern law and usages of war.
> Military necessity admits of all direct destruction of life or limb of armed enemies, and of other persons whose destruction is incidentally unavoidable in the armed contests of the war; it allows of the capturing of every armed enemy, and every enemy of importance to the hostile government, or of peculiar danger to the captor; it allows of all destruction of property, and obstruction of the ways and

130

channels of traffic, travel, or communication, and of all withholding of sustenance or means of life from the enemy; of the appropriation of whatever an enemy's country affords necessary for the subsistence and safety of the army, and of such deception as does not involve the breaking of good faith either positively pledged, regarding agreements entered into during the war, or supposed by the modern law of war to exist. Men who take up arms against one another in public war do not cease on this account to be moral beings, responsible to one another and to God.[6]

This interesting section says that nothing is apriori excluded, but uses undefined items such as "necessity," "indispensable," or "unavoidable." Perhaps the only real limit is the concept of "public" as distinct from "private." All use of military force for private gain or out of private motive is prohibited. But any distinction between combatant and noncombatant is significantly altered by the reclassification as armed enemy and unarmed enemy.

This instruction was the first of the modern type of field manual on the laws of war. Its most outstanding omission was the lack of a comprehensive treatment of the duties of belligerents toward noncombatants. Actually the omission probably reflected the general acceptance of established customs already in international law and military practice. But such customs were strained during the Civil War conditions, where propaganda on both sides warned of the rapacity of enemy soldiers, and marauding bands, the foraging of regulars, and organized raids behind enemy lines gave credence to the propaganda.

B. Military Necessity

One of the fundamentally troublesome elements in any positivistic approach to international law is the set of assumptions on the status of individual people. Since the rise of democratic theories, the people of a nation have been looked upon as the sovereign political entity at issue, with the government somehow as merely the instrument of the people. The problem here is that, as individuals, people have no international standing in the positivistic structure, only states do. War is an action of state, yet most of ius in bello thinking has made the effects on people of the physical violence of war an essential issue. One consequence is that the positivists premise any mention of ius in bello limitations with the priority of state sovereignty and military necessity.

Most positivistic efforts have sought to alleviate the sufferings caused by war. (Note: this is not the same as affirming any immunity status.) If military necessity involves doing things that are "harmful to the enemy" in the sense of physical force against life, liberty, or property, no infliction of sufferings on civilians may apriori be ruled out, but only those acts and practices mentioned at least in general terms by agreement.

The appeal to military necessity exemplifies once again the hypocritical imperative. Even if those making the appeal are not subjectively honest about it, the appeal itself evidences that there is an operative standard for limits to in bello destruction and discrimination. Given the ad bellum political judgment about going to war, the in bello military strategy, tactics, and activities have their proper objectives, targets, and dynamics. The appeal to military necessity is compatible with the traditional assumption of a hierarchy of values in which societal values are over individual values. It also might be seen as substantiation of Clausewitz's analysis of war as an instrument of policy. The fact that a state has elected war as an instrument of its policy would indicate that, insofar as going to war is justified, then whatever is necessary in the war on the in bello level is justified. Conversely, the need for the appeal indicates the acknowledgement that whatever destruction of life, liberty, or property is not necessary is not justified. As Marshall Cohen well notes, the principle of military necessity can only be understood in the context of the distinction of combatants and non-combatants.[7] But the principle implies that there may be proportional reasons that call for the use of military force against non-combatants, at least as a "second effect." There certainly were precedents in the tradition.

It is never lawful to kill innocent persons, even unintentionally, except when there is no other means of carrying on the operations of a just war.[8]

> If the end is lawful, the necessary means are also lawful. And so, in the entire course and duration of a war, virtually nothing can be done which contains injustice, except the direct killing of innocent persons. For all other damages are ordinarily judged necessary for attaining the end of war.[9]

> A just and unavoidable necessity makes anything lawful.[10]

> The first rule: In war the things which are necessary for attaining the end are lawful.[11]

The thrust here is that necessity can at times make doing physical evil moral. (This, of course, is different from the question of validating the actual necessity which, thanks to the hypocritical imperative, is not essential to the discussion here.) The appeal to necessity would involve two phases: that there is going to be a bad result with respect to some value; and that some action which will lead to that bad result is still reasonable to do because of some other value. These two phases would seem to suggest that the action is understood to be reasonable because of the application of either the principle of the double effect or the principle of the lesser evil.

However, as Cohen suggests, the concept of "military necessity" is much like the concepts of due process or fair price.[12] In other words, it is a formal concept that gains substantive content from people in action who make reasonable decisions guided by the ideal as well as generalizations from past sets of decision by similarly situated people. The formal concept is primarily attitudinal, that is, it signals an important value and prompts consideration of the value insofar as the value is proportional to other values involved.

The answer to the question "who decides" has in practice been the commanders on the scene or their superiors. This actually is an reflection back to the origins of in bello standards in the self-imposed standards of the knights. Out of their chivalric code they decided how to act nobly in reference to what

133

targets were valid. In time there came lists of classes specifying who were and who were not valid targets in war. The terms "nocent" and "innocent" named the two sets in the lists. But with the emergence of citizen involvement with the French Revolution and guerrilla war, and the theoretical responsibility and loyalty of all citizens in modern societies, the earlier guidelines have not always been adequate for commanders during a war. These developments called forth the principle of "military necessity". The claim of military necessity appeals to some ethical standard that pertains to the relation between in bello proportionality and discrimination. The major questions it confronts are: could the life, liberty, and property of unarmed citizens ever valid in bello targets; are there still some who belong to those sets of possible targets that are absolutely prohibited?

In the Army field manual of 1917, there is this expression of principles:

> First, that a belligerent is justified in applying any amount and any kind of force which is necessary for the purpose of the war; that is, the complete submission of the enemy at the earliest possible moment with the least expenditure of men and money. Second, the principle of humanity, which says that all such kinds and degrees of violence as are not necessary for the purpose of war are not permitted to a belligerent.[13]

In the Army field manual of 1956, there is this passage:

> The prohibitory effect of the law of war is not minimized by "military necessity" which has been defined as that principle which justifies those measures not forbidden by international law which are indispensable for securing the complete submission of the enemy as soon as possible. Military necessity has been generally rejected as a defense for acts forbidden by the customary and conventional laws of war inasmuch as the latter have been developed and framed with consideration for the concept of military necessity.[14]

134

The 1917 version clearly ranks the two values, the military necessity is always superior in any conflict between it and the principle of "humanity." This version does not seem to add anything to General Order No. 100 in this regard. The political objective justifies the military objectives, which in turn justify what activities are "necessary," and this necessity justifies the killing and destruction involved.

The 1956 version seems to add something new. It envisions a different relation, wherein the ranking of the two principles is the same except there are some measures and actions that have been set beyond appeal to present military necessity. It seems to say that external to the political objective - military objective - military necessity schema is a set of customary and conventional laws that cannot be overridden in the name of military necessity, and which laws add substantively to the limits on military killing and destruction. However, the last phrase suggests that the laws themselves were formulated with the demands of military necessity in mind. Apparently this indicates that whatever is of military necessity can be found appropriate by the laws.

But this should cause no surprise. For a presupposition of the conventional and customary laws is the sovereignty of each state, which includes the right of each state to decide its political objectives. It would be inconsistent for the international consensus to accept state sovereignty and self-help and yet call upon the same agent-states to refrain from doing acts necessary for political objectives. And military objectives are means to achieve such political objectives (in that thinking described by Clausewitz).

Comments by two contemporary writers are worthy of inclusion here. Michael Walzer correctly emphasizes that the normal phrasing of the principle of military necessity justifies "not only whatever is necessary to win the war, but also whatever is necessary to reduce the risks of losing, or simply to reduce losses or the likelihood of losses....In fact, it is not about necessity at all; it is ...a hyperbolic way of speaking, about probability and risk."[15] "Necessary" means "that without which another event will not occur." To advance, a soldier may have to kill an enemy soldier. To take this town,

the army may have to fight a battle. These are
necessities, but they are conditional, conditional on
the adoption of this tactic or this strategy. And
there is always a range of options in both. Unless
"military necessity" is vacuous as a guide, the
concept will authorize certain choices of means to a
particular military goal, but not others, certain
choices of strategy, but not others.

Walzer distinguishes two levels on which the
concept of military necessity works.[16] The one level
is that of strategy: the odds of victory will be
improved and lives saved if x operation is done. The
second level is that of the political value of victory
itself. Unfortunately, Walzer here restricts what
could be necessary about victory in war to that of
survival as an independent nation. Other values in
victory he thinks would be in the realm of
unnecessitated options for a military commander. Such
a position would mean that military necessity could,
on this level, authorize force against non-combatants
only if the survival of one's own nation were at
stake. This at best seems an intuitional ideal, but
it would eliminate use of military necessity as a
guide when other ius ad bellum justifications were
operative. And it omits the relation of the ad bellum
proportionality significance to the in bello risk of
killing of non-combatants. It is not part of the
tradition for wars other than for national survival to
rank non-combatant immunity at the status of an
absolute (apriori sovereign) value.

Thomas Nagel argues that military necessity is
limited as a justification by certain absolute
prohibitions which say that it is not allowable to do
certain things and "no argument about what will happen
if one doesn't do them can show that doing them would
be all right."[17] Thereby he joins others, such as
Elizabeth Anscombe, who advocate a new idea to the
tradition: the absolute limit on in bello
justifications from non-combatant immunity.

He accepts that, if those "certain things" are
not involved, then the utilitarian reasoning of
"military necessity" is valid. But those "certain
things" are apriori sovereign in any conflict with
military necessity. He warns that utilitarian
considerations are especially liable to violate the
"certain things" when the goal in mind is phrased in
terms of the "usual speculations about the future of

freedom, peace, and economic prosperity."

Nagel is writing toward the end of the U.S. involvement in the Vietnam war, but his position would also tell against revolutionary wars with goals of "justice, peace, and liberation."

Nagel identifies these "certain things" with the principle that "hostile treatment of any person must be justified in terms of something <u>about</u> <u>that</u> <u>person</u> which makes the treatment appropriate."[18] The principle, of course, is merely formal, for it itself it does not specify what about the person could qualify as making the hostile treatment appropriate. Much contemporary thought holds all citizens of an enemy country to be enemies just by being citizens of that country. Would that make hostile treatment appropriate? If not, what more about the person must there be? And how would one know where to draw the line?

He makes these elaborations of his formal principle:

"One consequence of this condition will be that certain persons may not be subjected to hostile treatment in war at all, since nothing about them justifies such treatment. Others will be proper objects of hostility only in certain circumstances, or when they are engaged in certain pursuits. And the appropriate manner and extent of hostile treatment will depend on what is justified by the particular case."[19]

This approach, says Nagel, treats others as persons even as one does hostile acts against them and avoids the moral despair of either pacifism or naturalism. It treats the others who are objects of hostile treatment as persons and not as merely means. But it does this by making the hostile treatment appropriate to some characteristic about them as persons.[20] But this returns to the question of what is to count.

In his analysis of the moral connection between the two levels of justification, Nagel has <u>in bello</u> putting limits on <u>ad bellum</u>: some kinds of acts are not permitted no matter the consequences. He rules out extrinsic justification of killing non-combatants.

The traditional position has generally been that the common good is above individual goods and that the military commanders on the spot are the best guides for any limitations. Nagel might have a precedent in the Chivalric tradition of the knight's refusal, no matter the consequences, to kill a defenseless, even if otherwise hostile, party, even if such a one is being used by an enemy (e.g., as a hostage to cover an escape). But today this may lead to consequences so much more severe to an entire group that a qualitative difference comes about (e.g., in charging Vietcong who strapped children to their chests).

One can see formally the distinction Nagel has in mind: to distinguish hostile acts against people as the most expedient or least costly or only possible way to achieve some goal, from hostile acts against people because of certain "real or presumed characteristics or activities of the person which are thought to justify" the hostile acts.

In sum, his position on the use of violence in war in terms of military necessity is curtailed by "the maintenance of a direct interpersonal response to the people one deals with is a requirement which no advantages can justify one in abandoning."[21]

Even if Nagel's absolutist principle could be used by individual soldiers, it would be inapplicable to strategical or even tactical decisions by commanders. And these are the more probable locations for decisions involving military necessity. Except in terms of ruling out indiscriminate attacks, the principle probably will not function.

His major omission is the failure to explain how the responsibility of citizens relates to his principle for appropriate treatment. Is being a citizen one of the "certain circumstances", or acting as a loyal citizen being "engaged in" one of the "certain pursuits" he acknowledges as identifiers of valid targets in war? Would there then be an "appropriate manner and extent of hostile treatment" justified by the responsibility of citizenship? Could the distinction made by Lieber and others between armed enemy and unarmed enemy be important for in bello discrimination? Nagel seems to keep elements of the earlier discrimination based on class role within society but yet hint in his formal principle the modern classlessness that comes from common citizenship.

The benefit of the use of international law was to give a more orderly way of thinking about international problems. Yet it has failed as a theory of international relations because "its own theoretical presuppositions have so little relevance to many of the more urgent and tragic problems of international society as a whole." For example, "It has paid too little attention to the intimate relation between political objectives or national interests and the willingness of nations to abide by principles and rules of law." Also, "It has been seen as a Western product, leading to its rejection by nations emerging from a status where legal principles allegedly worked against them."[22]

NOTES

(1) "Instructions for the Government of Armies of the United States in the Field," General Order # 100 of the Secretary of War, 24 April, 1863, sect. III, para. 68.
(2) Manual of Political Ethics (Boston: Little and Brown, vol. I, 1838; vol. II, 1839), vol. II, 657-658. Quoted in J. T. Johnson, Just War Tradition and the Restraint of War (Princeton: Princeton University Press, 1981), 299.
(3) Letter from Halleck to Rosencrans, "On the Treatment of Disloyal Persons Within Our Lines," Mar. 15, 1863.
(4) See J.T. Johnson, Just War Tradition, 300n.
(5) Johnson, Just War Tradition, 322.
(6) Gen. Inst. #100, sect. I, paras. 14-16.
(7) "Morality and the Laws of War," in V. Held, S. Morgenbesser, and T. Nagel, eds. Philosophy, Morality, and International Affairs (New York: Oxford University Press, 1974), 84.
(8) Francisco Vitoria, De Indis et de jure belli relectiones, ed. Ernest Nys, tr. John Pawley Bate (Carnegie Institute, 1917), 37. See also, 35, 41, 42, 52.
(9) Francisco Suarez, De bello, in De Triplici Virtute Theologica Fide, Spe, et Caritate, tr. by G.L. Williams, A. Brown, and J. Waldron (Oxford: Clarendon, 1944), VII, 6. See also, VII, 15-17.
(10) Alberico Gentili, De jure belli libri tres, tr. by John C. Rolfe (Oxford: Clarendon, 1933), III, 12. See also, III, 2 and 23.
(11) Hugo Grotius, De jure belli ac pacis libri tres,

tr. Francis W. Kelsey, et al. (Oxford, 1925) III, 1, 2, title. "We ought not to attempt anything which may prove the destruction of innocents, unless for some extraordinary reason and the safety of many." III, 11, 8.
(12) "Morality and the Laws of War," 75.
(13) U.S. Dept. of War, Rules of Land Warfare, para. 9 (1917) [War Dept. Doc. No. 467, Office of the Chief of Staff, approved April 25, 1914, 34. Quoted in Cohen, 72.
(14) U.S. Dept. of the Army, The Laws of Land Warfare, para. 3 (1956) [Dept. of Army manual FM 27-10], 34-35. Quoted in Cohen, 73.
(15) Just and Unjust Wars (New York: Basic Books, 1977), 144.
(16) Just and Unjust Wars, 240-241.
(17) "War and Massacre," Phil. and Public Affairs 1 (1972, 128.
(18) "War and Massacre," 133.
(19) "War and Massacre," 133-134.
(20) "War and Massacre," 136.
(21) "War and Massacre," 136. For a critique of Nagel, see Joseph Margolis, "The Concepts of War and Peace," Social Theory and Practice 6 (1980), 219-220.
(22) Kenneth Thompson, Understanding World Politics (Notre Dame: Notre Dame University Press, 1975), 168.

CHAPTER NINE

ANALYSIS OF JUST WAR TRADITION: I

Justum est bellum quibus necessarium; et
pia arma quibus nulla nisi in armis
relinquitur spes.[1]

There is no one theory of "just war" in Western
thought, but there is a tradition that runs through
the many different theories and arguments. And, as is
true of second-level principles generally, the content
in the specifications of the tradition has changed as
new situations and circumstances forced new moral
decisions. Thus it is appropriate to do an analysis
and a critique in order to uncover guiding questions
for an ethics of war and other international
relations.

Perhaps there never has been a totally just war.
But then perhaps there never has been a totally
virtuous person. Neither fact reduces the usefulness
of clarifying the standards involved or having them in
the first place. For intuitively we do morally
distinguish between persons and intuitively we, most
of us at least, do morally distinguish between wars.
The just war, like the virtuous person, is a more or
less reality.

One might note that the usual term "just war" is
slightly improper. What has always been at issue is
"justified war," that is, whether war can be ethical.
But the term is too settled in tradition to make it
worth the effort to change it.

Before taking up the elements that have occurred
rather continuously in the tradition, one might also
query what kind of justice is meant in the term "just
war." One can identify at least the following kinds.

There is contributive justice in the sense that
governmental decision makers owe the duty in justice
to all citizens to provide for the common good of the
nation, which would include both immediate defense and
long range conditions in the international situation.
Much of the tradition stressed it was reasonable to
use military force to prevent or curtail that wrongful
use of force which took life, liberty, or property on
a social scale.

There is retributive justice in that there was concern about setting right a wrong already suffered and punishing those who caused the wrong. The import here is to assert in actions that there are values which one state or the international system does not passively allow to be violated deliberately by an country.[2]

There is also contributive justice in the sense that each citizen owes duty in justice to act for the common good by cooperating with those official decisions to provide for the common good of the nation.

I. IUS AD BELLUM

The general theme in all ius ad bellum elements is that the recourse to military force in war is moral only if certain conditions of state are satisfied.

(A) AUTHORITY.

The consensus has been that only certain office holders may call the state to war. Reference ordinarily was made either to those in the office morally responsible for the public common good, or in the office that expresses the state's sovereign power. Always involved here has been the distinction between killing as a private individual and killing as a citizen who acts under the competence of one's office and is to act for the public common good.

In early feudal times, local bishops and local lords had seen their way to engage in military action on their own initiative for the sake of honor and power and prize. As a way to eliminate this bane in Western Europe, the Canon lawyers especially repeatedly insisted that it was required for a war to be called by a "sovereign," a hierarchical office "above the law." The pertinent authority could be either one of the princes or the pope, "who are competent to wage war because of their office."[3] This grounded the crucial distinction between bellum and duellum, and was the medieval assumption for the distinction between killing as a private individual, which was rather consistently forbidden except in immediate self-defense, and killing as a citizen, under the authority of the sovereign, either as public executioner or as military soldier.

For Aquinas, the political public good was hierarchically supreme among human goods.[4] The role of the hierarchical ruler, the prince, was to promote the common good. When this public common good was threatened, either by external aggression or internal disruption of order, the prince could marshall the forces needed to respond. This power, including political power over life and death, Aquinas termed "perfect coercive power."[5] The argument ran thusly: the good of the whole is rationally preferred to the good of the part when the latter threatens the former.[6] But only the prince, or someone authorized by the prince, could ethically intend the death of a human being for the sake of the common good.[7] Aquinas was quite aware that a bad prince could abuse such power for personal advantage. But he eventually argued that the public coercive power belongs to the office, not the person.[8]

In the early modern period, theorists such as Vitoria and Grotius extended the set of legitimate rulers to those beyond Christian Europe. And with the rise of state sovereignty, with each state conceived of as a "perfect society" complete unto itself, each prince was considered to be empowered to call a war on his own authority. This "competence of war" (competence de guerre) was not so much an expression of the prince as someone hierarchically authorized by the deity to promote the public good, but an expression that the state, as a whole, was in control of its own destiny through the office of the prince. Clausewitz's analysis that the fundamental rationality of war was as a political act of the state was external support for the requirement of proper authority. The "competence of war" was never disputed even in positivist efforts, by various pacts, to make going to war "illegal."

Three major ethical problems that occur today in reference to the _ius_ _ad_ _bellum_ authority element are the matters of contributive justice within a state, the matters of the distribution of responsibility for the collective acts of the state, and the matters concerning revolutionary wars within a state and external intervention in them. We have commented on the first in reference to pacifism. Here I would add only that the tradition favors the citizen's obedience to the decisions of the governmental in going to war.

Augustine argued that the soldier must obey the commands of superiors as long as moral evil is not evident in them, that is, if the war is not clearly against the law of God, or clearly is not against the law of God.[9] Throughout the tradition of justified war, this position is maintained that following legitimate civil authority is acting for the civil good and a duty of all citizens.

> If subjects in a case of doubt do not follow their prince to war, they expose themselves to the risk of betraying their state to the enemy, and this is a much more serious thing than fighting against the enemy despite a doubt.[10]

Suarez argued that the presumptive duty was to obey the prince because disobedience might entail "serious and general misfortune" to the state whereas the worst that could occur in obedience was the commission of a minor injustice.[11]

But the writers also make a distinction between the presumptive duty to obey and the obligation on the part of the private citizen to examine the justice of the cause of the war. This is important, both because of the question of the moral participation by the individual in the war and also because of the question of the responsibility of the individual for the war. Let's take the two in turn.

If one were able, by intellectual ability and access to adequate facts, then the individual was obliged to make a personal judgment on the justice of the war before one could participate. If one judged the war was unjust, then one had to follow one's judgment, even if one objectively were wrong.[12]

A word of caution is in place. Since many contemporary claims make an appeal to individual conscience to justify refusal to participate in a war, some important elaborations of this element in the tradition ought to be added.

First, the one refusing must have made reasonably thorough and open examination. One who held a position based one one-sided study, on easily counter-pointed premises, or, worst of all, on emotional slogans, would not qualify as one who had come morally to a judgment of refusal. In our day of visual images, the physical evils of war are more impressive than any proferred justice of the cause. This places a burden both on the leaders and on the individual citizens that they give honest consideration to whether the (ad bellum) cause and the (in bello) military targets are proportional to the physical evils of the war.

The appeal to conscience is valid only if the examination already has been adequate, for conscience generally has not been understood to supply content to the judgment itself about justness of the war. Conscience is temporally posterior to that judgment and is about consequent action by the individual. The import of the integrity of conscience is that one is obliged to act consonant with one's prior judgment on the morality of one's subsequent action (of participating).

It would be too extreme to say that individual citizens would never be in position to judge the morality of a war. But the weight of tradition says that one may not refuse to go to war when the reasons for and the reasons against the justice of the war seem equal, since this condition is one of "speculative" doubt only, and inadquate to refuse a command from a legitimate civil authority. However, the tradition also insists that one must avoid the "rash judgment" on the objective truth (subjective good faith on either side is not the issue) of either side. So unless the "doing of the act" is clearly wrong, the citizen is justified by the prima facie authority of the civil leader.

The tradition does not suggest that all in society can do such an examination. The tradition assumes a majority-minority class structure to be a truth about every society. Most citizens are incompetent to judge the objective justice of a war because of their undisciplined reasoning faculties and because it has not been possible to explain all the reasons to them.[13] But a minority of citizens are competent in varying degrees.[14] Since it is not possible ever to anticipate more specifically on who and when, Juan de Lugo concluded that the entire problem of citizen judgment is not resolvable in the theoretical order.[15]

Yet there is a balancing theme in the tradition on the responsibility of individual citizens for the war. Grotius held that, since modern states acted through their governmental leader, all citizens were responsible for their leader's action international actions. Nevertheless he rejected the concept of collective guilt, both because the citizens can support and act for the state from motives that in general are civilly virtuous, and because merit, as distinct from responsibility, belongs only to individuals, not to groups. Lieber held that all citizens in the enemy territory were of the enemy, even if some were unarmed. And the U.S. Catholic bishops assert: "In a democracy, the responsibility of the nation and that of its citizens coincide."[16] Yet the bishops immediately add: "Americans share responsibility for the current situation, and cannot evade responsibility for trying to resolve it." This certainly assumes an authority status for citizens, but it is ambiguous how the "sharing" exists and what is the range of feasible options for specific actions that the individual has in "trying to resolve" the "current situation."

In a democratic republic, such as the United States, the people as a collectivity at least theoretically are "sovereign." This means those who belong to the people are in some sense responsible for the actions, especially the international actions, of their government. But this has never been given satisfactory reflection. For instance, it would be an obvious fallacy of division to move immediately from an collective responsibility of the people to an individual responsibility for any particular citizen. Yet it is important to locate individual citizen responsibility in order to clarify what actions by the individual citizen are called for, and also what justifiable action by the enemy can be taken against the individual citizen. (This latter will be taken up under in bello discrimination.)

If a private citizen or office holder becomes convinced after open, non-partisan examination, that the country's war is essentially unjust, what should that citizen or office holder do? The question does not admit of any easy and single answer, since the circumstances determine the feasible options (e.g., public protest, cooperate somewhat out of valid patriotism while attempting to mitigate the evil, a private refusal to cooperate any further, flee the

146

country, etc.). Much depends on the level of responsibility for the individual, the reasonable options to try to effect some change, the other individuals who might be negatively affected.

We will take up matters of revolution and insurgency war a little later.

(B) JUST CAUSE

The element of _causa_ _belli_ is consistently required by authors from Cicero to contemporary positivists. On this element there is formal agreement, even though the consensus on what would count as a justifying cause has changed with historical circumstances. However, one point has become rather consistently held: the cause must be able to be phrased so that it may be evaluated by an independent party. Consequently, causes expressed in idiosyncratic ideology that is comprehensible and acknowledged only by one of the parties involved would not satisfy the traditional requirement. (James T. Johnson traces this consensus back to the European wars of religion in the early modern period.)

The basic formal concept is that there must be a serious value threatened that is higher on a public good hierarchy than the disvalues involved in taking military action. This grounds the _ius_ _ad_ _bellum_ level of "proportionality," and makes going to war a reasonable decision. Historically such items as protection from already initiated military aggression, restoration of rights wrongfully denied, reestablishment of just order (including retaliation for specific injury), reestablishment of secure balance of power, and the overthrow of internal tyranny against the people have been claimed as just causes by different theorists.[17] Except for the last item, there has been sufficient consensus on these by decision makers.

There has not been agreement as to whether a state may enter war solely in terms of its own interest or whether it may enter war when it is not directly interested as an individual state but for the sake of the direct interest of another state or for the sake of the broader international order. Some have seen a danger in accepting a going to war for the interest of another state, even if the other state has

147

a legitimate cause for war, since the action may serve illegitimate interests of the assisting state or may exacerbate disproportionately the international order. And it certainly intrudes on the principle of self-help. Bismark, for example, cautioned:

> Every great power which endeavors outside its own sphere of interests to bring influence and pressure to bear on other lands and to direct affairs, runs a risk in going beyond the sphere which God has allotted to it. It pursues a politics of power rather than the politics of interest, and makes a bid for prestige.[18]

Yet others argue that what is at stake in contemporary international relations is qualitatively different than in some former times. Specifically, in past times, the lives of ordinary people seldom changed as the result of victory or defeat in war. But the twentieth century phenomenom of totalitarian social structures and the methods for effective control of all major phases of the lives of a people perhaps would prima facie justify war much more than in the past.

As an example, a victory for a totalitarian social polity would entail the forcible imposition of an unjust social order on the defeated polity (e.g., Nazi Germany, Soviet Russia). This imposition would be a moral evil notwithstanding the fact that the character of some of the overcome polities could be judged less unjust only by comparison. Here it is important to avoid invalid analogies (e.g., "there is no difference between this unjust government and the conquering unjust government") by careful analysis of all the major social values involved and the aims of the conquerers and the conquered, not merely those matters in which they are similar (which would be an instance of "special pleading").

In positivist and international law thought, there is no significance in terms of how just or how representative a government of a sovereign nation is. Consequently, from the time of Vitoria and Grotius until World War II and later insurgencies, each state's competence de guerre satisfied the requisite of a just cause. This meant an "ostensive justice" on both sides, but Vitoria, Grotius, and Vattel argued that allowance for this tended to reduce the virulence

148

of a war.

In addition to the hierarchy of values involved, the just cause element has included the requirements of "hope for success" and "last resort."

The requirement of "hope for success" historically has varied in accordance with the situation. It has been claimed to be more a requirement for those already conquered who think of rebellion or for those engaging in war across boundaries for causes other than self-defense. Those who fight in self-defense may be able to justify fighting to near total destruction of their polity. Suarez denied that the requirement applied to wars of defense since to go to war in defense was not a choice.[19]

The requirement seems confusing since it entails the acceptance of an unjust situation in some situations but not in others. Nevertheless, it is the backside of the ad bellum proportionality requirement. It says that acting in a just cause may at times not be worth it, yet it always is worth it if the cause is immediate defense of the social polity. But the main point is that prudence traditionally has been the controlling societal virtue above justice.

The ranking of prudence parallels but is not identical with the later Clausewitzian position that bodies politic must familiarize themselves with the thought of defeat. Since war involves great uncertainty, to be able to accept defeat when the proportionate costs for continuing are too great is worthy of civilized leaders of states. The Suarezian position was that a state should not even go to war offensively if the "reasonable hope" is not met, but should fight to the end in defense because what is at stake is the body politic itself. Clausewitz placed such a criterion at many decision points within the course of the war no matter its character of offensive or defensive.

This topic, of course, brought to the surface the relation of justice and success in war. The publicists who touched on the topic generally denied that victory in war could be used as evidence as to which side bore the stronger case for justice.[20]

It has recently become more difficult to decide what counts as "success" because of the pluralism in horizons used to interpret war. A brief examination of three common horizons will help elucidate this.

The "new era" horizon functions for those who look upon war as the means to a better future. Examples in our century are numerous: American entry into World War I to make it a "war to end all wars"; the civilizing missions of Japan in the 1930's; the renaissance of the Empire by Mussolini; the peace and justice theme of contemporary revolutionaries. Lenin called for the support of all wars that furthered the cause of international democracy and socialism.

> The socialist revolution will not be solely, or chiefly, a struggle of the revolutionary proletarians in each country against their bourgeoisie. No, it will be a struggle of all the imperialist-oppressed colonies and countries, of all dependent countries, against international imperialism.[21]

The "civilization" horizon functions for those who look upon war as the means to save some or all of civilized humanity from disaster. They are convinced not that the body politic will gain positively from the war, but that the war removes some negative threat. Albert Einstein, a life-long advocate of personal pacifism as a way to combat what he saw as the rampant militarism in nations, made an exception in the case of Nazi Germany. In reply to a request for intervention on behalf of imprisoned conscientious objectors:

> Today we face an altogether different situation....Were I a Belgian, I should not, in the present circumstances, refuse military service; rather, I should enter such service cheerfully in the belief that I would thereby be helping to save European civilization.[22]

Both the new era and the civilization horizons tend to override _ius_ _in_ _bello_ restrictions.

The "political" horizon functions for those who look upon war as a rational instrument of national policy. In varying ways, this horizon operates in the present thought of the Peoples' Republic of China, in the Soviet Union, and in the United States and Western Europe.

In the past, the requirement that war be a "last resort" assumed time for diplomacy to settle disputes and more importantly, a system of shared values by the potential belligerents. Today disputes that cause wars often have their origins in differences so basic that they are soluble only by force or by the abandonment of fundamental convictions and values. (For example, communists and non-communists in the nations of Korea and Vietnam; the differing Arab groups among themselves and opposing Israel.) In today's intersocietal tensions, often all that can be achieved outside war are "intermediate resolutions" that always remain merely that, intermediate. They are not solutions that achieve even a brief span of peace, and will show how ephemeral they are as soon as one side has the will and the power to attempt to dominate. In such situations, leaders could, except for external political pressure, decide rather quickly that there can be no other recourse than war.

Also a problem for "last resort" is the reasonable requirement of "timing." In the past, it was possible to wait until after overt military action had taken place in order to establish that one's own nation had a just cause (defense, restoration, punishment). But today, if a nation waits until it is directly attacked or until it is cut off from supplies, it often would be too late. After praising those who seek first for a peaceful compromise as being not only often right morally but also from a practical standpoint, Winston Churchill cautioned, "There is no merit in putting off a war for a year if, when it comes, it is a far worse war or one much harder to win."[23] Machiavelli noted that the Romans were wise in the timing of their actions.

> They never allowed a trouble spot to remain
> simply to avoid going to war over it,
> because they knew that wars don't just go
> away, they are only postponed to someone
> else's advantage.[24]

And Douglas MacArthur insisted that most losses of life in military action could be attributed to action being taken "too late." So a nation must decide how far along must the adversary's tactics develop before it should take action to stop them. The consensus has been that, under the principle of self-help, each state has the right to decide on the timing.

(C) RIGHT INTENTION

In natural law theory from Cicero to Grotius, the ultimate goal in going to war was always to be the subsequent condition of peace. Thus from a standpoint of sound policy, it is unreasonable to engage in belligerent actions that unnecessarily endanger the prospects for the better peace. In the modern period (at least until World War I), the European powers had as the aim the penultimate goal of a satisfactory "balance of power." Bismark's policy, "Do not exact conditions which will compel your former adversary to await his time for revenge," tried to combine some of these elements and its absence in the Treaty of Versailles is evidence of its validity.

As Augustine long ago noted, different people have quite different understandings of "peace." So it would be worthwhile to describe various types of international situations that might be called ones of peace.

There is the peace of empire, which is that peace obtained by having many nations and peoples ultimately under one political control. This is a peace internal to the empire itself.

There is the peace of hegemony, which is that peace obtained in an area of several political states, all of which defer in certain important international matters to the leadership of one of their number because of its dominant military or economic power.

There is the peace of equilibrium, which is that peace obtained in an area of several political states because of a "balance" among groups of the states in military and economic power, which balance is based on the knowledge that military or economic aggrandizement will bring about international opposition that erases any advantage.[25]

There is the peace of "liberal states." Michael W. Doyle, who did a fine study of the phenomenon of peace between liberal states, defines them as those states with four characteristics: market and private

152

property economies, polities that are externally sovereign, citizens who possess juridical rights, and "republican," representative, government.[26] Since the early nineteenth century, there has never been a war between two such states.

From the standpoint of natural law, a nation would be unjust if it entered war motivated by hatred, vengeance, or greed. [Many in the tradition held that interior hatred of the enemy violated charity, but not justice.[27]] The requirement obviously faces a psychological problem for most people during the actual belligerency, especially if one side has provoked righteous anger. The requirement must not be referring to such things. Rather, it prohibits the translation of anger into overt behavior during the war that goes beyond its political bounds (which is a crossover to the in bello level). People may have cause to want to go without limit at an enemy, but this requirement says "don't do it." It does not say, "don't even feel like doing it."

Compliance with the requirement seems pragamtically verifiable if the animosity does not continue long after the war ends (e.g., reciprocal attitudes of the U.S., Germany, and Japan during and after World War II).

For the foreign policy horizon, Clausewitz expressed the intention in war very succinctly: "War therefore is an act of violence intended to compel our opponent to fulfil our will."[28] For the new era horizon, the intention in going to war is to further the coming of the new era of peace and justice. For the civilization horizon, a nation goes to war to stave off disaster.

As a final comment on this summary, one might note that there has not been in the tradition any evident hierarchy in the three ad bellum elements of authority, cause, and intention.

NOTES
(1) Livy, Ab urbe condita libri IX, 1.10 (written between 27 B.C.E. and 17 A.C.E.).
(2) Some have thought retributive justice might involve conflicts with distributive justice. See John Locke, Two Treatises on Government, II, sec. 180-185, esp. 183.

(3) Thomas Aquinas, Summa Theologiae, II-II, 188, 4 ad 2. See II-II, 188, 3 ad 4, and also the Quodlibetalis Quaestio on indulgences for a crusade, written at the same time as the Secunda Secundae, Quodlibetum II, 16.
(4) Summa Theo. II-II, 124, 5 ad 3.
(5) Summa Theo. II-II, 65, 2 ad 2; 67, 4.
(6) Summa Theo. II-II, 64, 2.
(7) Summa Theo. II-II, 64, 7.
(8) Summa Theo. II-II, 63, 3.
(9) Contra Faustum 22, 75; De Div. Dei I, 26.
(10) Vitoria, De jure belli, 31.
(11) Francisco Suarez, De bello, VI, 8-9, in Selections from Three Works, tr. Gwladys L. Williams Classics of International Law (Oxford, 1944). See Leroy Walters, Five Classic Just War Theories (unpublished dissertation, Yale, 1971), 333-334.
(12) E.g., Vitoria, De jure belli, 22, 23; Grotius, De jure belli ac pacis, II, 26, 3, 5. See Walters, Five Classic., 335-338.
(13) E.g., Vitoria, De jure belli, 25, 31.
(14) See Leroy Walters, "A Historical Perspective on Selective Conscientious Objection," Jour. of Amer. Acad. of Religion 41 (1973).
(15) Difficultas tota est in ordine ad praxim.... De justitia et jure I, 18, s. i, 21.
(16) The Challenge of Peace (1983), #326.
(17) In recent times, Pius XII and John XXIII have asserted that war is no longer justified by some of these traditional causes. See Pacem in Terris, n. 127; John Courtney Murray, We Hold These Truths (New York: Sheed and Ward, 1960), 256.
(18) Speech in the Reichstag, Feb. 6, 1888; in Horst Kohl (ed.), Die politischen Reden des Fuersten Bismark (14 vols.; Stuttgart: Cotta, 1892-1905), XII, 447; cited in Helmut Thielicke, Theological Ethics, Vol. II (Grand Rapids: Eerdmans, 1969), 106.
(19) De bello, IV, 10. But see Grotius, De jure belli ac pacis, II, 24, 1, 4, and 7.
(20) See Grotius, De jure belli ac pacis, Proleg. #27; Gentili, De jure belli, I, 6 and 14; Vattel, Law of Nations, III, iii, 38.
(21) V.I. Lenin, Collected Works (Moscow: Progress, 1964), Vol. 30, 159.
(22) Letter of July 20, 1933. In Einstein on Peace, ed. by Otto Nathan and Heinz Norden (New York: Avenel, 1960), 229.
(23) The Gathering Storm, Vol. I of The Second World

War (Boston: Houghton Mifflin, 1948), 320.
(24) The Prince, tr. Robert M. Adams (New York: W.W. Norton, 1977), III, p. 9.
(25) See Raymond Aron, Peace and War (New York: Praeger, 1968), 151-154. See also Michael W. Doyle, "Kant, Liberal Legacies, and Foreign Affairs," Phil. and Public Affairs 12 (1983), 205-235, 323-353, at 223-224.
(26) Michael W. Doyle, "Kant, Liberal Legacies, and Foreign Affairs," Phil. and Public Affairs, Part I: 12 (1983), 205-235; Part II: 12 (1983), 323-353, at 212. But for some doubts on the significance of Doyle's correlations see Bruce Russett and Harvey Starr, World Politics: the Menu for Choice, 2nd ed. (New York: W.H. Freeman, 1985), ch. 15.
(27) See, e.g., Bellarmine, Disputationes de controversiis christianae fidei, Tomus Primus, Quintae Contraoversiae Generalis, Liber III, De Laicis, c. xv (col. 1477c).
(28) On War, ed. and trans. by Michael Howard and Peter Paret (Princeton: Princeton University Press, 1976), I, 1, 2.

CHAPTER TEN

ANALYSIS OF JUST WAR TRADITION: II

IUS IN BELLO

The general theme in all ius in bello elements is that the right to use force in war is not unlimited. There are two major categories under the rubric of ius in bello: proportionality (one distinct from ad bellum proportionality), and discrimination. Historically these elements originated primarily from knightly nobility with its class distinctions, the disciplined control of early "common man" armies which in turn led to standards of professionalism, and the military standards manuals that are epitomized by the Union Army's General Order No. 100 from the Civil War.[1]

In the tradition there has been no consistent moral priority in the relation of ad bellum and in bello elements, but always a judgment on how the two sets balance in the historical circumstances.[2] The justice of the war has never been held to justify without qualification any in bello means that involved the killing of combatants, the indirect killing of noncombatants, or the destruction of property and social structures. But neither has the position been held that what activities count as satisfying in bello limits are absolutely decided, no matter the seriousness of the cause.

(A) PROPORTIONALITY

On the ad bellum or raison d'etat level, proportionality requires that the good to be achieved by war must be proportionate to the physical and social evils that come from going to war.

On the in bello level, the attention is to the means used in carrying out the war. That is, at issue are the military strategies and tactics and the political policies that these express in reference to the existential harm done to physical life and social and economic practices (liberty and property). But it is not that clear what is the referent by which to judge the proportionality. Some would argue that it is the formulation of the political ends in raison d'etat terms. Others argue that it is the

156

intermediate military goals (<u>raison</u> <u>de</u> <u>guerre</u>) that are the appropriate referents.

To refer all strategies and tactics (and the included harm done to life, liberty, and property) to the highest <u>ad</u> <u>bellum</u> ends gives scant guidance or justification for particular military alternatives. The consensus that there are limits to what military force justifiably can be used would be in danger when using "new era" or "civilization" horizons in the <u>ad</u> <u>bellum</u> cause. When Vietnamese forces "liberated" Cambodia, anyone who did not support them was thereby an enemy to freedom, an opponent of the just cause, and consequently a valid target.

However, there might be some <u>ad</u> <u>bellum</u> guidance in reference to "right intention". When the particular tactics touch on some sensitive international issue, so that employing them would endanger the postwar international situation, it would not seem reasonable to refer <u>in</u> <u>bello</u> matters to the <u>ad</u> <u>bellum</u> goals.

But, ordinarily, experience shows that a military practice or tactic could be proportionate (or disproportionate) to a legitimate military goal regardless of the legitimacy of the <u>ad</u> <u>bellum</u> (or <u>raison</u> <u>d'etat</u>) level as a whole.

The distinction is also important the other way around. There could be justification on the <u>ad</u> <u>bellum</u> or <u>raison</u> <u>d'etat</u> level, but morally questionable proportionate harm to life, liberty, or property on the <u>in</u> <u>bello</u> level. (When Lt. Calley's group killed Vietnamese villagers, his defense was that the villagers' deaths were called for as they, in the context, presented a probable threat to the security of his troops. His appeal, and the judgment against him, remained always in terms of what would be legitimate military interests.) It is one thing to assimilate controversial means into the total war effort and pronounce that the total war effort is proportionate to the justified going to war. It is quite another thing to justify particular military and other means used to carry out the war as proportionate to particular military ends. There are usually options for tactics and practices with respect to military goals. So it would seem that the morality of particular military operations should be judged in terms of their proportionality to intermediate

157

military goals as a matter of justice to military commanders who do not determine political strategy.

The following schema seems reasonable. According to Clausewitz, the ad bellum cause would guide the decision on the political objective in the war. This objective must be specifically articulated. For example, in the Korean War, it might have been phrased as "stopping the aggression of North Korea into the South and restoring the status quo ante." From that political objective, again following Clausewitz' logical connection, the overall military objective would have been "to remove the North Korean military forces from South Korea and to prevent them from re-entering." The military strategy would have been chosen among such options as gaining control of transportation routes, attrition or neutralization of the enemy's military forces, destroying the enemy's industrial strength, cutting off the enemy's supply routes and outside assistance -- all with the intent of weakening their will to resist.

It would have been in the next step, the one to specific military strategies, that in bello proportionality would pertain. There would be three possible grades of specific objectives: those conceivably connected with the overall strategy, those substantially connected, and those necessarily connected. I agree with Walzer that the category of "necessarily connected" is too dubious to justify major destruction. It is unlikely that we could identify any plan that would truly be necessary. But I am likewise wary of plans that are only "conceivably connected" with the overall military objectives. This category quite likely could accept almost any plan. With one side of the proportionality formula involving forceful destruction of physical and social life as well as property, there must be identifiable limits on what strategies and tactics are needed to justify it. Therefore, only those plans that are "substantially connected" in practice would be proportional. It is that guide I employ when interpreting references in the tradition to "necessary military means".

It is important to have this more refined understanding of "military necessity" because there has been in the tradition a thematic connection employing the concept between the ad bellum level and in bello proportionality: if a military means is judged necessary to fulfil the moral expression of ius ad bellum, then it is of the tradition that this justifies its in bello violence. The idea is that the values in terms of the common good on the ad bellum level justify whatever is necessary on the in bello level. At least in this relationship, the social dimension is morally superior to the private dimension when the values conflict. And this superiority justified both the direct (intended) killing of combatants and the indirect (unintended but risked) killing of noncombatants.

> If the end is lawful, the necessary means are also lawful.[3]

> The first rule: In war the things which are necessary for attaining the end are lawful.[4]

Vitoria had a typical position on the risk of killing noncombatants when using such necessary means. His argument ran thusly. Unless some killing of noncombatants were ethically permissible, it would not be possible to use some of the present weapons, such as cannons. Since the use of these weapons was permissible due to the relation of the just cause and military necessity, one had to adjust the limits of immunity if the noncombatants were in the immediate vicinity of a legitimate military operation that could not be conducted without harm to them.[5] This instance of what comes to be called "indirect killing" was based on the ad bellum justice of the war itself. Unless necessary military operations were permitted, Vitoria feared that greater evils to the common good would occur that outweigh the concomitant physical evils that occur to noncombatants during those operations.

The morality of the indirect killing of noncombatants was accepted by Gabriel Vasquez, S.J. (1551-1604). "Killing innocent persons accidentally in war is justified by the common good."[6] This again had an ad bellum reference. A concurring position was taken by Johannes Azor, S.J.(d. 1603) and by the Augustinian Basilio Ponce (1569-1629).[7]

Thus, in an application of the principle of the double effect, warriors may have to negate but not deny the acknowledged immunity of those held to be noncombatants in order to protect superior values of all, even those whose immunity is negated.[8] For the consensus was that there cannot be a moral prohibition against using a particular type of tactic or weapon which significantly endangered noncombatants if that prohibition would mean (in the reasonable judgment of military commanders) that the just cause would be sacrificed.

In another exception, perhaps more telling of his thinking, Vitoria allowed that letting troops sack cities, even when not directly necessary for military victory, may be moral if done either as a deterrent or as a spur to the courage of the troops.[9] While he acknowledged that this may open the way to cruelties (e.g., rape and slaughter of innocent persons, looting, etc.), he allowed there may be times when it could be permitted. "It is undoubtedly unjust in the extreme to deliver up a city... to be sacked without the greatest necessity and weightiest reason." That is, while it should be rare, such tolerance is not unquestionably evil, even if commanders foresee the likelihood of the killing of noncombatants, and even though the officers issue the ordinary prohibitions on this.

But there were some provisos in the tradition. First, one must determine whether the just cause supported only a limited war, which would mean, as Clausewitz averred, that a state has to weigh whether a military loss of the war would be less against the state's interests than the costs of a military victory, or even of continuing.

Also, since killing of noncombatants was permitted on the basis of the justice of the war itself, whenever there was doubt on the latter, or where there was considered "simultaneous subjective justice," the tendency was to argue that the war must be fought with more restraint.[10]

With respect to the operational standard by which to decide _ius in bello_ proportionality, the reasonable judgments by experienced persons seems the best available norm. And what is reasonable can only be judged in the specific context. However, patterns recur in situations for which common models of judgments may be anticipated. (This is the ordinary way we acquire moral rules in this area.)

(B) DISCRIMINATION

The formal level of discrimination is rather simply explained. The right to kill in a public capacity is limited with respect to possible objects since the right to kill in the public role is grounded on the need for certain actions to achieve a public good, given the reality of international affairs. And the consensus position in the tradition on which persons make up the set of possible objects for such killing in war is: those who are engaged in the war.

The two major questions are: who are included in those who are engaged in the war; and, is this an absolute limitation.

In the Just War tradition, the _ad_ _bellum_ justification for going to war did not of itself answer the question of what killings were justifiable because of the war. The thinking consistently was that there had to be specific grounds on the _in_ _bello_ level for justified killing, in other words, for valid targets. The three grounds most accepted in the consensus were that of retribution, that of military necessity to achieve justified military objectives, and that of defense while carrying out the war. Unless the killing could be connected to one of these, it was not justifiable under the rubrics of the Just War.

1. The Background and the Term "Innocent"

The historical origin of the _in_ _bello_ principle of discrimination seems to have been from the concept of noble action valued by the medieval knights. Discrimination in targets was for them both a matter of not degrading oneself by attacking those of another class, and also not degrading oneself by attacking those who unable to threaten them (for example, those who were not able to wield a sword).[11] For the knights, the point of discrimination was primarily concerned with what killings should not be done because they would be ignoble and unworthy.

When the Canon lawyers and theologians of the same era worked at the question, their concern was more about what killings could morally be done in time of war. They introduced the use of the moral terms "guilty" and "innocent" to designate the valid and

161

invalid target groups. The reference was to the moral guilt acquired by leaders and soldiers of one state as they made aggressive acts against the public common good of another state. Certain persons, usually identified by class, were outside the set of moral targets because, even though they were within the population of the morally guilty state, they did not have the occupation or social function of making war.

With justice only on one side (as was true in the position of Aquinas, but not in the position of Augustine), any killing of any person by the unjust side was by definition immoral. And killing by the justified side was to be restricted to those who were morally guilty, those who were doing immoral harm, the "nocentes". Those who were not doing harm were the non-nocentes, the "innocent".[12] The medieval use of "innocent" did two jobs. It named the class of those who were not valid direct targets in war, and it explained why the class's members qualified for immunity.

What this bit of history indicates is that in bello discrimination did not develop as if it were some ideal standard with timeless specifications. To hold that it did and, consequently, that it designates some absolute demarcation of the limits of what is eternally just is to ignore how substantive moral principles here were achieved. James T. Johnson writes that the consensus on subjects for immunity "originated principally in the intentionality and customs of military professionals...; this is a significant point not only for understanding the history of Western thought on war, but also for making a connection today between public policy and explicitly moral analysis based on just war tradition."[13]

By the early modern period, there developed the consensus (for example, in the positions of Grotius and Vattel) that, for evaluation purposes as well as for purposes of mitigating the destruction done in war, it would be better to start the analysis of justified killing in war with the premise of "mutual ostensive justice" for all the states in the war and to downplay the position that the just cause for the war can be only on one side. This, of course, entailed a problem with the continued use of the terminology of guilt and innocence. What happened was that the more operative distinction became that between combatant and noncombatant. To make an identification between noncombatants and innocents, as some did, ignored the difference between the two jobs of naming the class of those with immunity and the explanation of how individuals qualified for membership within that class. One might say that continuing to refer to noncombatants as innocent was mostly a matter of "extrinsic denomination".

However Grotius introduced a new aspect into the discussion: the responsibility of all the members of a society for the public actions of the leaders. He argued that the modern type of society only worked if the people gave either overt or tacit consent to the government. This had obvious implications for the matter of in bello discrimination, which Grotius did not hesitate to draw.

> The right of killing enemies in a public war ... extends not only to these who actually bear arms, or are subjects to him that stirs up the war, but in addition to all persons who are in the enemy's territory.[14]

Nevertheless, Grotius explicitly rejected, as did Francisco Vitoria, the suggestion of "collective guilt" and separated this concept of guilt from whatever made someone a proper object for killing in war. Vitoria held that, even in an unjust cause, most soldiers fought in good faith.[15] Grotius argued similarly that the "body politic" is a kind of being that has important distinctions from the kind of being an individual is. While in some matters it is appropriate to employ the concept of the people as a single body, this is not proper in the area of merit.[16] Merit, or desert, is something that belongs to individuals. Guilt only attaches to those individuals who have knowingly and formally cooperated with unjust actions.[17] Many in a state take part in the war for more general reasons which in themselves can be noble, such as compliance with the decisions of valid superiors, the presumption of goodness of the actions of one's own state, and so on.

In the eighteenth century, some new circumstances mitigated to some extent the problem of noncombatant immunity. These circumstances reduced the military necessity to be in or attack areas where there were many noncombatants. The style of war, epitomized by

Frederick the Great, required strict military discipline which facilitated restraints. First, the armies were tied to a network of magazines (fortified supply bases) by relatively short umbilical cords of wagons moving over bad roads. So the general military strategy was: attack the enemy's magazines. The shortness of the season for campaigning also made such a strategy imperative. Second, since the nation's economic needs meant having to use mercenaries in the army (or using captured enemy, or impressing the socially powerless), the soldiers had little intrinsic incentive. So harsh discipline was the rule. Thus, the disposition of the armies in battle was at least partially dictated by the needs to minimize the opportunities for soldiers to absent themselves. This entailed a restraint on what targets could be attacked, since the time of attack is the time when it is most difficult to keep track of the soldiers in one's command. Third, it was usually crucial for the armies to keep the economy of the area going.[18]

By the nineteenth century the military and political supports for discrimination changed even more with the advent of modern war and its varying degrees of "totalization." War became a matter of one people against another and the problem of discrimination shifted its focus away from who were the valid targets and concentrated rather on who were the necessary targets. Francis Lieber, author of General Order No. 100 promugated during the U.S. Civil War, argued that soldiers were only authorized to do that killing that was militarily necessary during a justified war. Lieber was solidly within the Just War tradition with the position that the right to kill in a war was limited since the soldier's right to kill is grounded on his role as a public agent and the need for certain actions to achieve a public good.[19] But he gave witness to a development in the tradition with his position that, in practice, this right to kill was guided in its targets by two considerations: what was necessary to achieve the valid purposes of the war and what was necessary for self-defense while carrying out these purposes.

Lieber raised few brows with his position that all in the enemy country were enemies; the only distinction was that some were armed, some were unarmed. It was now the case that even a noncombatant no longer would automatically be considered in the class of those with immunity.

Despite these historical changes, many still refer to a violation of the principle of discrimination as "an attack on the innocent". The most we are authorized to say about this usage of "innocent" is that it names the set of nonvalid targets for killing in war. It does not seem correct to claim that the property of being innocent explains why someone should be considered a member of the set.

After this summary, we can use three questions to set the problem of in bello discrimination. Who are to be classified as proper subjects to benefit from the principle? What sort of restraints count as fulfilling the principle (e.g., absolute, proportional, life only, life and property)? Why is there such a principle? Historical use indicates that none of the answers are self-evident. We shall treat them together as we look at the suggestion the principle should be absolute today, at the tradition on "indirect" killing, and at the claim that attacking the innocent violates the value of human freedom itself.

2. Who Does the Principle Protect Today?

As mentioned, there have been three specific in bello justifications for direct of "intended" killing during the war. The three have been "retaliation", "necessary targets in the process toward a legitimate military objective", and "self-defense of the soldiers and the many impersonal items important for carrying on military activities". (Justification for "indirect" or "unintentional" killing has always rested on the reasonable proportionality between the risk of killing nonvalid targets and the importance of making an attack on specific valid targets.)

Using the post Civil War classifications of armed, unarmed, and neutral enemy, the question of who are protected by the principle of discrimination today would come to this: might unarmed enemy be valid targets, and, if so, is it in terms only of their property and their social liberty, or is it also in terms of their physical life?

Elizabeth Anscombe, who retains the "innocent-guilty" categories, argues that to be a valid military target one must be engaged in an objectively unjust proceeding which the attacker has

165

the right to make his concern. Then the latter can attack with a view to stopping the proceeding. This means it is ethical to attack not only the soldier, but also the supply lines and armament factories.[20]

Anscombe then writes, "But people whose mere existence and activity support (the war activity) by growing crops, making clothes, etc., (even though they) constitute an impediment to (the attacker) ---such people are innocent and it is murderous to attack them, or make them a target for an attack which he judges will help him towards victory."[21]

What is the thinking here? Can we hold equivalent the set of innocent and the set of those who do "ordinary" societal activities during war? Certainly the people Anscombe classifies as innocent are cooperating in the support of the enemy society, and this cooperation is vital to permit the nearly total mobilization of that society for modern war. Is there a cutoff level in kinds of cooperation by citizens that makes those below that level "innocent" and those above "non-innocent" and thus liable to attack?

Perhaps the traditional distinction between formal and material cooperation could be used. Basically, the idea of the distinction is this: while anyone might contribute either by acts that positively supply something to the primary agent's goals or by failure to do acts that deter those goals, one might do either without consenting to and wanting the goals. If so, one is classified morally as a material cooperator. Only if one consents to and wants the primary agent's specific goals does one become a formal cooperator. According to the tradition, using the double effect distinction between the end of the cooperating agent and the end of the act, only the formal cooperator becomes personally "guilty" if those goals are improper. The material cooperator might become personally "guilty" if the reason one continued the cooperation was not proportional to the moral seriousness of the primary agent's goals. In Anscombe's approach, however, the material cooperation status seems to hinge not on consent to goals nor on the proportional reasonableness of the cooperator's continuing, but simply on whether the activities done are of those sorts which, even though supporting the war, were the same sorts of activities that those citizens were doing or would do without the preparation for or prosecution of the war. No matter how essential such material cooperation was to the war effort, those doing it would still be "innocent" and not involved in a cooperation which "the attacker has the right to make his concern".

Unfortunately, there are few who do not have some change in their lives because of a modern war, and also few who would not support their own country in time of war. Moreover, those who consent to the goals of the war probably would not fall neatly into classes or functions so that they could easily be distinguished by an attacker. Let me give examples of several degrees of cooperation within a society.

1) The actual governmental leaders, the top military leaders, the military leaders who plan the strategy;
2) the local military leaders who adopt tactics; the military personnel who fight;
3) the civilian formal cooperators who organize and capitalize the war;
4) the civilian formal or material cooperators who work in the specific production and distribution of war materials;
5) the civilian formal or material cooperators who work in production and distribution that is not specific but is essential to the war effort;
6) the citizens who formally cooperate by wanting the ends for which the war is fought but who work in areas only indirectly supporting the war effort.

Those in groups 3-6 would be noncombatant, but many in the same groups would be "guilty" in the sense of formal cooperators, since they want the specific goals of the war. (For example, those who supported the specific Nazi causes during World War II.) Others might be "responsible" in Grotius' sense because they want or do not oppose the general success of their country in the war. (For example, those Germans who supported Germany's side during World War II.) If these latter would also be called formal cooperators, it would have to be of a qualitatively different kind.

Anscombe's index of a change in life activity would indeed be a practical way to identify classes of valid targets given such commingling in contemporary societies. But there seems no basis to claim the reason for such distinctions is because of innocence.

167

Perhaps "guilt" and "innocence" are not by themselves sufficient to decide who is a valid target and who is an invalid target under the principle of discrimination. This conclusion is reinforced if we recall that the original basis for using the mark of innocence to decide discrimination among possible targets was that intended killing was primarily a matter of retaliation.

As time went on, killing during war was also justified in terms of essential steps to reach valid military objectives and defense of self, others, and various impersonal items important for military activities. Is it also possible in our day to extend the justified targets to include those who are noncombatants but who nevertheless are significantly responsible?

Let us begin this examination by an analogy. Some today speak of a kind of moral responsibility for "socially unjust structures" shared by those who belong to some class or power-block or country that systematically carries on actions that debilitate, denigrate, or destroy human beings as self-ordering individuals. The notion of "social structures" here refers to the ways the group, as a group, does actions in specific areas so that results are rather consistent, persistent, and pervasive.

Implicit in such social justice discussions is the distinction between an individual's personal responsibility and that same individual's social responsibility for the ways things are done in the society. The general drift is that, even though one personally does not make the decisions that set up or continue a wrongful way of doing things, one is still "socially responsible" and so "socially guilty."

Such an analysis does not sit well with those in the North Atlantic community who have come to assume that individuals, at least in some meaningful way, are primordially pre-social individuals who are only responsible for actions they individually have done, consented to, or somehow cooperated in. Yet the ancient Hebrews and Greeks, for instance, had ways to think about the share in the social guilt by those who were personally innocent. For them social guilt did not depend upon personal decision but upon social membership. Karl Marx also would probably have found this way of talking acceptable, as he considered the individual to be constituted both from one's personal decisions and also from the ensemble of social relations one had.

A blend of these two standpoints on the moral implications to the individual because of the harmful effects of social structures shows up in contemporary discussion of social responsibility. The reference for what makes individuals who are not social leaders share in a certain level of "social guilt" has not been to the actions that create the unjust structures or even to the (cooperative) actions that support them. Rather, reference has been to the failure of people to act to change the unjust ways of doing societal activities.

In reference to individual action, moral culpability for failing to do reasonably required actions is ordinarily acknowledged. Still, for one to have personal culpability for omissions, the individual had to have the power and the opportunity to avert the wrong act or the physically evil outcome, yet have failed to act. What of moral culpability for failing to act to change institutions? There is an obvious disanalogy here when one talks of social culpability for such omissions, since it is seldom true that an individual has the power to change social structures. [Karl Marx, one of the first to identify wrongful structures, rather consistently held that individuals as such could do nothing about structures.[22]] But it must be kept in mind that what is at issue here is "social" culpability, not "personal" culpability, for the social structures.

To assign guilt for wrongful structures to all members of a social group without more assumes a concept of humanism wherein only overt recantations on the part of each individual of the society's ways of doing things can break the web of each member's responsibility for the commissions and omissions of the group of which one is a member. It would seem that citizens are all responsible somewhat unless they do, by commission or omission, something to indicate that they reject cooperation or the social structures. This something must be from a set of options that are realistic for the specific country. Certainly these options would have to be feasible for people of ordinary human virtue.

Robert Harvenak has raised doubts on the applicability of the language of "cooperation" in the matter of the individual's social responsibility for wrongful structures.[23] I take him to mean that there really is a disanalogy between an individual's cooperation with another individual's wrongful action and an individual's membership in a social group that has wrongful structures. He correctly notes that the matter turns on the distinction between an individual as voluntary member of a privately formed group and an individual as an involuntary member of a societal group. In the latter case, the claim is that one is responsible for the way things are done within one's society. The language implies that this is a responsibility not restricted to being based only on formal intention. Indeed, it does not seem to require even active knowledge. Rather, by analogy with culpable ignorance in extending individual responsibility, the claim is that social responsibility is to be extended insofar as there is culpable ignorance of what ways the society to which one belongs is unjust.[24]

Now let us apply these concepts of personal cooperation and social responsibility to the question of who is a valid target for physical violence during war. The first application is that one can no longer use "innocent" and "noncombatant" as if they were synonyms. The civilian who urges on the national leader in a war is, even thought a noncombatant, certainly sharing (as a formal cooperator) in whatever guilt is involved, while a soldier who reluctantly but nobly carries out what seems the moral duty of serving the country might be seen as more innocent even though a combatant.[25]

Consequently, if one were to target both the personally innocent combatant and the personally guilty noncombatant or the socially responsible noncombatant for attack in war, the justification of the targetings would differ. The first would be in terms of self-defense against the immediate physical threat. Targeting the personally guilty because of formal cooperation would be in terms of punishing the one deserving retribution because of the abetting of the aggression.[26] What of the socially responsible noncombatant? To answer this, I would think it possible to draw a parallel with the formally cooperating noncombatant. To make this clear, let us examine a counterargument that protests targeting

170

those who formally cooperate.

The counterargument usually stresses that killing noncombatants cannot be justified because they are unarmed and so do not constitute the immediate physical threat.[27] Even if the unarmed would be considered "guilty", the most that could be justified would be force against their liberty or their property.

But such an exclusive emphasis on a self-defense justification itself has a problem. There is a disanalogy between self-defense in the continuing phenomenon of war, in the single battle within the war, and in the one event phenomenon of individual self-defense. The remote, necessary, and yet continuous cause of the war that comes from those who in various ways promote the war, is essentially involved in the physical threat that is the continuing war itself, and the defense is against that threat. When such remote, necessary, and continuous causes are noncombatants behind the lines, there might be no practical alternative besides that use of force which likely would kill some of them.

If noncombatants are formal cooperators, they would be "guilty" or responsible as individuals and deserve some retribution. Whether this would necessarily mean they would be valid targets for direct killing is a second matter. And whether this should come by military action during the war or by some penalty after the military action itself is a third matter. Robert K. Fullinwider argues against direct military targeting, not because these individuals do not merit attack, but because military targeting could not discriminate between guilty noncombatants and innocent noncombatants.[28]

Now what of those who are socially responsible even though not personally guilty? Recall, those who use such a classification say social responsibility is caused by omission of active objections to the wrongful societal activities? If those in the country are guilty on this social responsibility level, even if not on a personal responsibility level because of formal cooperation, may they be directly targeted also in terms of deserving retribution?

171

There are two questions. (1) Can moral responsibility be placed upon members of groups for the structural wrongs of the group? (2) Would this justify direct targeting of these people during the war, or, at least, affect the proportionality judgment in the risk of indirectly killing them?

To the first question, from the discussion above one might conclude that, while to make each individual as an individual blameworthy for wrongful social structures would be to commit the fallacy of division, it is not necessarily fallacious to make each individual blameworthy as a member of society.[29] To assume it was would be to ignore the dynamic of societies, in which relations that are necessary and sufficient conditions for the structures are independent of any individual's will and yet are the result of ways of relating socially in which all cooperate, at least materially (that is, they do some ordinary actions consistently that as done on the whole are the necessary social context for the structures). This seems the grain of truth in the contemporary talk about responsibility for "unjust social structures."

Certainly in those countries that have a decision method for social policy actions, which method at least indirectly (through representatives elected by universal suffrage) involves the people, it would be arguable to hold the people responsible (even the minority nay-sayers.)[30] The U.S. Catholic bishops went so far as to assert: "In a democracy, the responsibility of the nation and that of its citizens coincide."[31]

Consequently, insofar as the analysis of social responsibility is valid, one might conclude that to target socially responsible people is as acceptable as to target anything in war under the rubric of self-defense and perhaps even under the rubric of retaliation.involved in some types of nuclear deterrence.

What of countries that lack suffrage representation? To a lesser, but still to some, extent, it might be arguable to hold the people responsible, since even tyrannies, if they are to be stable, need some popular approval or apathy to continue. Yet, by an irony of societal dynamics, it may indeed be true, as Caspar Weinberger has stated, that with regard to such countries, the citizens are much less socially responsible than in democratic countries. Weinberger has spoken strongly against any "assured destruction" nuclear deterrence strategy since it seems to fail the moral retribution test. It is not justifiable, he said, to retaliate against the Soviet people for "an attack launched by the Soviet leadership, a leadership for which the Soviet people are not responsible and cannot control."[32] His reference to the lack of responsibility would be irrelevant unless one assumed that a presence of responsibility in citizens would validate their being killed during war in terms of retribution.

3. "Direct" and "Indirect" killing

We have already adverted to the fact that, in descriptions of justified killing of innocents, those in the tradition used terms as "direct/indirect" and "intended/permitted." The former pair echoed the second requisite of the principle of the double effect ("never let the existential evil be the means to the existential good"). The latter pair echoed the third requisite ("the evil outcome must not be intended, only permitted"). Both these pairs, obviously, have technical meanings. And these meanings have been, and still are, vigorously debated. But continuously in the various meanings have been some constants: the killing of the noncombatant is a grave existential evil; it may at times be morally done; and it must be regretted even as it is justifiably done.

One must keep in mind that the principle of the double effect came from analysis of real decisions in various contexts of conflicts. By this analysis, we have identified the formal elements requisite for the validity of conflict resolutions. The paradigmatic expression of the decisions in the conflict situation is as follows: "I knew that y existential evil would also be caused because of my action (and omission), but I had to (rational coercion) do it because x existential good was more important (rational hierarchy)."

As it stands formally after analysis, the principle is without specific content. It is not an apriori principle with specified limits that can be deductively applied. Consequently, its application properly is not as a univocal but as an analogous principle, and it must take meaning for its requisite

173

elements from the context of the conflict. (For example, killing under public authority and for public defense is not the same ethical context for decision as is killing in private self-defense.)

Now let us see how this might function in the context of killing innocents during a war. Why is the killing of the innocent or noncombatant considered a grave existential evil? Some say because the value negated by such a killing is of such qualitatively special rank that it is incommeasurable and so beyond proportionality with values other than physical human life. It is true that the life of innocent people is valued in a special way in the tradition, but it has never been considered apriori sovereign in a clash with other values. The very existence of the distinction between direct and indirect killing of the innocent, wherein the latter can be moral if there is a proportionate reason, is evidence of this.

Thomas Aquinas and others even argued that the direct and intentional slaughter of the innocent could be moral if it were commanded by God.[33] This, of course, is stipulative, not explanatory, and it wavers toward making the value of the innocent life based on God's will and not on any ontological status.

Aquinas held that life was valuable because it belonged to God. Therefore, one could kill in private self-defense, but one could not in the defense "intend" the death of the other.[34] Human life was a possession of God and to intend to kill as a private individual would be to usurp God's property. So one could directly intend to defend oneself, but the death of the other is "indirect" and "only permitted."

The analysis he used distinguished the end of the agent (_finis operantis_) and the natural outcome of the material act (_finis operis_). The material act could have a double effect, one of which would evince the end of the agent, one of which would not. The former effect of the material act would be "intended" in the sense of "wanted." The other effect could not be intended reasonably because it is not reasonable to want the negation of an existential good; this other effect the rational person could only "permit," and this would in turn only be reasonable to do if the intended effect secured a more important existential good.

Because he held public authority to be the instrument of God in social matters such as capital punishment and war, Aquinas could approve of direct and intended killing if it was done for the common good and ordered by public authority.[35]

Vitoria allowed the use of weapons that killed both innocent and aggressor as long as the intention was limited to the latter.[36] Antonius de Corduba held that if one does what is licit to defend oneself, the death of the innocent bystander was not intended.[37] (Of course, the use of the term "licit" begs the question somewhat, since it presumes a hierarchy of values that must be established. But Corduba held it had been.)

Certain examples themselves became part of the tradition here. In the one, an act of self-defense involves charging one's horse across a bridge, but there is a child on the narrow bridge and charging across risks the child's death. In another, an attacking enemy is using a child as a shield. (This latter example, of course, became very real for many U.S. soldiers in Vietnam as they faced enemy soldiers who had strapped children to their chests and then charged.)

The consensus in the tradition was that it was morally permissible to effect the death of the innocent in one's own self-defense. This is the more striking when it is noted that this was in the context of killing without public authority. So adding that authority, as in the case of soldiers in war, would only more strongly support the moral permissibility. The deaths of the noncombatants were classified as "permitted but not intended" since the actions that cause them are actions that "have to be done" to support a superior value yet are "regretted and unwanted" since the value of the lives lost is still respected. Quite likely, the "necessity" here is in the sense of "substantially connected".

Using again the evidence authenticated by the Hypocritical Imperative, the consensus testifies that the risk of indirectly killing noncombatants remains an operative moral guide. When the U.S. performed a "surgical strike" against Libya in 1986, the Secretary of Defense insisted on the military character of the targets hit and the efforts to reduce risks to others. The consensus standard even surfaces in some

statements of contemporary terrorists. It is true
that some terrorists appeal only to the ad bellum
level of their cause to justify doing anything they
think will advance that cause, and therefore in
principle they accept no limitation on targets. But
other terrorists begin with the conviction that their
enemy is the invasive culture of foreigners, and so
anyone who does not join with them by that very fact
supports the enemy culture and is thereby an enemy.
This at least acknowledges that the moral
justification of a specific target must be on the in
bello level.

The moral danger with all this about "indirect"
and "permitted but not intended" is that, despite all
the talk, nonvalid targets become the "means" to an
end. Elizabeth Anscombe warns that the
"direct-indirect" distinction can become a tool for
self-deception. She writes: "It ought not to be
pretended that rulers and their subordinates do not
choose the killing of their enemies as a means." She
has two points here. (a) Rulers have a right to kill
(external and internal enemies of society). (b) To
distinguish the act that kills and the intent to kill
here is dangerous. "Someone who can fool himself into
this twist of thought will fool himself into
justifying anything, however atrocious, by means of
it."[38] (This latter is always an important reminder.
Any particular action in the concrete has many
connections which bring about many states of affairs.
Thus, any action can be described by a number of
propositions. We must beware of selecting a
description that abstracts from some major set of
effects of the action done, and we must always beware
of thinking of any abstract description of a human act
as if it were a concrete human act.)

Anscombe's main thrust here seems to be against
the ethical significance of the distinction between
"direct" and "indirect" killing of non-valid targets,
especially insofar as the it comes from the
"intend-permit" distinction in the third element of
the principle of the double effect ("The evil outcome
may only be permitted, not intended"). Her objection
is that it is playing with words to claim one is only
"taking actions to end the threat while not intending
the killing (of innocents)." Her position does not
deny any of the potentially beneficial consequences of
such killing, but simply absolutizes as decisive the
innocence of the targets.

This absoluteness of the principle of discrimination has only surfaced in the twentieth century. The basis in the tradition for the possible overriding of the limits from discrimination was the premise that some values involved in a war for the public common good were more important. Consequently, if there was an apparent conflict with the values of the private sphere, the actions under military necessity serving the public common good could morally be done. (This was interpreted, after it was given general formulation as a second-level principle, as coming under some formal rule for the resolution of conflict situations, such as the principle of the double effect.) Anscombe must reject this and hold the premise that individual values of physical life are always above the values of the public common good.

Since discrimination itself is an inductively reached second-level principle of justice in war, its status, when it conflicts with other values in war, must come from decisions in the matter at hand, and eventually gain generalization as a principle. The tradition so far is that this conflict resolution principle allows the subordination of discrimination. It is certainly true that inductive principles can develop, as new decisions are needed in situations qualitatively other than those of the set from which the traditional principle was drawn. The difficulty here is that the assertion that the principle of discrimination enjoys an absoluteness is new. Yet without some distinction, as in the matter of levels of responsibility and cooperation, and without some clarification on how to resolve conflicts with reasonable military necessity, it does not seem likely to enjoy much of a consensus.

None of this suggests that the consensus denied that killing the noncombatant or the non-formal cooperator was a grave existential evil. The sovereign had the office of ordering activities for the public common good, and this included the "intended" or "direct" killing of those who acted in ways to threaten that good. In acting to carry out this directive, soldiers operating under the authority of the sovereign could morally risk killing non-valid targets, the noncombatants and the non-formal cooperators. This risk was justified by the importance of the public common good over the existential good of individuals. This risk could be taken knowingly, and since the value superiority justifies the indirect killing and does not merely excuse it. Only in the present century has the position been given some support that the value hierarchy should be inverted. But the support has not yet reached a consensus.

Consequently, "indirect" does not mean "not foreseen" (as some suggest is the way to interpret "not intended"). The justification of the deaths of the innocent in war is not dependent upon the ignorance of the agents. The point is not to excuse the agents from responsibility. Rather the point is to hold them responsible but to argue that their action is justified. In the traditional phrasing of the principle of the double effect the third element is that the existential evil is "permitted but not intended." The agent can knowingly bring about the evil and still be placing a moral act. Both what one intends and what one permits are voluntary and thus imputable. Otherwise, the entire principle of the double effect, and especially perhaps the fourth requisite element, that there be proportionate reason for causing the evil effect, would be vacuous.

Nor could "indirect" mean "not as a means to an end" (which perhaps fits Anscombe's objection). To understand this suggestion and the need to reject is we must rephrase the second requisite of the principle of the double effect. If one wills the end, one wills the means to that end. To demand that killing the innocent not be a means to an end seems to have this main idea: to make a person a means is to treat that person as an abstract thing we use for our exclusive values. One does well here to be precise on what is wrong with this. In most of our dealings with others, we treat them as abstract things we use for our exclusive values. Yet we think the aspect that permits these dealings to be moral uses of others is that we do not in the dealings deny, debilitate, or destroy the dignity of those we use. And how could we violate this dignity in the use of others? Precisely by having an effect on them by our use which negates a value for them that is superior to the value we are enhancing by our use of them. Such a use of them expresses a disdain for them as beings who have dignity, that is, intrinsic control over meaning and value. This dignity status is the point of the prohibition of using people merely as means.

Now what of the direct-indirect interpretation in the principle of discrimination? It does seem that the distinction itself echoes the "never use merely as a means," and "only permit but never intend" requisites of the principle of the double effect. But if proportionately superior values are at stake, as in war they can be claimed to be, why not simply balance the total net good of all those effected to decide among alternative choices, a straight utilitarian methodology with the possible exception of restricting the values involved to the number of humans killed? But that is the rub. Number means a quantification, and human dignity is always a unique, non-fungible reality, not numerable. In a real and important sense, each person is incommeasurable.

4. The innocent and freedom

The avoidance of a utilitarian analysis which considers people as abstract and quantifiable is the concern of Richard McCormick. He works to combine unconditional values with the context and consequences in moral situations, frames an argument to show what are the limits of using the device of proportionality to decide when there are conflicting values. He says the correct use of proportionality would not allow such examples as the decision by President Truman to drop the bomb "to save more lives than would die in a prolonged conventional war."[39] Using Paul Ramsey's formulation that the manner of protecting the good must not undermine it in the long run by serious injury to an associated good, McCormick sets up the following argument:

> Making innocent persons the object of bombing is a form of extortion in international affairs that contains an implicit denial of human freedom. Human freedom is undermined when extortionary actions are accepted and elevated and universalized. Because such freedom is an 'associated good' upon which the very good of life heavily depends, undermining it in the manner of my defense of life is undermining life itself.[40]

Insofar as war, according to Clausewitz, is the use of force to get an enemy country to do one's will, then all acts in war, according to McCormick's formulation, would be extortion. Since this is the point of war, even just war, why is the killing of innocent an extortion that contains an "implicit denial" of freedom that will undermine the very value defended by the action (of saving lives)? Would not every act even in a justified war be under the same condemnation? McCormick just prior to the above passage writes:

> For by killing (innocent people) to prevent others from unjustly killing (innocent people), one equivalently denies the freedom of these others (i.e., the ones prevented from killing). That is the very moral meaning of extortion. One supposes by his action that the cessation of others from wrongdoing is necessarily dependent on my doing harm. Such a supposition denies, and thereby undermines, human freedom.[41]

If I understand him, McCormick bases the nexus of extortion to "implicit denial of freedom" in that the "extortion" has as its structure "if I don't do this harm, this evildoer will do evil to so many more." And this is to claim falsely (=it is not true) or immorally (=it is true, but should not be because of the value of liberty) an inherent connection between the doing of the harm and the change of mind of the evildoer. "For those who hold the notion of free will in the doing of evil (and good), there is never an inherent connection between killing an innocent person and changing the murderous mind (of others)."[42]

But surely this is wrong. McCormick cannot mean that any act in war, including the killing of innocent, since it tries to force the enemy to stop the unjust aggression by inflicting harm, is thereby extortion. If it fits the definition, then the definition is inept. The assertion that "the very moral meaning of extortion" is "to deny the freedom of others" contains a false analogy and a crucial ambiguity.

Taking a clue from Gregory Kavka, one might argue that "actions taken to prevent others from going against my demands not to perform unjust actions" are not morally parallel to "actions taken to prevent others from failing to comply with my unjust demands."[43] The definition of "extortion" must include the "end of the agent" (_finis operantis_), and so these two kinds of actions differ morally.

180

(This would mean the principle "If it is wrong to do, it is wrong to intend to do x," which some hold rules out a deterrence posture of threatening, if we are convinced the actual use of nuclear weapons would be wrong, since it would inevitably lead to escalation beyond proportionality, errs also.)

The ambiguity is in the phrase "to deny the freedom of others." "To deny" can mean either "to say that x is not so," or "to act to prohibit the exercise of x." McCormick objects against acts that express the latter sense of denial, but he seems to support the objection by appeal to the former sense of denial.

Of course, McCormick is not arguing that all actions in war are immoral because they intend to be coercive. He is making an argument about killing the innocent in order to hasten the end of the war and save more lives overall. So he must define "extortion" in a way that excludes doing harm to military personnel and supplies.

But this is peripheral after all. For the heart of his argument is that killing innocent to force the enemy to come to terms undermines the value of life itself since it implicitly denies the associated value of liberty. And why so? Because it expresses the conviction that the first must happen before the second will happen. This in turn expresses a false connection of the harm to the changing of the will of the enemy, <u>since there is in reality human freedom</u>. That is, there is no necessity of doing the harm. The enemy can change its mind freely without such an external cause. Now doing harmful acts in war (which for now let us stipulate may include killing the innocent) may be immoral, but they cannot be immoral because they deny the reality of human freedom, for they do not do that. The harmful acts are done in war expressly because of the conviction that, even though the enemy could otherwise stop doing the evil aggression, the enemy will not stop unless we, by the harmful actions we do, make them see that it is the sensible choice.

McCormick writes of freedom here as a Sartrean, stressing that at any moment any person can freely do an about face. But the just war tradition is based on the experience of human character, which Sartre at best undervalued. As John Stuart Mill read it, one only changes one's character because of the experience

of admiration of a noble other or because of the
experience of the painful consequences of the actions
flowing from one's own present character. Thus, the
"extortion" of the actions in war acknowledges this
kind of property of freedom, but does not deny the
freedom.

NOTES

(1) James T. Johnson, Can Modern War Be Just (New
Haven: Yale, 1984), 14; and Just War Tradition and
the Restraint of War (Princeton: Princeton
University Press, 1981), ch. 6.
(2) See Johnson, Can Modern War Be Just, 31.
(3) Francisco Suarez, De bello, in De Triplici Virtute
Theologica Fide, Spe, et Caritate, tr. by G.L.
Williams, A. Brown, and J. Waldron (Oxford:
Clarendon, 1944), VII, 6. See also, VII, 15-17.
(4) Hugo Grotius, De jure belli ac pacis libri tres,
tr. Francis W. Kelsey, et al. (Oxford, 1925), III,
1, 2, title. See also: Francisco Vitoria, De Indis
et de jure belli relectiones, ed. Ernest Nys, tr.
John Pawley Bate (Carnegie Institute, 1917), 37, 35,
41, 42, 52; Alberico Gentili, De jure belli libri
tres, tr. by John C. Rolfe (Oxford: Clarendon,
1933), III, 12, 2, and 23.
(5) Vitoria, De jure belli, 35, 36, 37.
(6) Opuscula moralia, De restitutione, Lib. 3, par.
1, dub. 7, n. 27.
(7) Azor, Institutiones Morales, Pars 3, lib. 2, c.
3, no. 22; Ponce, De sacramento matrimonii, Lib.
10, c. 13, n. 2.
(8) Compare James T. Johnson, Just War Tradition..,
223, 304, 305.
(9) Vitoria, De jure belli, 52.
(10) James T. Johnson, Just War Tradition.., 94-103,
201.
(11) See James T. Johnson, Ideology, Reason and the
Limitation of War (Princeton: Princeton University
Press, 1975), cc. 1, 5, and 7; Just War Tradition
and the Restraint of War (Princeton: Princeton
University Press, 1981), ch. 5.
(12) On Aquinas, see Leroy Walters, Five Classic
Just-War Theories, unpublished dissertation, Yale,
1971, 159-162.
(13) "Historical Tradition and Moral Judgment: The
Case of Just War Tradition," Jour. of Rel. 64
(1984), 306.
(14) Grotius, De jure belli ac pacis, III, 4,6; and
see III, 4,8.

(15) Vitoria, De jure belli, 48.
(16) Grotius, De jure belli ac pacis, III, 11, 16.
(17) Grotius, De jure belli ac pacis, II, 21, 7 and 21; III, 11, 3 and 16.
(18) See James T. Johnson, Just War Tradition..., 204-212.
(19) Francis Lieber, Manual of Political Ethics (Boston: Little and Brown, vol I, 1838; vol. II, 1839), vol. II, 657-658. Quoted in James T. Johnson, Just War Tradition and the Restraint of War, 299.
(20) "War and Murder," in Wasserstrom, War and Morality (Belmont: Wadsworth, 1970).
(21) "War and Murder," 45.
(22) See, for example, Capital, Preface to the First German edition (New York: International Publishers, 1967), 10.
(23) Robert Harvenak, "The Reluctance to Admit Sin," Studies in the Spirituality of Jesuits, 9 (St. Louis: American Assistancy Seminar, 1977), 163.
(24) Mark Twain wrote of "the lie of the silent assertion," that is, "the silent assertion that there wasn't anything going on in which humane and intelligent people were interested." "My First Lie and How I Got Out of It," The Complete Short Stories and Famous Essays of Mark Twain (New York: Collier, n.d.), 567.
(25) See George I. Mavrodes, "Conventions and the Morality of War," Phil. and Public Affairs 4 (1975), 122-123. He is doing a critique of the "immunity theorist," such as Elizabeth Anscombe.
(26) See Robert K. Fullinwider, "War and Innocence," Phil. and Public Affairs 5 (1975).
(27) But see Lawrence A. Alexander, "Self-Defense and the Killing of Noncombatants: A Reply to Fullinwider," Phil. and Public Affairs 5 (1976), 410, 412, 415.
(28) "War and Innocence," 96.
(29) See Peter A. French, "Morally Blaming Whole Populations," in Philosophy, Morality, and International Affairs, ed. by V. Held, S. Morgenbesser, and T. Nagel (New York: Oxford, 1974), 280; Richard A. Falk, "The Circle of Responsibility," in Crimes of War, ed. by Falk, G. Kolko, and R.J. Lipton (New York: Random House, 1971); Michael Walzer, Just and Unjust Wars, 296-303. For the responsibility of noncombatant officials see Walzer, 287-296 and Sanford Levinson, "Responsibility for Crimes of War," Philosophy and Public Affairs 2 (1973), 244-273.

(30) See Virginia Held, "Moral Responsibility and Collective Action," in Peter A. French, ed., Individual and Collective Responsibility (Cambridge: Schenkman, 1972), 101-118.
(31) U.S. Catholic Bishops Letter, The Challenge of Peace (Washington, D.C.: U.S. Catholic Conference, 1983), #326.
(32) Casper Weinberger, "U.S. Defense Strategy," Foreign Affairs 64 (Spring, 1986), 681.
(33) Summa Theo. II-II, 105, 3 ad 4.
(34) Summa Theo. II-II, 64, 7. John Connery calls this "a difficult thesis to which authors have offered different explanations." Abortion: The Development of the Roman Catholic Perspective (Chicago: Loyola, 1977), 126.
(35) Summa Theo. II-II, 64, 7.
(36) De ablatorium restitutione, Lib. 2, c. 3.
(37) Quaestionarium Theologicum, q. 38, dub. 3, cited in Connelly, Abortion.., 126-128.
(38) "War and Murder," 45n.
(39) "Notes on the Literature," Readings in Moral Theology #1 (New York: Paulist, 1979), 334. The Truman quote can be found in Wasserstrom, War and Morality, 83.
(40) "Notes..," 334-335.
(41) "Notes..," 334.
(42) "Notes..," 332.
(43) See his "Some Paradoxes of Deterrence," Jour. of Philosophy 75 (June, 1978), 285-302, esp. Sect. II., and "Nuclear Deterrence: Some Moral Perplexities," in Douglas MacLean (ed.), The Security Gamble: Deterrence Dilemmas in the Nuclear Age (Totowa: Rowman and Allanheld, 1984).

CHAPTER ELEVEN

JUST WAR REVIVAL AND NUCLEAR WEAPONS

The lack of an acceptable theory of natural law or just war proved troublesome at the war crimes trials after World War II. Those trained only in positivistic international law could do no better than to invent new laws during the trial (e.g., "crimes against humanity"). But the sense of need gave impetus and importance among theorists to the postwar writings of some major just war theorists. Two representative early writers in this revival were John Courtney Ford and John Courtney Murray. The one began applying the tradition to problems of contemporary war, especially the problems of air attacks and nuclear weapons, from the in bello perspective. The other first worked out moral guidelines for a contemporary foreign policy and only then turned to the causes that would justify war as a means of policy which, in turn, would set limitations to war's proportionality.

A. John C. Ford

Even though he saw the distinction between norms for international policy and personal ethical standards, and even though he wanted to investigate justified war in the present international situation, John C. Ford did not totally avoid one significant positivistic influence. If we recall how ius ad bellum analysis had more or less evaporated under the sun of European ideas of sovereignty and international law, it is not surprising that, while Ford was most influential in getting just war theory back in attention, he brought it in upside down.

Ford put at the center of his analysis the ius in bello principle of discrimination, but he did it in such a way as to make it more personalistic and more absolute, less political and prima facie, and to reduce the encroachment by in bello proportional allowance of "indirect" killing. Moreover he phrased it in the medieval terminology of "the innocence of noncombatants." From such an approach, he had to condemn the strategy of "obliteration bombing."

> Obliteration bombing... is an immoral attack on the rights of the innocent. It includes a direct intent to do them injury.

Even if this were not true, it would still
be immoral because no proportionate cause
[obviously here he means a military target
of _in bello_ proportionate cause] could
justify the evil done; and to make it
legitimate would soon lead the world to the
immoral barbarity of total war.[1]

It was not difficult for him to see that this
could entail the condemnation of all modern war, since
modern weapons lacked any assurance of effecting such
discrimination.[2] But Ford backed away from that
logical entailment. Instead, he insisted that modern
war could be made moral if it were made non-total,
that is, if it followed the _in bello_ rules of
discrimination and proportionality in its targets.

These two points were repeated in his analysis of
the use of nuclear weapons. First he argued that
hydrogen bombing of cities could not qualify under the
proportionality test alone and justify killing
innocents "only indirectly." It also had to face the
test of discrimination.

But it may be urged that the hydrogen
bombing of cities could by justified
because there would be no _direct_ intention
of killing the innocent.... It would
merely be the reluctantly permitted
side-effect of a good action, the
destruction of military targets.... There
comes a point where the immediate evil
effect of a given action is so
overwhelmingly large in its physical
extent, in its mere bulk, by comparison
with the immediate good effect, that it no
longer makes sense to say that it is merely
incidental, not directly intended, but
reluctantly permitted.[3]

The good effect here is thought of exclusively as some
in bello military objective, not as an _ad bellum_
cause. What Ford did was to assert that numbers may
shift where _in bello_ proportion justifies encroachment
of targets protected by the principle of
discrimination. He was putting forth a new judgment
call, aiming at a new consensus, on the basis that
nuclear weapons are a significantly new circumstance.

One recalls that in the tradition the response to any new and terrible weapon was to say that an <u>ad</u> <u>bellum</u> cause could be so important that, in terms of <u>ad</u> <u>bellum</u> proportionality, the hierarchy of values in terms of the public common good justified using the weapon on the principle that "otherwise injustice may win." An approach along these lines was taken by Ford's good friend, Gerald Kelly, in the early 1950's.

All of us would undoubtedly agree that atomic weapons should be outlawed. Yet in the supposition of the conflict between theistic, peace-seeking nations and atheistic, aggressive forces, such a compact is hardly possible. The atheist would choose his own weapon. Granted this supposition, I agree... that the use of the hydrogen bomb by the defensive nations can be justified. I also agree that when such a weapon is directed toward a military target, the damage to civilians can be explained as indirect, even though it be terribly devastating. Finally, I think that (one) is wrong in saying that there can be no proportionate reason for permitting this devastation; for, in the supposition I am making (which is certainly not unrealistic), there is a question of preserving the lives, as well as the religious and civic liberties of more than half the world. I think that this is a sufficient compensating reason for almost any amount of damage indirectly inflicted on the citizens of the atheistic, aggressor nations.[4]

I also agree... that, once the United States was certain of an imminent attack by an aggressor with an atomic bomb, our government would have no obligation to await the attack before using atomic bombs on the military targets of the aggressor nation. In fact, I should think that there would be an obligation not to await such an attack.[5]

Kelly thus had taken the position prior to Ford's paper on the hydrogen bomb that if the weapon is used to attack many individuals, some of whom are legitimate targets, then it can be interpreted that the killing of the innocent people is indirect. In addition, if it is because of the number of these killed that one claims a different moral judgment, the claim actually rests on proportionality and not on the principle of discrimination. Therefore, in the context of Kelly's "supposition," the ad bellum cause would support both the use of nuclear weapons against military targets and also "terribly devastating" albeit indirect damage to "civilians."

Ford, however, argued that the ad bellum cause and its proportionality element were insufficient to balance off the in bello disproportionality in the damage done to innocent lives.

> It is illegitimate to appeal to the principle of the double effect when the alleged justifying cause is speculative, future, and problematical, while the evil effect is definite, enormous, certain, and immediate.[6]

As a boost to this, he added the ex semel licita caution of the moralists.

> Furthermore, if this kind of warfare were once conceded by moralists to be legitimate, it would mean the practical abandonment of any distinction between innocent non-combatants and guilty aggressors.[7]

He admitted that deciding what counts to make someone a legitimate target in a mobilized industrial society is quite different from past qualifications. But he seemed to draw the line somewhere in the area of "essential" material cooperation.

> But stretching the term combatant to the very limit and beyond all reasonable limits, and including in it all the employees of all manufacturing industries of every kind, and all those engated in public utilities, in transportation, in communications, and in contract construction in that whole area (New York-Newark in 1951), they would all together constitute less that 25 percent of the total ten million inhabitants. Three-quarters of that population, seven

and one-half million people, are innocent human beings, innocent of the one thing which in our theology would make them legitimate targets of direct violence, namely violent warmaking, or sufficiently close cooperation in violent warmaking.[8]

Tactically, it is important to distinguish the many levels of contribution involved in technologically advanced societies whose members have been mobilized. Significant reflection is needed to settle the ethics of whose contributions to the war effort make them valid targets for attack. Are the persons who work to make the troop trains run vulnerable to ethical attack? What of those who work in munition factories? In steel factories? Those who mine the ore? What of those who work in communications centers? It misses the point if one insists upon using categories that were given content before the times of the mobilization of all major societal sectors for a state's "war effort." Likewise, it abandons the discussion if one despairs with appeals such as "Well, at least there are the children." An ethical assumption is that "ought implies can." But there is no way in our times to attack a mobilized nation without disrupting the lives of all therein, and that entails attacking the lives of children. And we have seen above that Ford drew back from the conclusion that the unavoidability of attacks on the innocent was so abhorrent that all modern war was ruled out. The question then is: did his interpretation of the principle of discrimination on the in bello level in fact disqualify even the minimal means necessary to have a chance to act successfully for a just cause? One can here see how troublesome it is to try to work out a just war theory starting on the in bello level.

One may question whether Ford attended sufficiently to the political differences between the medieval kingdom and the modern state in respect to the responsibilities of citizens. If we take the concepts of "guilt" and "innocence" to refer to the dimension of responsibility, there can be many different mixtures of guilt and innocence in nearly all the people in a modern nation. Clausewitz was touching upon an important fact when he said that the "will of the people" is one of the most important targets if one's war efforts were to be successful. Such was not true in medieval times when the identification of innocent and noncombatant was made in the many lists of classes of those who were not ethically vulnerable in war. Ford held that any intention to "destroy enemy morale" was simply a euphemistic phrase for "killing and maiming innocent non-combatants in order to frighten the resistance out of those who survive."[9]

Neither does it help to talk of "guilt" or "innocence" in reference to the dimension of moral guilt. As we have seen, the publicists from Vitoria and Grotius on saw it was seldom easy to identify objective moral guilt or justice in international struggles. Perhaps better would be to seek out the facts in each case of who contributed, and how (actively, passively) to the policy decisions that led to the beginning and the continuance of the war. Again Clausewitz's identification of the "will of the people" is very pertinent. Perhaps the many levels of contribution in today's various types of societies would make the old lists of classes (e.g., farmers, fishermen, foresters, teachers, priests) misleading.

No theorist has ever denied that some discrimination in targets in war is an ethical requirement. Even the positivists held that only "necessary" killing was justified. But when Ford gave new life to the just war tradition in the 1940's and 1950's, he did it in such a way that in bello discrimination became the principal moral problem of war. Not only is this something new in the long tradition of justified war thinking, but it tends to dilute assistance from the tradition to the many different kinds of wars and crises today. If nations have the right to defend themselves by violence if necessary, then the ad bellum level and the proportional physical evils that it necessarily entails must be kept in the analysis of in bello level violence.

B. John Courtney Murray

John Courtney Murray, from the 1940's to the 1960's, worked on problems connected with justified war within a theory of contemporary international relations. After an initial euphoria with the possibility of institutions expressing a true, international community analogous to the institutions of a single society, Murray shifted to the "ability to conduct reasoned discourse" as basic to international relations. That is, he urged a commonality of language of natural law which would involve agreement on meanings of terms to identify values and goals. Out of this came a consistent theme of his later years, the requisite for people to keep lines of dialogue open with opponents. Finally, by the 1960's, Murray had concluded that the central problem of international politics was "the moral problem of the use of force as an instrument of policy."[10] He was one of the first to recognize, with little explicit reference, that Clausewitz's thesis is the international premise most in need of moral guidelines.

He discerned three major factors hindering clear thought on this use of force. First was the gulf in the American psyche between individual and collective morality. A mainstream interpretation of morality, one that led to pacifistic isolation or idealistic disapproval of the use of power, refused to acknowledge societal moral standards. Murray rejected this interpretation of morality as voluntaristic, subjectivistic, and individualistic.[11]

It is voluntaristic in that it sees morality as identical with the will of God as expressed in the Christian scriptures. It insists expressions as "resist not evil" or "turn to the other cheek" are to be taken literally. This kind of morality denies any intellectual examination since it holds that acts are right or wrong solely because of the will of God.

It is subjectivistic in that it sees morality as primarily a matter of the sincerity of one's interior motive, especially the motive of love. This kind of morality denies moral approval to any expression of national self-interest such as involved in some uses of power in relations.

Finally it is individualistic in that it sees morality solely as a matter of interpersonal relations of individuals. It denies any difference in moral standards that obtain for societal institutions from those that obtain for private individuals.

The other two hindrances grow out of this voluntaristic, subjectivistic, and individualistic mindset. The one is the problem of the tension between the dynamic of a state acting in its self-interest, which dynamic is *handicapped by the

American morality tenet that acting in self-interest for an individual is a primal evil. Murray responds:

> The obligatory public purposes of society and the state impose on these institutions a special set of obligations which, again by nature, are not coextensive with the wider and higher range of obligations that rest upon the human person.... In a word, the imperatives of political and social morality derive from the inherent order of political and social reality itself, as the architectonic moral reason conceives this necessary order in the light of the fivefold structure of obligatory political ends--- justice, freedom, security, the general welfare, and civil unity or peace.
>
> It follows, then, that the morality proper to the life and action of society and the state is not univocally the morality of personal life, or even of familial life.[12]

The third hindrance was that the issue of power upsets the American psyche since it has, since the early Nineteenth century, held the idealistic position that the state should avoid any use of power (military, economic, or diplomatic) in foreign affairs. Murray insisted that state force is an instrumental means which necessarily coerces life, liberty, and property, but only for the sake of some justifying goal. (Murray thereby employed the Principle of the Double Effect, which accepts that the end justifies the means, but not any expedient means, only one whose cost in values sacrificed is proportional.)

> Force is the measure of power necessary and sufficient to uphold the valid purposes both of law and of politics. What exceeds this measure is violence, which destroys the order both of law and of politics.[13]

By holding that the end of politics and law is order, Murray adopted the Augustinian position of a spectrum of justice in the nations of <u>Civitas</u> <u>Terrena</u>. Recall, Augustine proposed that one can judge the relative justice of such nations by their intention and success in respect to controlling avarice and the lust of domination.

If the power that comes from technology is to be ethically handled, the goals and direction must come from human choice by political decision makers. That is, only those moral principles that have come from induction from the decisions of persons involved in concrete international reality can be correctly applied to political decisions. This is sound methodology.

But it is here that Murray, along with others, found the United States greatly lacking.[14] It had no doctrine of a world order or legitimacy, and so interpreted each crisis as of ultimate significance. There was absent a set of intermediate categories in which to formulate the multiple situations in international relations today. Not only the Washington administration, but also the media and the people were unable to nuance the ebb and flow of events in reference to the public common good, but rather categorized everything in foreign relations as "victory" or "defeat." There was little patience with slow or long range developments. Persuasive sounding slogans abounded for Americans whose disposition it is to simplify. Constantly the demand was to settle problems in some final manner, and then "get out." (Things have not changed much in the past two decades.)

Murray therefore insisted that a usable ethical theory respond to an honest appraisal of the political realities of the day. There must be a "dialectical process, an alteration between principle and fact," each stage clarifying and modifying the interpretation of the other.[15]

For Murray himself, there were three facts of the international scene that specified the present era. The first was the possibility of a nuclear total war.[16] The second was the reality of the communist threat to the values of the North Atlantic civilization. (One might recall here that Albert Einstein made an exception to his strong pacifistic convictions in reference to the radical threat to human values he found in the Nazis.) Murray wrote:

> [The Soviet state] is an imperium, a mode of rule guided in its internal and external policy by a comprehensive systematic doctrine that contradicts at every important point the tradition of the West.

Only Soviet doctrine makes Soviet power a threat to the United States. Only Soviet doctrine explains the peculiar nature of Soviet imperialism.[17]

The Soviets have given some cause for such a judgment. In a reply to a Chinese challenge in the Sino-Soviet difficulties in the early 1960's, the Communist Party of the U.S.S.R. said in an open letter:

We fully support the destruction of capitalism. We not only believe in the inevitable death of capitalism but we are doing everything possible for it to be accomplished through class struggle as quickly as possible.[18]

The third fact is the "existence" of an "international organization which is committed by its charter to the preservation of peace by pacific settlement of international disputes."[19] Perhaps Murray let his hope exceed his experience on this last fact and interpreted the creation of the United Nations as indicative of widespread aspirations for new ways to settle international problems. Others have since interpreted it as the last phase of the international law approach, expressing a European temperment, which looked to charters and treaties to control international affairs.

From this sketch, we might construct the schema Murray had in mind for an ethical approach to foreign policy.

The first step would be to define the problem to be handles. The definition would be done by identifying with value judgments the boundaries of what is acceptable and what is not in the matter of any specific international series of events. For example, given Murray's list of the major facts of the present scene, the U.S. might decide that the problem to be handled was "how to limit the Soviet success in fostering Communist world order."

The next step would be to define the goal to be achieved by policy. Probably this would be in rather formal terms at first, such as "containment". So the process cannot stop there but must go on to specify what actual situation would count as containment in the present world relations.

194

Finally there would be approval and rejections of various means to bring about the solution and the goals. One model Murray himself brought forth was the model of a "limited nuclear war"; the war possibility itself was required by ad bellum causes, its limitation was required by ad bellum proportionality.

> [F]orce is still the ultima ratio in human affairs. . . its use in extreme circumstances may be morally obligatory ad repellendam iniuriam. The facts assert that today this ultima ratio takes the form of nuclear force, whose use remains possible and may prove to be necessary, lest a free field be granted to brutal violence and lack of conscience. The doctrine then asserts that the use of nuclear force must be limited, the principle of limitation being the exigencies of legitimate defense against injustice. Thus the terms of public debate are set in two words, "limited war."[20]

The creation of such a possibility Murray saw as a work of intelligence, which was to take place on many policy levels (political, diplomatic, military, technological, scientific, fiscal, etc.), with the very important inclusion of public opinion and public education. The creative solution would be in three stages. The first would be the conceptual analysis phase of the construction of a model of the limited war, a phase wherein Murray, without acknowledgement, gave concurrence to Clausewitz.

> Its value consists in making clear the requirements of limited war in terms of policy on various levels. Notably it makes clear that a right order must prevail among policies. It makes clear, for instance, that the limitation of war becomes difficult or impossible if fiscal policy assumes the primacy over armament policy, or if armament policy assumes the primacy over military policy, or if military policy assumes the primacy over foreign policy in the political sense.[21]

The next stage would be to question the situational possibilities.

The question then is, where and under what circumstances is the irruption of armed conflict possible or likely, and how is the limitation of the conflict to be effected in these circumstances, under regard of political intentions, as controlling of military necessities in situ?[22]

Finally, the policy decision conjoins the first two stages.

Policy is the hand of the practical reason set firmly upon the course of events. Policy is what a nation does in this or that given situation. In the concreteness of policy, therefore, the assertion of the possibility of limited war is finally made, and made good. Policy is the meeting-place of the world of power and the world of morality, in which there takes place the concrete reconciliation of the duty of success that rests upon the statesman and the duty of justice that rests upon the civilized nation that he serves.[23]

Murray, a man of his time, took the communist threat as the focal ad bellum cause. He did not investigate formulae to interpret other possible causes that could arise with the present multiplication of ethnic, religious, and revolutionary agitation in the world.

NOTES

(1) "The Morality of Obliteration Bombing," Theo. Studies 5 (1944), 308-309.
(2) "The Morality of Obliteration Bombing," 267; "The Hydrogen Bombing of Cities," Theo. Digest 5 (1957), 6.
(3) "The Hydrogen Bombing of Cities," 7.
(4) Gerald Kelly, "Notes on Moral Theology: 1950," Theological Studies 12 (1951), 58.
(5) Gerald Kelly, "Notes on Moral Theology: 1951," Theological Studies 13 (1952), 66.
(6) Ford, "The Hydrogen Bombing of Cities," 8.
(7) "The Hydrogen Bombing of Cities," 8.
(8) "The Hydrogen Bombing of Cities," 6-7.
(9) "The Hydrogen Bombing of Cities," 7.
(10) We Hold These Truths (New York: Sheed and Ward, 1960), 90.

(11) "Morality and Foreign Policy," in _Between Two Cities: God and Man in America_, ed. by Davis, Campion, and McHugh (Chicago: Loyola, 1962), 109-130, esp. 110-111.
(12) "Morality and Foreign Policy," 122.
(13) _We Hold These Truths_, 288.
(14) See also Kissinger, _American Foreign Policy_ (New York: W.W. Norton, 1977), 32-33.
(15) _We Hold These Truths_, 270.
(16) _We Hold These Truths_, 249.
(17) _We Hold These Truths_, 228.
(18) "The Soviet Reply to the Chinese Letter," letter of the Central Committee of the Communist Party of the Soviet Union, _Pravda_, July 14, 1963; cited in _The Current Digest of the Soviet Press_, XV, 28 (Aug. 7, 1963), p. 23; also in Kissinger, _American Foreign Policy_, 36.
(19) _We Hold These Truths_, 250.
(20) _We Hold These Truths_, 270.
(21) _We Hold These Truths_, 271.
(22) _We Hold These Truths_, 271.
(23) _We Hold These Truths_, 271-272.

CHAPTER TWELVE

DETERRENCE, NUCLEAR WEAPONS, AND THE JUST WAR

It appears that the question of the use of nuclear weapons is intuitively on the in bello level, but it reaches the ad bellum level also. The in bello aspects are the problem of proportionality and the problem of discrimination. The ad bellum aspect is the proportionality component of the just cause.

The in bello proportionality problem arises as leaders attempt to concentrate any use of nuclear weapons solely on military objectives and make every effort to minimize the indirect killing of noncombatants, the destruction of non-military property, and the disruption of the ordinary social order. The discrimination problem arises for those such as John Ford who judge that the enormous destructive power of nuclear weapons cannot but be considered to have noncombatants as their direct target. Finally, the ad bellum problem is whether any cause is so important as to make such destruction of life and property proportional.

Those who hold the use of nuclear weapons to be immoral on the in bello proportionality account emphasize that such use against military installations, weapons, or personnel would have side-effects so devastating, either immediately or over a time, that no military objective could be proportionate to the physical harm done to all lives, both combatant and non-combatant.

Those who hold the use of nuclear weapons to be immoral on the in bello discrimination account emphasize that certain groups in any society are morally immune from direct attack, e.g., children, hospital patients, the elderly, those who cooperate simply in maintaining the regular life of the society, those who cooperate merely in some "material" way to the war effort, etc. But nuclear weapons, which attack all in the area, would attack many in such groups. The claim is that this would amount to direct attack upon the innocent. This position seems to assume that the prohibition of direct killing of the innocent is an absolute, apriori sovereign principle.

We have discussed earlier the non-identity of innocent and noncombatant. Many noncombatants actually could be more or less formal cooperators in contemporary nations, especially after their government had controlled the information and analysis of the war situation. That is, they would at least support the ad bellum action of their country, even though they may not be formal cooperators who support many in bello aspects. Likewise, there seems to be some basis for a social responsibility simply from being a member of the society.

Nevertheless, this ambiguous status of noncombatants is not peculiar to the matter of nuclear weapons. What is peculiar is this. The ethician has difficulty getting a purchase on the nuclear weapons disputes because, for the first time, the arguments are occurring beforehand. There has not yet been a nuclear war. Even though there have been two wartime uses of nuclear devices, we must expect that there would be morally important differences between these two instances in the past and any future war wherein the use of nuclear weapons would be intrinsic to an overall policy.

So we might well separate three questions: what of the present prewar strategy on future wartime use; what of the present use as a deterrent prior to war; and what of any actual use in the future. The first two questions connect with existing decisions. The last has only a speculative basis.

The popular understanding of how nuclear weapons are intended for use (and, consequently, how they function as a deterrent) is that they are targeted against the society of the potential enemy. This is analogous to holding all the people of the enemy's cities as hostages, and is termed the countervalue strategy.[1] Nuclear attacks would "directly" kill many nonmilitary citizens of the enemy's country. This seems prima facie to violate the principle of discrimination. It was articulated by Defense Secretary Robert McNamara in his budget speech in 1968 and became identified as the Mutual Assured Destruction (MAD) or Balance of Terror strategy. It is effective for mutual deterrence on the condition that one's enemy has the same strategy.

Actually the most likely major nuclear enemy of the United States, the Soviet Union, never committed itself to that strategy, but has consistently examined and prepared for war with limited use of nuclear weapons. The book, Marxism-Leninism on War and Army, written by a group of Soviet authors, listed in the Great Soviet Encyclopedia as a basic reference for the subject of military doctrine, and intended for Soviet officers studying doctrinal teachings on war, has this in reference to how policy would control and thus limit the use of nuclear weapons:

> As regards [nuclear war's] essence, such a war would also be a continuation of the politics of classes and states by violent means. Politics will determine when the armed struggle is to be started and what means are to be employed. Nuclear war cannot emerge from nowhere, out of a vacuum, by itself.... Armed struggle with the use of nuclear missles and other weapons will ultimately be subordinated to the interests of a definite policy, will becomes a means of attaining definite political aims.[2]

In 1973, the head of the propaganda department of the military daily Red Star wrote:

> No weapon can change the political essence of war. It has been and remains a continuation of the policy of the state and classes by violent means. The nature of a given war, that is, whether it is a just, liberation, aggressive, or reactionary war, depends on what political aims are pursued in it.[3]

For the official Soviet planning tenets, the suggestion that the reality of nuclear weapons turns war into something that no longer is limited by the framework of policy is "theoretically incorrect and politically reactionary."[4]

By the mid 1970's, the U.S. announced that it had shifted to a counterforce strategy, with only military targets for the use of its nuclear weapons.

One may have doubts about these official policies, but, for the immediate discussion, let us stipulate the seriousness of these official limitations. The fact is indubitable military targets are often around or even within cities, and so nuclear attacks would "indirectly" kill many nonmilitary citizens of the enemy's country. This pertains to _in bello_ proportionality. For example, a nuclear attack on a valid military target which borders on a medium sized city might "indirectly" kill many thousands of nonmilitary citizens.

Those who hold the use of nuclear weapons to be immoral on the _ad bellum_ level claim that no cause for war itself could justify the resultant physical evils to civilized life that would occur during the course of the war. This is a claim that no rational purpose for going to war could outweigh the disadvantages to all the societies affected by a war using such weapons. Even more starkly, some worst case scenarios claim that the necessary conditions for those values the defense of which one would enter war in the first place would be annihilated. Thus a nuclear war would be self-contradictory.[5]

The annihilation would occur subsequent to one of two developments: there would be an inevitable escalation of the use of nuclear weapons (Clausewitz's Absolute War dynamics), or there would be, even after a limited use, an ecological breakdown that would be universal and devastating (a "nuclear winter").

This premise of an inevitable escalation must at present remain pure speculation since we have no experience on which to base it. It envisions Clausewitz's absolute war without Clausewitz's real world political constraints. It presumes a loss of minimum rationality on both sides. Certainly there is evidence that political activities and human viciousness may well lead those with nuclear capabilities to acts of military aggression in the limited manner usual in the past, as long as it promises to be of political benefit.[6] But all indications are that no major power is willing to fight to the end, taking all down with it if necessary. (The outstanding exception to this was Hitler's attitude toward the end of World War II.)

Likewise the threat of an ecological breakdown, even if a nuclear war was limited but went past a "threshold" level, seems to have been downgraded from the status of certain to that of speculative or even doubtful by more sophisticated and less controversial scientists.[7]

On the supposition of rational limitation of nuclear weapons in war, one can face what used to be the first element in judging a war: the justice of its cause. What ad bellum causes in our day could justify the limited use of nuclear weapons? It would have to be a cause that would substantiate a qualitative superiority to the enormous existential evils involved in such a war.

Acting to achieve the presence of a situation is justified, even though there is the risk or the certainty of a second effect that is existentially evil (values are somehow negated), by the qualitative superiority of the human values to be achieved over the values to be negated in the second effect. (This is the core of the principle of the double effect.) Acting to achieve the absence of a situation is justified, even if there is the risk or the certainty that existential evils will be brought by the performance, by the qualitative superiority of the human evil to be prevented over the evils that are accepted or effected by the performannce. (This is the core of the principle of the lesser evil.)

Using the former principle, one regrets the concomitant evil but finds it reasonable to do the performance to achieve the superior good. Using the latter principle, one regrets the evil brought about but finds it reasonable to do the performance to prevent the greater evil.

Both principles are needed in a complex and flawed human world. Both principles are species of the end justifying the means. But there is no apriori moral difficulty with that. Nothing else but the end could justify the means. And there would be no intelligibility in using the term "means" at all except as related and subordinated to an end. The moral question only troubles us as we acknowledge that an end seldom justifies every expedient means. Reason demands a qualitative (and not merely a quantitative and utilitarian) proportionality. That is the point of the "qualitatively superior" qualification above.

The second new question engendered by nuclear weapons is the question of their use as a deterrent. This also is a question about a set of policy decisions already being carried out, and there is a dispute whether the use of such weapons as a deterrent can reasonably be separated as a distinct moral question from that of their use in war.

Let me set out a formulation of those elements that seem requisite for a policy of nuclear deterrence and which would be matters for moral evaluation.[8]

1. The intended end of nuclear deterrence is to prevent an act of aggression. (It is a tautology to talk of "an unjust act of aggression.") That an agent-state has this intended end is within the tradition of justified defense.

2. For the agent-state to use nuclear deterrence as the means that causally achieves this end is to impose a threat of death and destruction on a great number of individuals, many of whom, by an stipulation here of innocence, are not legitimate targets of such a threat.

3. Carrying out the threat is conditioned on the activities of the agent-state considered the potential aggressor. If it does not commit certain aggressive acts, the threat will not be carried out.

4. The agent-state intending deterrence does not want to follow this causal path of imposing a threat, and it would achieve the intended end in some other way if such were judged equivalently effective. The point here is that it is not a matter of selecting the cheapest, or the swiftest, or the most expeditious means, but rather a matter of selecting an available, morally proportionate means to achieve the intended end.

5. The agent-state adopts a public plan to activate the causal link between the means (the imposition of the threat) and the end (the prevention of the aggression).

Some want to identify the moral question of having nuclear weapons as a deterrent with the moral question of using nuclear weapons in actual war. These then go on to argue that, since the use of such weapons in war may not be envisioned, therefore having such weapons for deterrence likewise is morally unacceptable. The principle cited is that "If it is wrong to do an action, then it is wrong to intend (to threaten) to do the action."

As a preliminary to examining the matter of nuclear deterrence as a threat or as an intention, let me make a few comments on this principle, "If it is wrong to do an action, then it is wrong to intend (to threaten) to do the action." A model instance of how this principle works would be where Egbert intended to rob a bank but was prevented from carrying out the robbery because of uncontrollable circumstances. To judge that Egbert's intention itself was a morally wrong action makes sense because Egbert wanted to do the morally wrong robbery. As this model shows, the principle assumes that "to intend" an action includes "wanting" to do the action.

However, to apply the principle to a matter of deterrence brings out an ambiguity hidden in the phrase "intend to do". It might be used in reference to quite different decisions: (a) one may categorically intend to do the action in the future; (b) one may conditionally intend to do the action as soon as one finds the circumstances favorable, the time right, and so on; (c) one may conditionally intend to do the action unless someone else pre-empts the the possibility of doing the action; (d) one may conditionally intend to do the action unless someone else pre-empts the need to do the action to realize some goal; or (e) one may conditionally intend to do the action unless someone else performs in some way to relieve the need to rectify a situation.

The first four, (a), (b), (c), and (d), intentions clearly can be measured by the principle "If it is wrong to do the action, it is wrong to intend (to threaten) to do it". In all four cases the agent, by the intending, wants (positively wills) to do the action and is only delayed or prevented from doing it.

The fifth, (e), is the general form of the deterrence intention. Here it is unclear whether the agent wants to do the threatened action, and so it is at least unsettled whether it can be measured by the principle, "If it is wrong to do it, it is wrong to intend to do it."

Gregory Kavka argues that, even though actual use of the nuclear weapons is wrong, the threat to use them, which is the essence of the deterrence policy, may be morally permissible under certain circumstances.[9] Kavka admits that, if to do x action would bring about enormous amounts of physical evils, and therefore would be judged a morally evil action, then the intention to do that action would ordinarily receive the same moral judgment. However, the deterrent threat to do that x action, that is, the intention to do x action conditioned on the aggressive act of another, also brings about enormous good consequences: namely, the prevention of aggression which would of itself bring about enormous amounts of physical evils. Since these good consequences involve important human values, intending them as goals is rational. To achieve these good consequences (the intended end of #1 in the deterrence policy outlined above), the agent-state using nuclear deterrence accepts the risk that, if the aggression still takes place, it would apply the sanction. Therefore, given the alternatives of having the deterrence policy or not having it, the likelihood of maximizing the good consequences (the utilitarian criterion) favors having the policy.

But what if one holds that more is involved in the moral quality of an action than the good or evil "existential" consequences, a "more" that might refer, for instance, to "treating all persons affected as self-ordering ends in themselves" and not treat some "merely as means" (that is, the action destroys or debilitates some individuals' abilities to act as self-orderers) for the intentions of some others.

The principle of the double effect traditionally has been identified as the principle used by people when they settle those conflicts in moral decision where good is intended but the (risk of) evil to individuals is foreseen as an "unintended" effect of the action that will achieve the good effect. But in the paradigm case for the principle, the killing in self-defense, people so far have judged it reasonable

to intend to defend oneself (or others) if attacked
(and so to arm oneself beforehand) only if the act
taken to defend, the stopping of the aggressor, is
taken against the aggressor (and not against, say, the
aggressor's children). In the paradigm case, the
death of the aggressor is the second effect that is
foreseen as a risk as one arms oneself beforehand. It
is risked, but not intended (afterwards one can
truthfully say, "I didn't want to kill him, but I had
to"). In a second case, also in the tradition, the
risk of injury to, or death of individuals other than
the aggressor because of one's defense ("indirect
killing") has been judged as a moral second effect
that is foreseen, risked, but not intended if there is
qualitative proportionality between such a risk and
what is being defended.

The question on nuclear deterrence then is: is
conditionally intending to carry out a threat to do
action x, which action involves a risk of enormous,
even though "indirect", existential evil for an
unusually large number of individuals who, for the
sake of the question may be stipulated as
non-aggressive, able to be justified. Could people
reasonably judge that the conditional intention (to
use the weapons) is a moral means to prevent some
aggression that is qualitatively new to history? Many
ostensibly good people do make that judgment, and
there is no evidence that they are more than
ordinarily self-deceivers.

So can one uncover what in their understanding of
the context of the question of nuclear deterrence they
use in their judgment? I suggest the clue is in the
conditionality of the intention and in the paradox
that, the more publicly firm the intention, the less
likely the condition of aggression will occur.

First of all, these people see "conditional
threats made to prevent others from going against the
reasonable demand not to perform unjust actions" (=
deterrence) as morally different from "conditioned
threats made to prevent others from failing to comply
with certain unjust demands" (= extortion). The moral
difference cannot be in the fact that there is a
coercive threat, for that is true in both cases. And
it cannot be in the fact that the threat is
conditioned, for that is also true in both cases. The
moral difference is in how the conditionality relates
to the "end of the agent" (finis operantis). The one

end is to force others to refrain from doing unjust actions; the other is to force others to cooperate in unjust actions. Even if the actions threatened conditionally in deterrence and extortion would if done bring about enormous existential evils including perhaps existential evils that effect non-legitimate targets, so that both threats are thereby morally suspect, they are not equally morally suspect. Many good people judge that the one threat must morally be rejected, but they accept the other, albeit reluctantly.

If we add to this the paradox that, the more publicly firm the intention, the less likely the condition of aggression will occur (which non-occurrence precisely is the end of the deterrence intention), then it makes more sense why good people can judge nuclear deterrence to be morally acceptable. The policy, of which the conditioned threat is an essential part, is judged to be the best chance to prevent the existential evils in the anticipated aggression.[10]

The major moral problem for nuclear deterrence is that the condition which would bring about the carrying out of the intention is, apparently at least, not up to many individuals who are put at risk by the deterrence intention. This makes it quite different from the conditioned threat of justifiable homicide as part of a intention to prevent unprovoked aggression, or the conditioned threat of punishment intended as part of a policy to prevent crime.

There is an often commented upon contradiction in the position taken by the U.S. Catholic bishops that holding nuclear weapons (for the sake of deterrence while working for a more permanent solution) is morally permissible, but any use of nuclear weapons can never (as least as they now foresee) be morally permissible, because they accept the premise that there will be inevitable escalation to unlimited use.[11] The contradiction arises since the suasiveness of deterrence rests on the option to use such weapons.

We have commented on the inevitability of nuclear escalation. Here we might add that, even if it is wrong to threaten to bring about existential evils disproportionate to the existential evils prevented by the threat, it is not wrong to threaten to bring about existential evils proportionate to the existential evils prevented by the threat. What is needed here is a premise that there are values that could be important enough for a war that uses nuclear weapons. One might suggest as the moral end of the use of nuclear weapons as deterrents the protection of the independence of states and certain basic cultural values such as political liberty within at least some of these states. But even more important than specifics here is that this kind of proportionality is properly on the ad bellum level.

Perhaps the question "are nuclear weapons admissible means or not?" is the wrong way to phrase the question. If the ad bellum cause is there, would any nation not use weapons that are necessary, with the proper limitation for the sake of survival? Not using would equal renouncing the ius ad bellum, which would be a prima facie violation of the duty of governmental office holders.

A better question than "are nuclear weapons an admissible means" might be "what are admissible ends in the nuclear age?"

Examining the morality of the use of nuclear weapons, John Connery starts with the assertion that morality does not pertain to any weapon as such but only to its use.[12] He then takes in turn the question of the use of nuclear weapons as a deterrent and the question of their use in actual war. He starts by noting that the possession of nuclear weapons usually is justified by comparison with the cost of the war the weapons presumably prevent.

Locating the central moral problem in nuclear deterrence in the "intention to use," Connery acknowledges that the actual full scale use of nuclear weapons for the total destruction of an enemy would be immoral. And the immorality of such actual use would entail the immorality of the intention to use in this way, that is, for total destruction. So Connery proposes that the deterrent effect need not come from the intention to use after all, but from the "threat to use, without prior intention." This means that "the deterrent factor would really arise from the possession, or buildup, of the power" alone. Nothing more would be needed, save the undoubtedly permitted ambiguity about one's actual intentions in the minds of the leaders of a potential aggressor nation. Would this "threat without prior intention" be a moral policy?

Connery begins his examination proper by noting that the just war tradition stresses that actual war should be only the last resort, and, insofar as a strategy can prevent the military violence of war, it is prima facie moral, if the values at stake warrant such drastic action. The difficulty with nuclear weapons as a deterrent to war is that the possession of nuclear weapons "may in itself lead to the very violence it is meant to prevent." Connery nods here and mixes up cause and effect. As many have noted, the existence of military weapons has never been the cause but at most one necessary condition for a war. The tensions and animosities that obtain internationally are the causes of weapons, not vice versa.

Of course, it is true that no leaders could use or intend to use nuclear weapons if they did not possess them. But this is not an interesting moral point, since some leaders may intend to use them when eventually they have them. So it is clear that the possession is a condition and not a cause of the morally evaluated action.

Connery, however, is on track when he assumes that possession increases the danger of an immoral use. And he then asks: "Is there an alternative that would be as effective, but less dangerous, in preventing the use of nuclear weapons?" (As an aside one might note that the closest the major powers came to using nuclear weapons against each other was in 1962, when both their nuclear holdings were in many ways smaller than today.) Obviously, he says, mutual nuclear disarmament would be a safer kind of deterrent. Again, this is misspeaking slightly. The absence of a certain kind of weapon on each side is a condition that prevents either side from using that kind of weapon. But the situation cannot be called one of deterrence. In any case, disarmament of both strategic and tactical nuclear weapons is not a feasible goal in the near future.

If the prevention of nuclear war is a valid goal for policy, then the debate that must be entered, and not circumvented by slogans, is: what is the best way to prevent nuclear war?

Citing the only wartime uses of atomic weapons as support, Connery rejects unilaterial disarmament as an alternative that would lessen the danger of future use. Mutual nuclear deterrence probably is closer to a peaceful situation than any kind of unilaterial disarmament.

In his direct analysis of the use of nuclear power in war, Connery notes that, since the advent of nuclear weaponry, many advocates of the just war tradition have held that the destruction involved in contemporary war (that is, war using nuclear weapons) made it impossible to justify an offensive war. Heretofore the tradition accepted several causes as justifying war, one of which was, for example, to restore some important conditions of justice. But now many in the tradition argue that *in bellum* proportionality can never be approached due to the destruction probable with nuclear weapons.

But a war in defense (either of one's own country or of another) can still be justified. To forego self-defense, Connery says, has three aspects of irrationality: it is too burdensome for the ordinary person or for a country to observe; it gives an advantage to the unjust aggressor and thus weakens the cause of justice; and, in some cases, it may violate certain obligations that demand resistance to unjust attacks.

With this preparation, Connery turns to the question of the moral use of nuclear weapons in a defensive war. He sets up a range of scenarios.

If the enemy has launched an all-out attack (counterforce and countervalue) that could not successfully be intercepted, "there would be virtually nothing to defend in a second strike." Any striking back, he argues, could not be "defense in any true sense.... If, therefore, only self-defense can be justified, it is impossible to speak of a just response to an all-out nuclear attack."[13]

If the enemy has launched a selective nuclear attack (at least one of counterforce and perhaps also countervalue), something would be left to defend. In such a scenario, Connery holds that counterforce use of nuclear weapons might be a valid defensive action, even though some distinction between combatant and noncombatant must be observed.

210

This gets Connery into the murky matter of the possibility of a discriminative nuclear response. In limited use, he argues, there is some reason to think that the problem of fallout (and afortiori other collateral damage) can be within the limits of in bello proportionality, especially if the use is restricted to tactical weapons.

A third scenario emerges in a 1983 article wherein Connery again faces the use question: if conventional weapons are judged inadequate in a justified defense against an aggressor nation which has already initiated military attacks, may a nation employ nuclear weapons tactically in that defense?[14] The alternative, of course, would be to forego the justified defense. Could the moral duty of a nation in such straits be to surrender? If the aggression itself is limited (at least temporarily) to some incremental shift in control of territory of people, could the defending nation reasonably forego fighting and judge the use of nuclear weapons disproportionate?

One might object that this seems to violate the duty under contributive justice of the governmental office holders. Connery, however, does not take this tack. Rather he suggests that foregoing nuclear defense would mean that material destruction would be confined to only the victim country and, in addition, injustice would be permitted to succeed.

All this indicates, as many have pointed out, that the question of the use of nuclear weapons must not remain on the in bello level but must include also the ad bellum level of cause.[15] The ad bellum proportionality between the overall destruction of people, property, and institutions must be judged against the alternative, the avoidance of which makes going to war itself reasonable. Put negatively, if one judges that some particular use of nuclear weapons is not reasonable, one would have to accept a clear-headed estimation of the consequent costs to human beings in terms of their freedoms and dignity that have to be paid if the war is lost. If people will be killed either way, then it is not unreasonable for a government leader to choose the option that will bring a lower number of deaths. But this lower number of deaths is a matter of proportionality, not of the justice of the cause, which has the logical (but not moral) priority. Once there is war from a just cause, it is the duty of governmental leaders who represent a people to choose the alternative that will save more lives of that people (a stronger obligation) and more lives of all people (a weaker obligation).

In terms of _in bello_ proportionality, the tactical use of nuclear weapons (including their physical residue) could be reasonable in certain situations. But there is no experience to estimate how reasonable opposing leaders will be to restrict use to tactical areas. This problem is termed the danger of escalation and is a crossover problem between _in bello_ and _ad bellum_ proportionality.[16] The problem is exacerbated with the likelihood of the breakdown of the command, control, communications, and intelligence systems needed to keep such use limited.

To say that no direct but only indirect killing of the innocent is fundamental to the principle of discrimination is an interpretation that has received much recent debate even beyond the level of _in bello_ killing. That the killing of the innocent is a grave existential evil seems accepted by all sides. Pacifists argue that modern war is always immoral because it inevitably involves the violation of the absolute principle of discrimination. But it is begging the question to assert that the principle is absolute. It has not been absolute historically. It developed independently of _ad bellum_ analysis and through the centuries the major writers qualified it, at least by instruments such as the direct-indirect killing distinction and the proportionate reason modification. And it has not been considered absolute even in our century.[17]

On discrimination, William O'Brien has a four-step analysis. (1) An absolute application of the principle against direct intentional killing of noncombatants in the sense that no such killing would be foreseeable with a weapon's use is incompatible with warfare waged in any environment that includes noncombatants and civilian targets. Consequently, the absolute application makes the principle incompatible with any contemporary war. (2) It is meaningless to affirm a right to legitimate self-defense and yet prohibit the means necessary to make that right efficacious. (3) The traditional principle of the double effect distinctions of "direct" and "intentional" are not readily accepted as helpful. (4) So the principle must be understood to be not an absolute but a relative principle, that is, it "enjoins us to concentrate our attacks on military objectives and to minimize our destruction of noncombatants and civilian targets.... the standard... is proportionality."[18]

His point seems to be this: what means actually will best protect the innocent. If there are only alternatives wherein some innocents will be killed or lose their liberty and respect in the social environment, the reasonable choice is the one that will minimize such human evils. This is an application of the principle of the lesser evil. It is consequentialist in itself, which bothers some people. But it need not, for the principle is only reasonable when one is looking for a resolution for a problem after one has already identified important human values at stake, which values were not identified by means of some consequentialistic procedure. Here, for example, the principle is only used in the <u>ad bellum</u> proportionality after the cause has been established.[19]

NOTES

(1) The comparison of nuclear deterrence policy and the exchanging of hostages is often drawn. One of the first to use it was Thomas Schelling, <u>Stragegy of Conflict</u> (New York: Oxford University Press, 1960), 239. Recent usage is by Christopher W. Morris, "A Contractarian Defense of Nuclear Deterrence," and Steven Lee, "The Morality of Nuclear Deterrence: Hostage Holding and Consequences." Both articles are in the special issue on nuclear deterrence of <u>Ethics</u> 95 (April, 1985), 479-486 and 549-566.
(2) <u>Marxism-Leninism on War and Army</u> (Moscow: Progress, 1972), 28-29.
(3) Colonel I.I. Sidelnikov, <u>Krasnaya Zvezda</u>, Aug. 14, 1973, 2-3.
(4) See the November, 1975, issue of <u>Communist of the Armed Forces</u>.
(5) See Peter Moody, "Clausewitz and the Fading Dialectic of War," <u>World Politics</u> 31 (1979), 417-433.
(6) See T.N. Bjorkman and T.J. Zamostny, "Soviet Politics and Strategy Toward the West: Three Cases," <u>World Politics</u> 36 (1984), esp. 198-207.
(7) See, for example, Starley L. Thompson and Stephen H. Schneider, "Nuclear Winter Reappraised," <u>Foreign Affairs</u> 64 (1986), 981-1005. The original thesis was: Richard Turco, O. Brian Toon, Thomas Ackerman,

James Pollack, and Carl Sagan, "Nuclear Winter: Global Consequences of Multiple Nuclear Explosions," Science (Dec. 23, 1983), 1283-1292.
(8) I am in debt in this section to the article by Gerald Dworkin, "Nuclear Intentions," Ethics 95 (1985), 445-460.
(9) "Some Paradoxes of Deterrence," Journal of Phil. 75 (June, 1978), 285-302, esp. sect. II; and "Nuclear Deterrence: Some Moral Perplexities," first printed in Douglas MacLean, ed., The Security Gamble: Deterrence Dilemmas in the Nuclear Age (Totowa: Rowman and Allanheld, 1984). See also Michael Walzer, "Nuclear Deterrence," in Morality and Practice, James P. Sterba, e. (Belmont: Wadsworth, 1983), 315-323; and James P. Sterba, "Between MAD and Counterforce: In Search of a Morally and Strategically Sound Nuclear Defense Policy," Social Theory and Practice 12 (1986), 173-200, esp. 180-189.
(10) Dworkin, "Nuclear Intentions," 458.
(11) For more on the "intending-using" relation in moral judgments, see George Sher, "The U.S. Bishops' Position on Nuclear Deterrence: A Moral Assessment," in MacLean, The Security Gamble (see note 9), 78; and Robert W. Tucker, "Morality and Deterrence," Ethics 95 (1985), 476.
    For the position that the bishops' principle should have led them to nuclear pacifism, see Susan Moller Okin, "Taking the Bishops Seriously," World Politics, 36 (1984), 527-554. An interesting exchange in what the bishops did and did not say between Bruce Russett of the bishops committee and Keith Payne is in Orbis 27 (1983), 535-543, 28 (1984), 401-408.
(12) "The Morality of Nuclear Warpower," America (July 17, 1982), 25.
(13) Connery, "The Morality of Nuclear Warpower," 27.
(14) "The Right to Self-Defense in the Nuclear Age," America (Apr. 16, 1983).
(15) For example, William O'Brien, "Just War Doctrine in a Nuclear Context," Theological Studies 44 (1983), 200.
(16) See O'Brien, "Just War Doctrine," 208-209: also, James T. Johnson, Just War Tradition and the Restraint of War (Princeton: Princeton University Press, 1981), 196-224.
(17) See William O'Brien, The Conduct of Just and Limited War (New York: Praeger, 1981), 44-45, and notes 14 and 17.
(18) "Just War Doctrine," 210-212; see also his The

214

Conduct of Just and Limited War, 44-45.
(19) See James T. Johnson, Just War Tradition.., 223,
on Vitoria.

CHAPTER THIRTEEN

PRINCIPLES OF FOREIGN POLICY

Every statesman must attempt to reconcile what is considered just with what is considered possible. What is considered just depends on the domestic structure of his state; what is possible depends on its resources, geographic position and determination, and on the resources, determination and domestic structure of other states.[1]

The moral issue, in a nutshell, is to act with moral discrimination and judgment in an essentially immoral world. Moral choices are made in an atmosphere of trial and error, never once and for all. Moral decisions, as the great moralists have proclaimed, are made not in the abstract but in context, measuring the endlessly complex array of forces that are part of every moral choice.[2]

In chapter one we adverted that most thinking on the morality of international practices has grown out of thinking upon practices in war. The Just War tradition might plausibly be seen as moral thinking at the extreme along a spectrum of various international relations. But some consensus of what is proper in foreign policy decisions all along this spectrum has emerged and shifted and emerged again over time. It is perhaps important to reflect over some of the elements of this art of foreign policy before we turn to the contemporary matters of intervention, revolution, and terrorism.

I. Elements of Foreign Policy

George Kennan suggests that we begin with the premise that "the conduct of foreign relations ought not to be conceived as a purpose in itself for a political society, and particularly a democratic society, but rather as one of the means by which some higher and more comprehensive purpose is pursued."[3] Foreign policy is a means, and it is distinctive for each state because each state materially conceives its own international purposes in a unique way.

Yet the means states use to accomplish their purposes includes the employment of, or response to, power. The power is of many kinds (e.g., economic, military), but it may be described formally as: "the exercise of significant choice expressed through organizations which results in control, by means of sanctions, of the decisions and actions of others in respect to values, which decisions and actions these others would not otherwise make or do."

(#1)The first element of foreign policy, consequently, is that the decision makers are to understand clearly to what ends their society exists as a political entity. Only from this will the decision makers understand the values and interests that are to be served by their decisions in the matters pertaining to foreign policy. They must know what they want.

Consonant with the principle of subsidiarity, the national government represents the interests and values of the people in relations with other nations. But this is a formal requirement only and lacks any substantive content directives. These values and interests must have at least enough specification to permit decision makers to know what foreign policy objectives and which means would be beyond proper bounds. A society that valied political participation, for instance, should consider support of foreign dictatorial governments suspect.

Presently, the differing states vary so much in their foreign policy purposes that, even though there are areas of attention common to many states at any time, there is little evidence that the values in those areas are at all commonly agreed upon. There is no real basis for concluding that there is any content in the notion of an "international Common Good" around which to talk of a "society of states."

In the Nineteenth century, European states looked upon themselves as the aristocentric standard for the civilized world. The other nations were viewed as only marginally developed and in needing to be taught how to live as members of the European household of nations.[4] In this worldview, the European states in some matters thought of themselves as part of a "society of states" pursuing at least some goals in common.

Since World War II, some groups have tried to promote the view that there can be and should be world planning (e.g., the push to bring about a "New Economic Order"). But experience continues to grow against a model of international relations involving an association of states which promotes substantive goals through deliberate cooperation, and of whose resultant benefits and burdens each member can justly claim a fair share. Experience rather supports the model of a system, an association of sovereign states, each with its own purposes, but conditionally consenting to abide by a procedural rules, to which each appeals, from which each can exempt itself by a further appeal, and of which newer states gradually learn the importance.[5]

Whether or not it may be "more reasonable" for the system to grow into an "international community" is not immediately an issue. A leader must make decisions relative to the actual political situation.

(#2)In order to work effectively toward the state's purposes, decision-makers must have a plan and a doctrine. "Being of good will" or "being sincere" are not substantive elements in foreign policy decisions. Without a plan with clear goals and several alternatives to respond to chance, friction, and the actions of other states, foreign policy agents bob along episodic waves of crises resolutions. Without a doctrine, foreign policy agents must paddle constantly to hold up their heads in a sea of immediacy.

> Those who are possessed of a definite body of doctrine and of deeply rooted convictions upon it will be in a much better position to deal with the shifts and surprises of daily affairs.[6]

The doctrine and the convictions enable a decision-maker to comprehend and evaluate the farrago of daily facts with some degree of wisdom. This body of doctrine would include an articulated theory of international relations, and specifically would in some way situate the power elements as characteristics (and not aberrations) in the scheme.

(#3)Consequent upon the first two elements, a state must attend to those world conditions that might affect its citizens and must plan how to act in reference to the actions and practices of other states, as well as the phenomena of friction and chance, that cause those conditions. This is the grounds for the use by the government of its many powers in long-term international relations. The acceptance and use of such powers is a reasonable corollary to the reasonableness of foreign policy as an institution. Insofar as possible, a state correctly acts in foreign affairs to maintain control over its future. Since other states act on the same premise, some sort of balance of power is a reasonable goal. Each state acts to maintain a scope for its future actions.[7]

It is common procedure, under the principles of independence and sovereignty, that one state does not ordinarily judge how just or how representative another state is internally. The attention is primarily on the actual foreign policy of the other state. This may be the promotion of political hegemony, conquest, economic expansion, an ideological ideal, or the enhancement of some tribal way of life.

Experience in the distant and in the recent past gives evidence that expansion and aggression often are the dynamics of states which discern weakness in others.[8] It is part of the duty of foreign policy decision makers to reduce this temptation. And with today's technology, the question is not whether a state will affect other states, but how it will affect others. Among other things, this means that decision makers must not be confined in their options to military force only as some last recourse. There have been over 100 wars since World War II, and none of them has been a total war. So a nation's leaders must have principles and forces for limited operations countering the dynamics of expansion and aggression.

However, one must note that "resisting aggression" is not properly a goal of foreign policy, but only a means employed in the overall process of achieving one's foreign policy's purposes. (This is the Clausewitzian formula from the top down.)

(#4) It is the constitutive duty of decision makers in the institution of foreign policy to serve the state's common good, and this is only possible with (that is, it is a necessary condition to have) existence as a political entity. The members of the society, to act in their varied ways for the common good and their private good, require as one minimum circumstance either the absence or at most the symbiotic influence of foreign military and political interference. Some have consequently concluded that the primordial responsibility that is central to foreign policy decisions is the survival of the complex integrity of the society.[9] This can be summarized under the rubric of "national security."

But certainly security is not properly a purpose, but rather a necessary condition. The leaders may not morally opt for those actions or policies that put the society as such at risk. This may mean in today's world a compromise or even cooperation with those nations whose governments have values incompatible with one's own.

Consequently, it is proper to indicate that there is a disconnection for foreign policy between survival and the use of military force. To employ the means of military force for justifiable political ends makes sense both militarily and morally. (Again, that is the message of Clausewitz's maxim: "War is the continuation of policy by other means.") But to make survival one of those ends tempts thinking to reduce all justifiable ends to that base alone. The Soviets, for example, with their insistence on the Clausewitzian theory of war, have all but removed survival from the list of possible issues at stake in the use of military force. Thereby, they can plan for limited war for limited political, economic, and ideological gains as part of a coherent policy. But the United States still remains troubled by its Nineteenth century ideology that this country should be beyond power politics in international affairs.[10] It has not yet clearly thought out what its military force is meant to accomplish as an instrument of foreign policy. It has not yet clearly defined its stategic purposes so that it can employ its military forces in limited, and therefore reasonable, ways. This is a serious fault when all its potential military adversaries, including its major adversary, find waging a limited war part of a sound strategy.

This confusion paradoxically opens to a very un-Clausewitzian premise that war itself is a matter of "either clear victory or defeat." From his writing, research, reflection, and teaching at the War College in 1946, George Kennan writes that "the most significant appreciation" he came to was that the unspoken assumption Americans held about the normal objective of war would have to be changed.[11] From the Civil War through World War II, the government, military, and people of the U.S. assumed that the objective of war was the total destruction of the enemy's ability and will to resist (Clausewitz's "absolute war"). This would open the way to the unhindered realization of the country's political objectives.

But in the post-World War II situation, this approach could no longer work. Kennan elaborates that today's total war, given nuclear weapons, forces us to return to concepts about the objective of war that help prior to our Civil War, that of limited war for limited political objectives (Clausewitz's "actual war").

Unfortunately, Kennan does not avert to the consequent problem of morale arising in the governmental, military, and civilian segments because of the limited objectives and limited results of such a war, a problem that became pertinent in the U.S. experiences in Korea and Vietnam. The people and the military lack awareness of what is involved and how to interpret the pursuit of limited political objectives by limited war.

(#5)The fifth element in a foreign policy for a democracy is that the actions and practices should be grounded in the values within the society they are designed to protect and promote. To claim any value as a human value is to claim it is such for all, and, consequently, the practices as means cannot contradict the values supported as the goal.

> If history teaches anything it is that there can be no peace without equilibrium and no justice without restraint. But I believed equally that no nation could face or even define its choices without a moral compass that set a course through the ambiguities of reality and thus made sacrifices meaningful.[12]

The irreducible human concern with morality in terms of which a democracy practices foreign policy is necessary to gain the support of the people who must see themselves expressed in those practices. But there are two cautions here. First, experience shows the troubles that arise as one nation tries to force its values without compromise into international relations. (This may be seen as a "cultural imperialism.") Second, leaders must be cautious and not try to base their policy on very general and ill-defined ideals rather than on specific goals and means. Kenneth Thompson calls this the principle of workability, and cites a recent leader who, in the world of sovereign nations each with its own national interests and its share of irrationality, tried to promote abstract and pure objectives that led, he thinks, to more harm than good to actual people in various countries.[13]

(#6) The sixth element is that leaders are not only to know what one's own country wants, but are to know what each country one deals with wants. This element assumes that the other country has its own policies, its own strategies, and its own purposes. The other country is not a "mirror-image" of one's own country.

There are four major divisions in the kinds of purposes other nations may have. Many other nations are seeking their purposes with a "decent regard for the interests of others."[14] But some nations hold some "positive aspirations, and one's that they regard as legitimate, more important to them than the peacefulness and orderliness of international life."[15] Still others show signs of seeking their interests in ways that disregard the interests of others.

In our day we may distinguish two types of disregard in the ways nations seek their interests. The first type has been described since the time of Thucydides, Plato, and Aristotle. It is the disregard of tyrants who act unjustly in striving to rule over others because of their passions for fame, wealth, glory, power, and dominion.

The second type of disregard historically is quite new. It is the disregard that grows from an ideology of an elite (e.g., Nazism) or an ideology of the process of history (e.g., Leninism). These ideologies logically demand, as a public practice, expansion of territorial or political control.

What is at stake in foreign policy in the context of this institutionalized type of disregard is more than the ordinary conflicts of diverse interests and values or even the conflicts with aggressive tyrants. Henry Kissinger said,

> We must understand the difference between governments making universal ideological claims and countries which do not observe all democratic practices---either because of domestic turmoil, foreign anger, or national traditions--- but which make no claim to historical permanence or universal relevance.[16]

There is something qualitatively different about an ideologically totalitarian society. An ideology eventually becomes so implanted into governmental structures that it affects all its actions and practices. Its leaders use terms that heretofore had referred to values and interests shared by many nations, but they still indicate by their actions and practices that their reference for such terms is equivocal to historical uses.[17] Ideological principles are expressed in words and phrases that connote commonly held moral values but are so unrelated to behavior as to be the exemplar of propaganda jargon. Eventually such jargon kills sensitivity to the truth.

The bases for the qualitatively different attitude toward the ideologically totalitarian society, then, is the pervasiveness of the equivocal use of ideas and the commitment to impose those distortions on other societies.

Given the fact that there are unjustly aggressive nations, given the principle that unless certain elements are present an international condition that obtains may not be peace at all, and given the exprience that non-violent tactics have only worked against Western democratic governments, a government must have policies to employ force reasonably.

(#7) In connection with this matter of ideological distortion, the seventh element of foreign policy is to know with whom one is dealing.[18] That is, policy makers must ascertain the character of the leaders of other nations based on their historical record at home and abroad. For example, have the

Soviet leaders consistently shown some character trait that would have significant repercussions on the effectiveness of, say, "countervalue" nuclear deterrence?

(#8) Finally, the eighth moral element is to know one's own country's strengths and handicaps. And the major handicap for foreign policy in a democracy is the fact that it is a democracy.

> Foreign politics demand scarcely any of those qualities which a democracy possesses; and they require, on the contrary, the perfect use of almost all those faculties in which it is deficient. . . a democracy is unable to regulate the details of an important undertaking, to persevere in a design, and to work out its execution in the presence of serious obstacles. It cannot combine its measures with secrecy, and it will not await their consequences with patience. These are qualities which more especially belong to an individual, or to an aristocracy.[19]

In today's international mix, the foreign policy institution of a democracy has both its traditional and some uniquely contemporary handicaps. The traditional handicaps, such as open internal discord intensified by partisan use of slogans and idealistic phrases in the legislative branch undermine the confidence by other nations in the timeliness and consistency of the policy by the democratic nation, have been exacerbated by the contemporary phenomena of the unprecedented proliferation of new states with various cultures and with quite different levels of development, and the ideological aggressiveness of a world superpower.[20] The former have no foreign policy tradition and the latter can put peculiar albeit indirect pressure on a democracy, especially in negotiations between states. The totalitarian state agents have no need to "reach an agreement" with agents of democratic states. But the latter are constantly and publicly examined to "show their sincerity" by accomplishing something precise and highly visible. This difference usually puts the agents for the democratic state, and eventually the democratic state itself, at a disadvantage.

The conduct of foreign policy seems to have two structural requirements almost impossible to obtain in a democracy: continuity and a measure of secrecy. In a democracy the office holders generally have a short tenure, and in a democracy the contemporay interpretation of freedom of the press as an adversarial watchdog of the government impels it to uncover the covered.

Unfortunately, this impelling can lead to abuses, since the duty in contributive justice for the press involves more than informing the people and watchdogging the leaders. Members of the press have a moral responsibility in their adversarial role not to perform it in ways that undermine the possibility of decision makers to act and react continuously and prudently in foreign matters. Journalists must not put such media pressure on that the leaders are unduly forced into immediate, emotionally satisfying but ahistorical solutions and episodic political showmanship.

The media's milieu is the "now." This is not the milieu for effective foreign policy, which is rather a milieu wherein "Events happen from day to day but they all happen as a result of long chains of causation which one must bear in mind if one is to see where the next link comes in or closes."[21] Kenneth Thompson puts it well. The concept of "foreign policy by continual referendum" misconceives the nature of the foreign policy process and its problems.[22]

This need not mean there will be no examination or criticism of foreign policy by the press, but it does mean that it is neither reasonable nor moral for the press to employ practices which subvert the very item that is to work in this area for the public good. To have the federal representatives daily answerable to popular summary denies the requirements of long-term progress.

Once again the disparity between democratic and totalitarian governments intensifies the problem. The totalitarian rulers do not have their foreign policy actions constrained by even analogous practices within their countries. In a democracy, the free and independent press can both inform the people and serve as a watchdog over their liberties. But the media in totalitarian nations serves solely as a propaganda instrument under rigid state control to indoctrinate rather than to inform.

Finally, in a democracy the journalistic media's concentration on the present action makes it difficult for them (especially T.V.) to convey certain things to the people which that people need in order to make intelligent judgments on the performance of their government's foreign policy. For example, during time of war, the T.V. journalists can show some aspects of the <u>in bello</u> performance, but they have often been unsuccesful in situating the <u>ad bellum</u> dimensions, even if they tried.

II. Three Functional Concepts of Foreign Policy

> On the other hand, occasions often arise when acts that seem preeminently worthy of a just individual and of the individual we call good reverse themselves and become their own opposites.[23]

I have argued that political ethics does not derive its substantive, second-level principles from the same sources as does personal ethics.[24] I have also argued that moral principles generalized from past decisions of good people are only as applicable to the present situation inasmuch as elements in the present belong to the set of elements from which the past generalizations were drawn. From our historical review, we can identify three concepts that always function in foreign policy moral decisions: power, utility, and necessity.

Power here is "the ability to act effectively for the true interests of the state on the international stage." Acquisition and maintenance of power thus is a necessary task because it is the omnipresent, even though never the exclusive, means for securing and promoting the morally required (under contributive justice) interests of the state. This will never be power for its own sake, but always power as needed to act in reference to the actual international conditions and the status of one's own country (e.g., is it a "great power"?) in the system of states.

Utility is "the choice of actions that are in the interests of one's state." Decision makers are to act as agents of the interests of the state, not as agents of justice in the world in some disinterested way, nor as some "world historical figure" on which the future will turn.[25] These interests are not formal ideals, but objectives so articulable that what counts as satisfaction of them can be specified.

Necessity is "the spectrum of choices limited by historical conditions of how to apply available power to actions to advance interests." That the spectrum of choices is limited by conditions implies that the goals one can actually plan to attain also are limited. But there is usually a spectrum of choices, and that makes room for political morality. Henry Kissinger writes:

> Yet there is a margin between necessity and accident, in which the statesman by perseverance and intuition must choose and thereby shape the destiny of his people. To ignore objective conditions is perilous; to hide behind historical inevitability is tantamount to moral abdication; it is to neglect the elements of strength and hope and inspiration which through the centuries have sustained mankind.[26]

As these three concepts function in the statesman's decision, it is inevitable that there will come times when that decision will conflict with the stateman's personal morality. Yet, by "necessity," the statesman will "have to" make the decision that overrides the call of personal morality. Today this is sometimes called "the problem of dirty hands."[27] Probably the most notorious summary of the dirty hands problem comes in Machiavelli:

> Any man who tries to be good all the time is bound to come to ruin among the great number who are not good. Hence a prince who wants to keep his post must learn how not to be good, and use that knowledge, or refrain from using it, as necessity requires.[28]

Lord Acton often said, "Great men are almost always bad men," and quoted Horace Walpole's saying that "No great country was ever saved by good men, because good men will not go to the lengths that may be necessary."[29] I suggest there is a moral pith hidden in these dicta that on the surface seem to recommend the abandoning of morality. This pith grows so dramatic because of the historical evidence that

those who acknowledge a moral duty to perform their
office well must at times do actions that cannot be
morally justified on the personal ethics level. What
Machiavelli said was that, if other states were
habitually virtuous, in both the personal and the
civil sense, then one's personal moral virtues quite
possibly could be employed to promote one's own
society's welfare. But in fact other states are not
so, and will not be so in this world.

Two points need expansion: (1) this is not an
advocacy of "might makes right" or a consequentialist
ethics in a utilitarian mold to secure some list of
arbitrary and subjective values; (2) this being "not
good" in reference to the level of personal morality
can be understood as either "excused" because of some
"necessity," or "justified" because of some more
important values that are in conflict with the
personal level values.

(1) "Might makes right" conveys the position that
there are no ethical values or virtues independent of
effective power used for the arbitrary self-expansion
of any state. But that one "must learn how not to be
good" implies precisely that it is morally virtuous
for the state leader to act thusly. The actions are
for the sake of morally compelling values to a state
office-holder, even though to act thusly is to act
contrary to what would be of personal virtue. It is
reasonable as well as virtuous to respect the value
hierarchy of one's office.

(2) In both "justification" and "excuse" there is
conveyed the idea that "doing something bad" can be
morally defended by insistence on a fuller description
of the event in its context.[30] If one justifies
"doing something bad," one accepts responsibility for
an act that does existential evil (harm), but denies
that it is actually bad (injurious in a legal or moral
sense) in the context (e.g., "justifiable homicide").
If one excuses "doing something bad," one admits that
the act actually is bad but qualifies the degree of
responsibility (e.g., "he hit me first"). There is
some existential evil that is not justified but from
which some significant circumstance diverts the force
of the _prima_ _facie_ moral judgment.[31]

In a sense, the basic concept of "necessity"
suggests that the leader can claim an excuse for
negating a personal level moral value. Yet in another

sense, the basic concept of "utility" suggests that the leader can claim a justification.

In neither sense is there denial that the act contains an existential evil, the doing of which on the personal morality level would be (very likely) morally wrong. And on that personal level there is no justification, there is only excuse. Machiavelli wrote: "When the act accuses him, the results should excuse him."[32] Machiavelli was not a "consequentialist" here proposing the principle "the end justifies any means." He did not say that the good results for the state justify an action that, on the personal level, would be wrong to do. The moral justification is on the political moral level. The higher value of the public common good justifies the means taken at the office level. But this necessity of office excuses on the personal level the means taken, "because virtue acts by necessity in confronting the uncontrollable chance."

Why does the superior relation of the office to the personal level only excuse and not justify the action on the personal level also? The immediate answer is: "the judgment does not say this to the one deciding." Most office holders who have expressed themselves on such decisions report the ambiguities of judgment that contribute to the label "dirty hands." The principle, then, comes from the actual decisions of people and is not imposed from an ideal which no leader has ever been able to use.

Machiavelli not only was quite insistent on a moral standard for the political level, but was equally insistent that acting on principles from personal morality would bring ruin to the state. For a morally good individual, it thus is necessary to learn, reluctantly, "how not to be good." This character trait, as Isaiah Berlin argues, is crucial for the good of society, and so it is a political virtue.[33]

Such a person uses some expression of the principle of the double effect in these conflicts. According to the principle's third requisite, the evil effect is "only permitted, not intended." This best is explained in the following form: "I had to (excuse from necessity) because of value y (justification from higher, morally compelling political value), but I didn't want to (regret because still respect personal level value)."

In international relations, the regret is often exacerbated because the activities of other states and the effects of chance dilate the degree of uncertainty.[34]

NOTES
(1) Henry Kissinger, A World Restored (Boston: Houghton Mifflin, 1957), 5.
(2) Kenneth Thompson, Understanding World Politics (Notre Dame: Notre Dame University Press, 1975), 202.
(3) Realities of American Foreign Policy (New York: W.W. Norton, 1966), 4.
(4) See Terry Nardin, Law, Morality, and the Relations of States (Princeton: Princeton University Press, 1983), 27-29; Elvin Hatch, Culture and Morality (New York: Columbia University Press, 1983), 13-34; Harold Nicolson The Evolution of Diplomacy (New York: Collier, 1962), 100-107.
(5) See Terry Nardin, 18-50.
(6) Winston Churchill, The Second World War: The Gathering Storm (Boston: Houghton Mifflin, 1948), 210.
(7) See Henry Kissinger, Arthur P. Salomon lecture, Sept. 25, 1977.
(8) See Emerich Vattel, Law of Nations III, iii, 42 and 47.
(9) See Henry Kissinger, American Foreign Policy, 3rd ed. (New York: W.W. Norton, 1977), 204.
(10) See Arthur Schleisenger, "Foreign Policy and the American Character," Foreign Affairs 62 (1983), 2-4.
(11) George Kennan, Memoirs: 1925-1950 (Boston: Little, Brown, 1967), 307-311.
(12) Henry Kissinger, White House Years: I (Boston: Little, Brown, 1979), 55.
(13) "The Ethical Dimensions of Diplomacy," The Review of Politics 46 (1984), 367-387.
(14) See Kenneth Thompson, Understanding World Politics, 210.
(15) George Kennan, American Diplomacy: 1900-1950 (Chicago: University of Chicago Press, 1951), 96.
(16) Arthur P. Salomon lecture, Sept. 25, 1977.
(17) Stanley Hoffmann notes, "A community of vocabulary is not the same thing as a community of values. . . . Behind the common grammar there are competing ideological logics." Duties Beyond Borders (Syracuse: Syracuse University Press, 1981), 20.

(18) See Carl von Clausewitz, On War, ed and trans. by Michael Howard and Peter Paret (Princeton: Princeton University Press, 1976), I, 1, 22.

(19) Alexis de Tocqueville, Democracy in America (New York: Knopf, 1945), I, 234-235. See also Harold Nicolson, The Evolution of Diplomacy, 21-25; and George Kennan, A Cloud of Danger (Boston: Little, Brown, 1977), 4.

(20) See Adam Weston, Diplomacy (New York: McGraw-Hill, 1982), 221.

(21) Winston Churchill, Parliamentary Debates, Vol. 458, Dec. 1, 1948, pp. 2019-20. Quoted in Kenneth Thompson, Winston Churchill's World View (Baton Rouge: Louisiana State University Press, 1983), 100.

(22) Understanding World Politics, 165-166. Harold Nicolson has this comment: "The theory that 'diplomacy should proceed always frankly and in the public view' had led to negotiation being broadcast and televised, and to all rational discussion being abandoned in favour of interminable propaganda speeches addressed, not to those with whom the delegate is supposed to be negotiating, with to his own public at home." The Evolution of Diplomacy, 120.

(23) Cicero, De officiis, I, 31.

(24) Helmut Thielicke has an interesting analysis of Bismarck, who had an analogous separation of political and personal ethics. See his, Theological Ethics, Vol. II: Politics (Grand Rapids: Eerdmans, 1979), 92-113.

(25) Thieliche makes the analogy of the difference between a player in the orchestra and the conductor. Theo.Eth., II, 103.

(26) White House Years: I, 55.

(27) See Michael Walzer, "Political Action: The Problem of Dirty Hands," Phil. and Public Affairs 2 (1973); reprinted in Cohen, Nagel, and Scanlon, War and Moral Responsibility Princeton: Princeton University Press, 1974).

(28) The Prince, tr. Robert Adams (New York: W.W. Norton, 1977), ch. 15.

(29) History of Freedom and Other Essays (1907), reprinted by Books for Libraries Press, 1967, 219.

(30) The locus classicus is in J. L. Austin, "A Plea for Excuses," in his Philosophical Papers (Oxford: Oxford University Press, 1961), 123-152.

(31) See Dante Germino, "Second Thoughts on Leo Strauss' Machiavelli," Jour. of Politics 28 (1966), 794-817, esp. 803-807.

(32) Discourses, I, ch. 9 (New York: Modern Library, 1940), 139. I take a slightly different approach to

interpretation here than does Walzer. See his, "Political Action: The Problem of Dirty Hands," 77.

(33) Isaiah Berlin, "The Originality of Machiavelli," in _Studies_ _on_ _Machiavelli_, ed. Myron Gilmore (Firenze: Sansoni, 1972), 147-206.
(34) See Walzer's note on Maurice Merleau-Ponty, "Political Action: The Problem of Dirty Hands," 74n.

CHAPTER FOURTEEN

FOREIGN POLICY AND JUSTIFIED INTERVENTION

I. Earlier Theory

The notion of intervention covers any activity of one state in which it deliberately acts to affect the internal or external affairs of another state in such a way as to reduce the independence, sovereignty, or self-help qualities of the target state. Since the activity is done deliberately and done for the sake of at least the interest of one's own state, if not also for the sake of some international good affecting other states, it obviously is an effort to "impose one's will" upon the affairs of another state. This makes it part of the spectrum of foreign policy of which war is the extreme.

But intervention is not war, strictly speaking, and need not involve military activities at all. Even if it does involve military action, it should, for clarity of thinking, either not be called a war, or should be identified as a war of a special kind.

Its essence is to act using some sort of material power, as distinct from moral persuasion, in order to affect what the other state does so that the other state does, in some important area, what the intervening state wants. If the intervention is military, it might involve the physical entry by military of one state into the political territory of the other state. It could also involve the movement of military forces by the intervening state to a proximity of the target state, but never actually into it.

There could be economic intervention, wherein the intervening state enters into economic arrangements with the target state and attaches conditions to the arrangments with the design to affect the target state's activities. This would be in matters of trade, aid, or travel.

Political intervention could take place when one state makes deliberate intrustion into the target state by means of propaganda, by support other than military of a revolution, or by refusal of recognition of the existing government.

233

The question of the ethics of intervention arose only gradually with the evolution of the ideas of sovereignty, independence, and self-help in the relations of states. Grotius, for example, made no distinction between war and intervention.[1] Moreover, since he still recognized some sort of universal community of persons, he did not consider that only states were the members of international society. Consequently, he approved of the action by one state to intervene in another state on behalf of the citizens of that other state.[2]

Over a hundred years later, Vattel held that states alone were agents within the international system. And with emphasis on the principles of sovereignty and independence, he insisted strongly on nonintervention.[3] The only exceptions he allowed were for helping on the just side in a civil war, and for restoring the balance of power.

In the Nineteenth century, the absolute position against intervention became identified with the arguments of Richard Cobden, Liberal-Whig M.P. in the British Parliament between 1840 and 1870. He applied the laissez-faire principle from economics to international relations.

The problems which arise to prevent social cooperation on the international scene, Cobden insisted, all come from interferences by the various state governments. Governmental interferences impede both economic trade and political peace and do it both within a country and internationally. These international interferences are ingenerate to governments who conceive of the relations between states sheerly in terms of force, either as exploitation, supremacy, or, ultimately, war.

Conversely, economic trade is the activity that best draws people together. People enter naturally into systems of social cooperation because they have a natural harmony among their varied, individual interests. As they experience the mutually achieved benefits to their individual interests, people develop a common interest in overcoming all barriers to trade. With complete freedom of trade, peace would be a reasonably anticipated corollary.

In addition to the argument that the long range consequences of peace between peoples develop in inverse proportion to governmental interferences, Cobden argued against political intervention from the undesired consequences of precedent which rationally implies consistency in similar cases.

I maintain this Government has no right to communicate except through the Government of other countries; and that, whether it be a republic, a despotism, or a monarchy, I hold it has no right to interfere with any other form of Government. Mark the effect of your own principle, if you take the opposite ground. If you recognise the principle of intervention in your Government, you must tolerate it in other nations also.... I say, if you want to benefit nations who are struggling for their freedom, establish as one of the maxims of international law the principle of non-intervention. If you want to give a guarantee for peace, and as I believe, the surest guarantee for progress and freedom, lay down this principle, and act on it, that no foreign State has a right by force to interfere with the domestic concerns of another State, even to confer a benefit on it, without its own consent.[4]

Cobden's two main consequentialist arguments why a nation should not have a policy of intervention were: that free trade between people is the best way to advance peace between states; and that any deliberate intervention would set a precedent that made for the insecurity of all nations. The only proper activities of international affairs, besides economic trade, were those of trying to influence other states by example and persuasion.

The major problem for an absolute non-internventionist position such as that of Cobden, a problem already noted with respect to pacifism, is that there is no moral standard for acting when the rule is broken by another state. To say it is unjust to intervene deliberately means that one must judge the action of intervention by another state as unjust. But then to do nothing in response would mean that one values one's "clean hands" more than justice.

John Stuart Mill, a Liberal-Whig contemporary of Cobden, came at the problem from the other direction. Instead of insisting on an absolute position, no matter the circumstances, Mill asked: "what are the grounds for justifiable intervention in the present world situation."[5]

If one accepted the guidance of International Law, argued Mill, then one must acknowledge that the rule of non-internvention applies differently to civilized (generally, European) states and to barbarian states. These latter were not accorded all the rights of states that were accorded to the former. (This distinction in law seems correct for Mill's time.) Perhaps interventions into barbarian lands offended against some more basic moral principles, but such actions could not offend against any legal principle of non-intervention.

With respect to inverventions into the affairs of civilized states, Mill focused his analysis on the matter of civil war. In such a matter, is it just to take one side over the other? Mill set up three scenarios and answered by various tactics, sometimes appealing to the customary law of nations, sometimes to moral rules, and sometimes to principles of sound policy.

If the civil war in a country was so protracted as to be troublesome to other nations, then, Mill argued, "the admitted doctrine" of nations is that it is correct to intervene to insist that the conflict cease.

If it is a civil war wherein people are struggling against their government to gain their liberty, then, Mill argued, it was not correct to intervene at all. It was precisely a people's willingness and ability to effect a successful revolution that tested and developed their fitness for a liberal republican form of government. "(T)he only test... of a people's having become fit for popular institutions is that they, or a sufficient portion of them to prevail in the contest, are willing to brave labor and danger for their liberation." People cannot, insisted Mill, be given liberty. In a civil revolutionary struggle, intervention cannot serve the purposes of liberty. (Generally, Marx's position on revolution would concur; however the official Soviet doctrine, as in their 1977 constitution and Brezhnev

Doctrine, commits them to "support wars of national liberation.")

The third scenario is that in which a third state has already intervened in the civil war. Here Mill, in contrast to Cobden, says it is a morally good action to "counter-intervene." This counter-intervention act could be morally justified by the principle of non-intervention itself, since the counter-intervention redresses the imbalance created by the unjustified intervention of the third state. Otherwise justice would submit to injustice since it would say: it is wrong to help one side, but nothing can be done about it. However, Mill cautions, "Intervention to enforce non-intervention is always rightful, always moral, if not always prudent."[6] He does not here place some rule of expediency above morality (albeit his use of the word "prudence" is other than as referring to the moral virtue). Rather he means that the justice of the counter-intervention cannot be abstracted from the duties of office that include the integration of such an action into a more comprehensive world analysis.

Mill's position has influenced appeals for justification made in many post World War II revolutions, by both sides. Those who justify the intervention of socialist states into revolutions within presently non-socialist states appeal to Mill and cite past "colonial" intervention or present "imperial" intervention which are being counterbalanced. Those who justify the intervention of western states into revolutions cite the public doctrine and (often secret or indirect) practice of the socialist states.

Even though he wrote much, Guiseppe Mazzini (1805-1872) was a political activitist more than a theorist. He saw the revolutionary call in terms of the forces of good versus the forces of evil. Consequently, he had little use for compromise with opposing viewpoints.[7] The call to revolution was a duty (not a right) based on a moral law that stood above the state's competency. The agent of the revolution was not the class or party but the nation, which was the basic unit into which people organize themselves in terms of values, practices, and traditions. Mazzini insisted that nationalism was essential to a true humanism because people were neither atomic individuals nor simply members of the

237

one human race. Yet a nation is not necessarily identifiable by means of the contingent political boundaries, which quite often disfigure the natural nations.[8]

Unfortunately, the use of the principle of non-intervention in the nineteenth century had often shown that it had become an instrument of suppressing the dynamic movement of peoples. The leaders of the present order of states invoked the principle to protect their own interests.[9] That is, the principle allowed rulers set in place during the Restoration after the Congress of Vienna to do what they pleased with the people within their political borders. It thus became a principle that supported the status quo against revolutions by the people. It forbade cooperation by people of other states in the overthrow of the despotic rulers of the target state.

But Mazzini did not reject the principle completely. Rather he set out three conditions under which it would be a good rule. First, similar to Cobden, he insisted that it would have to be adhered to absolutely. That is, if other states held to it and refrained from helping out the side of revolutions, they should also hold to it and not give aid to put revolutions down and be ready to recognize successful revolutions as legitimate. Second, similar to Mill, he insisted that the rule, as a rule of justice, demanded compensation for previous violations. "The same theory which proclaims non-interference as the first law of international politics, must include, as a secondary law, the right of interference to make good all prior infractions of the law of non-interference."[10] This supports counter-intervention.

For the third condition Mazzini threw in a new dimension: the principle applies between nations, not between states. A "nation," he held, was a group of people with a distinct approach to life and a distinct mission to fulfil in the world. But states with their present political boundaries jumbled nations, either splitting them or mixing them.[11] Interestingly, this idea of "mission" opened to Mazzini's assertion that certain nations (especially the Italian nation) were to be the source of the world revolution of nations. This would entail actions (by Italy and other European nations) to civilize the nations of Africa and Asia.

Mazzini held that it would be a duty of nations to act against some blatant violation within a state of a government against its people. And the appeal here would be to a law above the law of states.[12]

Mazzini has had much influence in the revolutionary thinking of the twentieth century, perhaps especially in terms of conceiving the struggles as ones between forces of good and the forces of evil, and in terms of identifying the revolutionary groups as those with shared values and experiences, whether these groups be nations or classes.

II. Soviet Practice of Intervention

Karl Marx held a complex judgment on international intervention. Approaching it under the rubric of colonialism, Marx held that many evils were done by the colonial powers against the target states, but that the general practice served the purpose of the dialectical movement in history.[13] In other words, Marx had approved colonialism as the needed stimulus to move static non-European countries upward toward the bourgeois stage. The main part of that stimulus was that European colonialism introduced the practice of private property. Marx, following Hegel, thought that the "world historical individual" acted against the morality of the time but in a manner essential to moving history. This contribution to history was independent of the actual subjective motivations of the particular individual or group who in fact was acting in the "world historical" manner.

Lenin modified this acceptance of the need for an external stimulus and advocated the rule of national self-determination for nonindustrial countries. But in contrast to those who press for the equality of nations and the right of peoples to national self-determination as part of a "peace philosophy," Lenin saw equality and self-determination as conditions for the facilitation of the process of the differentiation of the proletariat appropriate to each country. This in Marxian theory is necessary prior to successful proletarian class revolutions. To hold absolutely to the rule of self-determination would be to abandon those oppressed by present class structures to their own devices.[14]

Consequently, Lenin also advocated that the rule of self-determination be subordinate to any needs of class internationalism. For the sake of restructuring the bourgeois world order into a socialist world order and for the sake of achieving the liberation of oppressed peoples, it was crucial not to distort the concept and policy of self-determination so as to prohibit rendering practical assistance. The socialist movement aimed at bringing about a condition wherein all people would be citizens of the world with allegiance primarily to their class, not to their several nations. Thus, the principle of non-intervention was both advocated and denied by the Soviets.

The Soviet revolutionary level, which rejected the rule of non-intervention, was given formal expression in the creation, in 1919, of the Communist International (Comintern), which explicity subordinated the national interests of each state to the interests of the international revolution.

However, because of the weak position of the Soviet state in relation to other states, its leaders wielded a split-level foreign policy from the 1920's to the 1950's.[15] The Soviets advocated the principle of self-determination because of their need to provide for the security of the Soviet Union in an hostile international system. Yet their premise of the leadership of the Soviet Union in the world's socialist revolution, which was the basis for the legitimacy of the CPSU as the government of the Soviet Union, required Soviet power be used to support that revolution in other states.[16] Depending on the situation during those years, the Soviet leaders and the Comintern stressed one or the other arm of this duality.

An entirely new foreign policy problem opened for the Soviet Union after the Second World War. When Communist governments took over in Eastern European states and in China, the Soviet leaders had to work out new rules for intervention. Now there were not only communist parties in different states, there were different communist states. The problem was how the Soviet Union, the leader of the socialist revolution, was to relate to them. The principle of self-determination, urged by Lenin because of the necessity of a bourgeois revolution prior to the proletarian revolution, did not fit, since none of these other communist governments arose by means of the Marxian stages. Yet a simple continuation of a "leader-follower" principle, based on the priority of the Soviet communist party in international communism, conflicted with sentiments of national pride in China and Eastern Europe.

The solution, worked out over several years, was a modification of both principles. The Soviets acknowledged the nationalism insofar as they accepted the sovereignty of each communist state. Yet the Soviets maintained that, precisely because these other communist governments did not arise in the pure Marxian manner, they were still at a less advanced stage of the revolution. Consequently, the Soviets' ideological superiority would justify some kinds of intervention.[17] The Comintern was dissolved and replaced by the Cominform in 1947, which was to assist the cause of international revolution by informational exchange and not by leadership.

At the Twentieth Party Congress of the CPSU, Nikita Khrushchev put forth the principle of "peaceful coexistence" for Soviet foreign policy. This principle could be seen as an effort to combine the principles of self-determination and internationalism in relations to non-communist states. The meaning of the principle was that the Soviet Union would achieve eventual revolutionary success against the other states by achieving superiority in its own economic activities and not by military activities against the other states. However, there was still a danger that capitalist nations might resort to war for the sake of their own survival. By the Twenty-First Congress in 1959, Khrushchev suggested that war might be excluded from international relations even while capitalist states still existed. In Peking later that year, he disturbed the Chinese communists with the proposal that self-determination be the guiding principle for when a people in any country moves toward socialism.

While there is no doubt that Khrushchev's thinking had many aspects, such as the necessity of taking action against the possibility of nuclear war, lulling the western states to lessen military buildup, and sending a message to hesitant African and Latin American peoples, the response of the Chinese gives credence to the judgment that it was not all merely for non-communist consumption.

241

Stressing orthodox Leninism, the Chinese insisted that Clausewitz's premise that war is a valid expression of policy was good as long as capitalistic imperialism was still around. They did not rule out times of "peaceful coexistence," but they held closer to the earlier dual approach which placed advancement of international revolution as more important. This would be especially significant in giving support to wars of "national liberation" against imperialistic oppressors. This ranking could not be abandoned because such wars were "just wars." Mao Tse-Tung had insisted on the distinction. "Just war are wars furthering the revolution; unjust wars are those opposing the revolution." Khrushchev in 1960 modified the new Soviet position to permit support of nation liberation wars in terms of precluding or countering the intervention in areas of revolution by Western powers.

The next major challenge to Soviet foreign policy on intervention came with the Czechoslovakian "spring" in 1968. The result came to be known as the "Brezhnev Doctrine." In Czechoslovakia, the government itself had led the move to innovations in political and social experimentations. (This makes the situation different from the Polish workers' 1980 Solidarity movement.) The innovations were not acceptable to the Soviets, but seemed to come within the principles of sovereignty and Leninist self-determination.

The eventual justifications of the intervention of Soviet and other Eastern bloc military forces to overthrow the Czech government were these:

1. The peoples of socialist countries and the Communist parties therein have the freedom to determine their way of development.
2. However, if any decision of theirs damages the socialism of their countries or the basic interests of other socialist countries or the international movement in the struggle for world socialism, such a decision violates the responsibility they have to all such countries and to the international Communist movement.
3. No people or party can place sole emphasis on its own autonomy and independence.
4. No people or party can fail to take into

account such a decisive fact of our time as the struggle between the two antithetical social systems of capitalism and socialism.

This "Brezhnev Doctrine" justifies intervention in order to prevent an already socialist state from changing over to an imperialist state. The Doctrine holds that technically this is not an interfering in the state's internal affairs. It is rather the defense against such outside intervention that would cause deviation from Marxist-Leninist principles. Thus intervention by the arbiter of the limits allowed under such principles actually was not a violation of the sovereignty of the target state, but, since it was a socialist state and part of the international communist revolution, it was actually a support of that sovereignty. This argument then was analogous to the Millsian justification of counter-intervention. To verify that it truly was a counter-intervention, however, it needed to assume that anything that would cause deviation from Marxist-Leninist principles had to be the result of intervention from outside.

At a Polish party congress in June, 1986, Mikhail Gorbachev indicated that the Brezhnev doctrine is still in place.

> (S)ocialism now manifests itself as an international reality, as an alliance of states closely linked by political, economic, cultural, and defense interests. To threaten the socialist system, to try to undermine it from the outside and wrench a country away from the socialist community means to encroach not only on the will of the people, but also on the entire postwar arrangement, and, in the final analysis, on peace.[18]

III. U.S. Non-Intervention Policy

In a message to Congress on December 2, 1823, James Monroe laid down two principles (that show clearly the influence of John Quincy Adams) that came to be known as the "Monroe Doctrine." The first is that:

> the American continents, by the free and independent condition which they have

243

assumed and maintain, are henceforth not to
be considered as subject for future
colonization by any European power.

The second is that:

we should consider any attempt on their
[the allied powers of the 'Holy Alliance']
part to extend their political system to
any portion of this hemisphere as dangerous
to our peace and safety. With the existing
colonies and dependencies of any European
power we have not interfered and shall not
interfere. But with the governments who
have declared their independence and
maintained it, and whose independence we
have, on great consideration and just
principles, acknowledged, we could not view
any interposition for the purpose of
oppressing them, or controlling in any
other manner their destiny, by any European
power in any other light than as the
manifestation of an unfriendly disposition
towards the United States.[19]

Originally, then, the Doctrine stressed two
points: the "hands off" signal to European powers
telling them that the Western Hemisphere was no place
for them to carry on their balance of power struggles;
and the support signal for nascent republics of Latin
America. (In part, the principle that rejected
colonization was provoked by actions by Russia on the
West Coast of North America. But the specific
compromise worked out later on this matter was not
influence by the Doctrine.)

Neither non-intervention principle received
favorable reading either in Europe or in the U.S.
Against the first principle, it was the consensus by
the European powers at that time that any "civilized
political power" could colonize any land that had not
been colonized, or at least claimed in some realistic
manner, by another. At the time it would have been
hard to support the position that all the land in the
Western Hemisphere was already clearly belonging to a
civilized political power.

The second principle arose out of indications
that members of "the Holy Alliance" were considering
intervention based on the notion that colonies could

not separate themselves unilaterally from an absolutistic (European) political power.

In the nineteenth century, the most the U.S. did with the Doctrine was to talk about preventive intervention by the U.S., for example in Hawaii (1843), in Yucatan (1848), in Mexico (the late 1850's and 60's).

In the early twentieth century the U.S. activated the Doctrine by a "hands on" policy of hegemonic control over the internal affairs of Latin American states and engaged in various interventions between 1903 and 1934. The thinking was, in Theodore Roosevelt's message to Congress, that a "chronic wrongdoing or an impotence which results in a general loosening of the ties of civilized society" in some Latin American state requires intervention as a kind of "international police power." This Roosevelt corollary to the Doctrine was used by Roosevelt in the Dominican Republic, by Taft for "dollar diplomacy" in Nicaragua, Honduras, and Guatemala, by Wilson in the occupation of Haiti, and by Coolidge to quell political disturbances in Nicaragua. As Dexter Perkins sums up the period, the U.S. motives for the interventions were both noble and base, the provocations for intervention substantial but not compelling, and the effects in the countries themselves both positive and negative for the target state itself and for U.S. interests.[20] Yet these instances aroused such resentment that the Doctrine still conjures up mixed feelings both in Latin American states and in the U.S. itself.

A major shift in U.S. policy took place with President Truman. When the British announced on February 21, 1947, that they were cutting off their aid to Greece and Turkey, Truman decided the U.S. should replace the British support. By this move, he changed U.S. policy into one of a permanent world power agent. In a message to Congress he set forth the following rationale.

> At the present moment in world history nearly every nation must choose between alternative ways of life. The choice is too often not a free one.
> One way of life is based upon the will of the majority, and is distinguished by free institutions, representative

245

government, free elections, guarantees of
individual liberty, freedom of speech and
religion, and freedom from political
oppression.
The second way of life is based upon the
will of a minority forcibly imposed upon
the majority. It relies upon terror and
oppression, a controlled press and radio,
fixed elections, and the suppression of
personal freedoms.
I believe that it must be the policy of
the United States to support free peoples
who are resisting attempted subjugation by
armed minorities or by outside
pressures.[21]

In 1947, George Kennan published an article
treating "the nature of Soviet power as a problem in
policy for the United States."[22] In this article
Kennan used the image of "a fluid stream which moves
constantly, wherever it is permitted to move, toward a
given goal." Soon after, people connected the article
with the Truman Doctrine and, because of the Kennan
imagery, they began using the metaphor of
"containment" as the Truman Doctrine's policy toward
of Soviet foreign activities. The objective embodied
in the model was to contain Soviet expansion of
control by the application of counteraction "at a
series of constantly shifting geographical and
political points, corresponding to the shifts and
maneuvers of Soviet policy."

Kennan later wrote that it was a serious
deficiency in the article not to make clear "that what
I was talking about when I mentioned the containment
of Soviet power was not the containment by military
means of a military threat, but the political
containment of a political threat."[23] Likewise it
was deficient not "to make clear that the
'containment' of which I was speaking was not
something that I thought we could, necessarily, do
everywhere successfully, or even needed to do
everywhere successfully, in order to serve the purpose
I had in mind.... My objection to the Truman Doctrine
message revolved largely around its failure to draw
this distinction."[24]

Obviously the Truman Doctrine and its model of
containment implied that the U.S. would intervene in
other states with a new understanding of

counterintervention. Heretofore intervention as counter-intervention had been justified for the sake of the target state's independence and self-determination. Because of the historical circumstances, these were now interpreted to involve the style of government and liberty within the state. Any political agitation toward a communist "way of life" was interpreted as a Soviet intervention to be countered by the U.S. And this countering was to be effected anywhere in the world.

In practice, the U.S. acted on this Doctrine to give economic and other aid to states who in various ways were opposed to or threated by Soviet influence or Soviet supported forces. This at times entailed U.S. support of governments that were quite oppressive and authoritarian but which were not communist.[25] Among many countries who at least overtly advocated a status of non-alignment with respect to either the Soviet Union or the United States, the Truman Doctrine contributed to the impression that the U.S. was exercising "imperialistic" power.

IV. Contemporary Theories

Agreeing with J.S. Mill, Michael Walzer insists that "intervention is not justified just because revolution is."[26] The legitimacy of a government as an instrument of its own people has different criteria than the legitimacy of the state confronting other states. The state (which he understands as the conjunction of a people and its government) has territorial integrity and political sovereignty in respect to other states. Even though the ideal government is a republican (elected representative) type, other types may fit the people in the given historical circumstances. Walzer consequently advocates accepting a "pluralism" in types of state governments for purposes of judging the justification of intervention.

But he argues that the justification of revolution is otherwise, since he holds a dual reference for the legitimacy of a government. While outsiders are morally bound to presume the legitimacy of the existing government, the people may judge that legitimacy on other grounds. The presumption on the part of outsiders correlates with the principle of self-help of the people themselves. It is the only way to respect the rights of the people of a state to act with community integrity.

However, Walzer allows that the ban against intervention is not absolute. Another state may unilaterally suspend it in three cases, forming what he calls the "rules of disregard" at those times when respecting the ban does not seem to serve the purposes of the ban.

(1) If it becomes obvious that there are two or more political communities within the state's present boundaries, and one of these is in some large scale military struggle for independence, another state may disregard the ban.

(2) If another foreign state already has intervened, Walzer, like Mill, finds it moral to counter-intervene to balance off and thereby allow the internal struggle to settle itself.

(3) If violations of human rights within the state are so terrible that it is incongrous to talk of "community" and "self-determination," then another state may intervene.

These "rules of disregard," he notes, would indicate that there are justifications for wars that are not fought in "self-defense," or "against aggressors" in the strict sense. (He restricts "aggression" to attacks across political boundaries.)

Intervention in situations other than described by these three rules would violate the rights of citizens within the state to decide for themselves how the tensions with their government balance against their civic loyalties and their prudence.

Likewise the state considering intervention must employ prudence and proportionality in its decision whether to intervene when, under the "rules of disregard," it may do so. The external state must weigh matters such as the "probable consequent harm to those involved and to other parties," and the "hope of success." While it may be morally an option, there can be no moral obligation to submit one's own state or even third party states to risks judged so large as to be disproportionate.

Historically, this prudence and proportionality factor has most often deterred intervention in matters of Walzer's third rule: massive violation of human rights. The list is long even in our time: Cambodia under Pol Pot, Uganda, Equitorial Guinea, Hungary, Afghanistan.

It is his position on respecting "pluralism" in the kinds of states in the international system that is at the heart of most criticism against Walzer today.

David Luban objects to Walzer's principle that one state must treat another state as legitimately governed unless one of the "rules of disregard" applies.[27] Luban objects to the stress on the ignorance of foreigners and the requirement that the non-fit between government and people be "radically apparent."

To support the presumption of legitimacy in the international system, Walzer calls attention to the lack of knowledge needed to make a proper judgment on the fit. Luban finds such an assertion of ignorance not plausible today because of the many sources of information now available. Walzer's position is part of what Luban calls "the romance of the nation-state," which promotes the idea that one cannot adequately know an association unless one belongs to it. Luban suggests that this is analogous to the position that one cannot understand a woman unless one is a woman (or a black, unless one is a black, etc.). But since one cannot live and apply this principle in these analogous situations, to use it for a government's presumptive legitimacy opens one to the charge of inconsistency.

But Luban himself is somewhat incomplete here. Exactly what would count as the information needed for someone to judge the fit within a foreign state? Commercial television's news reports? Supplemented by Public television's documentaries? Supplemented by weekly news magazines? Supplemented by talk's given by exchange students? How much would be needed before someone could "know enough" to judge the non-fit in a foreign country?

Moreover, Luban ignores that verifiable information about the other country presumes some political openness of that other country, and dissemination of that information in one's own country presumes some political openness in one's own country. As a result, Luban's claim would seem to be true, if at all, only about less totalitarian target countries and only true within countries truly with a free press. (This is part of the explanation why all of Luban's examples are of non-fits in non-socialist countries.)

Luban's second point is that Walzer has too high a threshold before a non-fit is to be called "radically apparent." He suggests that ordinary dictatorship is clear enough. His premise is that human rights set a limit to the acceptable pluralism in the international system of state governments. Thus if a government systematically violates basic human rights, intervention is permissible. To wait for the state's own people to rise in revolution ignores that these people may choose not to revolt more from fear than from prudence or loyalty.

We must keep in mind here that the argument is over intervention. This covers not only military action. Economic sanctions or other governmental pressures also must be justified. The difficulty with Luban's premise concerning human rights is that intervention under this rubric falters under a double standard: it is less risky to intervene into countries that are not totalitarian. Not surprisingly, most political agitation for intervention has been in respect to countries that have less, albeit severe, systematic violations of human rights than those totalitarian countries. But this undermines the premise of the value of human rights.

Stanley Hoffmann suggests more attention be given to a "fourth rule of disregard": military intervention to establish or restore "democracy."[28] If counter-intervention is permissible for the sake of self-determination, why is intervention not permissible for the sake of self-government? Walzer's stern doctrine of self-help (in which he follows Mill) assumes the antipaternalistic position that one people cannot make another people become free.

Hoffmann notes that Walzer's critics have two main paths of argument against the stern doctrine of self-help. First is the categorical position that governments who keep their people unfree thereby make their states lose the right of political sovereignty, since this right is grounded in the consent of the governed. Second is the utilitarian position that modern governments have a formidable power of repression, and so the Mill-Walzer doctrine is out of date.

Hoffmann offers a mediation. Since Mill's restriction for self-help allows for intervention in the struggle for self-determination against an alien ruler (e.g., colonialism), could there not be rulers so oppressive as to be analogously alien (e.g., the "police-state")? Yet, Hoffmann notes, as in any analogy, there is also a difference, which Walzer had elaborated as the "dual reference for the doctrine of legitimacy," which in turn is behind his principle that "intervention is not justified whenever revolution is."

What is needed is a moral guideline for military intervention, and Hoffmann admits that abandonment of Walzer's principle is not likely to enhance impartiality. The small number of democracies lead one to worry that the consequences of a less severe principle would encourage tyrannical regimes to intervene almost at will. So it is not likely that most external powers would intervene impartially.

> Given the small number of democracies, and the fog that surrounds the claims to an application of the principle of self-determination, to allow military interventions on behalf of either is a formula for generalized war and hypocrisy.[29]

Yet Hoffmann proposes several mitigations, because of his conviction that "the international legitimacy of states depends ultimately on the principle of national self-determination, that internal legitimacy depends on the principle of self-government, and that there are cosmopolitan concerns that transcend states rights." He would allow some kind of international policy of human rights that would justify nonmilitary efforts to modify deplorable internal conditions. He would distinguish military intervention in a revolution from the provision of military assistance to those fighting for "a liberation from tyranny." He would permit "humanitarian" intervention when it could clearly be established that the purpose was the vindication of the principles of self-determination or self-government against large scale atrocities committed by a regime against the people. And in the matter of counter-intervention, Hoffmann would go beyond the neutrality of Walzer and Mill and allow the outside state to judge which of the internal forces was on the side of self-government and self-determination. This judgment may be a more or less matter, if the revolution is against a nondemocratic but authentically national regime and is carried on by those who wish to replace it with a nondemocratic satellite regime.

It is important to recognize after this brief review of analyses of the inductive principle of justified interventions, that there is no clear consensus on when intervention is morally permitted. But there is consensus that any decision to intervene bears the burden of justification. And there are certain consensus categories for this justification. Walzer's "three rules" are in these categories, but they do not exhaust them. Hoffmann's suggested "fourth rule," and the actual policies of the U.S. (the Monroe Doctrine, the Truman Doctrine) and the U.S.S.R. (the Breshnev Doctrine) are examples of finding justification beyond the "stern doctrine of self-help." Interestingly, all the categories involve the moral justification of the negation of some values for the sake of some more important values. Once again we encounter the tracks of the principle of the double effect.

NOTES

(1) See R. J. Vincent, Nonintervention and International Order (Princeton: Princeton University Press, 1974), pp. 22-24.
(2) E.g., Grotius, De jure belli ac pacis, Bk. I, ch. v, sect 2, para 1; Bk. II, ch. xxv, sect 6,; and Bk. II, ch. xxv, sect 8, para 3.
(3) Vattel, The Law of Nations, Bk II, ch. iv, para 54.
(4) Speech in the House of Commons, 28 June, 1850, in Speeches by Richard Cobden on Questions of Public Policy, ed. by J. Bright and J.E.T. Rogers, 2 vols. (London, 1870), 211-229..
(5) J.S. Mill, "A Few Words on Non-Intervention," in Dissertations and Discussions, Political,

Philosophical, and Historical, 3 vols., 2nd ed. (London: Longmans, Green, Reader, and Dyer), 1867. Vol. 3, pp. 153-178.
(6) ibid., p. 176.
(7) The Duties of Man and Other Essays (London: Dent, 1907), pp. 3, 29.
(8) ibid., p. 52
(9) See Life and Writings of Joseph Mazzini, London, 1891, Vol 6, Appendix on "Non-Intervention," p. 300.
(10) ibid., p. 305.
(11) ibid., pp. 302-303.
(12) ibid., pp. 307-308.
(13) See "The British Rule in India" (written June 10, 1853) and "The Future Results of British Rule in India," (written July 22, 1853) in Shlomo Avineri, Karl Marx on Colonialism and Modernization (Garden City, NY: Doubleday, 1969), pp. 88-95, 132-139. Avineri addresses this point in his introduction, pp. 14-24. Alan Gilbert argues that Marx may have later changed his mind. While Marx distinguished the immoral motives and existential evils of colonization from the dialectical impetus given to the historical advance of both the colonized and the colonizing countries, Gilbert finds that Marx thought that even the historical benefits were lost in the situation of the British in Ireland, since the colonizing fostered antagonisms among the proletariat itself. "Marx on Internationalism and War," Philosophy and Public Affairs 7 (1978).
(14) See, for example, his "Report on the Party Program," March 19, 1919, in V.I. Lenin, Selected Works, 3 vols. (Moscow: Progress Publishers, 1977), III, 112-129, esp. 117-121; also, "The Socialist Revolution and the Right of Nations to Self-Determination: Theses," and "The Discussion on Self-Determination Summed Up," in Collected Works (Moscow: Progress Publishers, 1964), XXII, 143-156, 320-360, esp. 323. See also, Konstantin Zarodov, "Leninism and Some Questions of Internationalism," World Marxist Review 25 (April, 1982), 8-15.
(15) See R.J. Vincent, Nonintervention and the International Order, ch. 4.
(16) See E.H. Carr, The Bolshevik Revolution 1917-1923, 3 vols., Harmondsworth, 1966, Vol.3, 32-33.
(17) See Zbigniew Brzezinski, The Soviet Bloc, rev ed. (New York: Praeger, 1965), 25-36, 108-110.
(18) Pravda, July 1, 1986. Quoted in Dimitri K. Simes, "Gorbachev: A New Foreign Policy?" Foreign Affairs 65 (1987), 487.

(19) Message of Dec. 2, 1823. Reprinted in Dexter Perkins, A History of the Monroe Doctrine (Boston: Little Brown and Company, 1963), 391-3.

(20) Perkins, A History..., 269-271.

(21) Dept. of State Bulletin, Vol. XVI, No. 403, March 23, 1947.

(22) This is the famous "X" article, "The Sources of Soviet Conduct," Foreign Affairs, 1947. His reflections on the misapplication of ideas in his article to the Truman Doctrine are in his Memoirs: 1925-1950 (New York: Bantam, 1969), 373-387.

(23) Memoirs, 378.

(24) Memoirs, 378.

(25) Memoirs, 338.

(26) Just and Unjust Wars, p. 89; "The Moral Standing of States," Phil. and Public Affairs 9 (1980), 214.

(27) "The Romance of the Nation-State," Phil. and Public Affairs 9 (1980), 392-397.

(28) Duties Beyond Borders (Syracuse: Syracuse University Press, 1981).

(29) Duties Beyond Borders, 69.

CHAPTER FIFTEEN

REVOLUTIONARY WAR AND JUST WAR CATEGORIES

Ethical and legal reflection has not yet caught up with the strategy and tactics involves in revolutionary war. There are unsettled questions about the application of the _ius_ _ad_ _bellum_ and _ius_ _in_ _bello_ traditions, either directly, with revolutionary warfare being but an instance of the more general categories, or analogously, with enough similarities to make the categories of the just war tradition still appropriate.

Prior to 1688, there were no revolutions in the modern sense, that is, as a fundamental innovation in the way of things in a state, rather than as resistance to, or elimination of, the tyrant.[1] The first use of the term "revolution" in the modern sense came with the beginnings of modern science, whrein it was used to designate how changes in astronomical phenomena relaxed to decisive changes in political and social realms.[2] The analogy with _De_ _Revolutionibus_ _Orbium_ _Celestium_ led people (e.g., Hobbes) to interpret political and social revolutions as a cyclic turning away from accumulated evils and a restoration of an earlier, more orderly situation wherein there was less oppression of the powerless and more security for all individuals. It was only gradually during the Seventeenth century that the term began to take on the meaning of "mutation," a transition to new conditions, and often (as for Hume) as a unique historical event that embodies for the first time certain fundamental and universal principles.

Revolutionary war today usually combines with the strategy and tactics of guerrilla war. The phenomenon of "guerrilla war" is quite old, but a continuity in strategy and tactics in such war dates from the resistance of the Spanish peasants to Napoleon. Carl von Clausewitz described it as the technique of using "irregular" troops to harass a more powerful enemy until it quits. Guerrilla "irregulars" were coordinated loosely with regular armies during the American Civil War. Guerrilla operations that were nearly independent, because of nationalistic sentiments, were constant sources of troubles for the German armies of occupation during World War II.

In today's revolutionary war, the enemy usually is the upper class in society, especially the landed aristocracies, who are in the revolutionary's doctrine often connected with the North Atlantic industrial capitalism of the "First World." The important theoretical contributors to this doctrine have been Lenin, Mao Tse-Tung, Ho Chi Minh, Amilcar Cabral, and several people in Latin America. However, there is some evidence that "revolution cannot be successfully exported," that is, there is no single theory combined with strategy and tactics that is universally successful.

I. IUS AD BELLUM Requirements

A. Competent Authority for Revolutionaries

Treason doth never prosper; what's the reason?
Why, if it prosper, none dare call it treason.
                    Sir John Har(r)ington

The ethician cannot rest with Sir John's implied solution to the question "who may call a revolution," and for two reasons. First, and most obvious, it would say that "success makes right." Second, less obviously but more to the basic problem, it would say that no ethical judgment on the justice of undertaking a revolution could be made until it is over.

The problem has two aspects: how to distinguish brigands and gangsters from genuine revolutionaries who merit moral and legal standing; and how to designate who these latter are in order to validate their use of physical violence in the name of the public common good. Perhaps all we can do here is exploratory reflection without promise of a general solution for the various revolutionary situations of our time.

Historically, in Just War theory, attention first came to this requirement of competent authority to call people to a war as a result of the politically troublesome battles carried on by medieval knights. Local bishops and local lords made it a practice to engage in military action on their own initiative for the sake of honor and power and prize. As a way to eliminate this bane in Western Europe, authoritative

256

writers, especially Canon lawyers, repeatedly insisted
that it was required for a war that it be called by a
"sovereign," either pope or prince. This emphasized
the crucial distinction between bellum and duellum,
and was the medieval assumption for the distinction
between killing as a private individual, which was
rather consistently forbidden except in immediate
self-defense, and killing as a citizen, under the
authority of the sovereign, either as public
executioner or as military soldier.

Aquinas, for example, argued that the$_3$ political
public good was supreme among human goods.^{3} The role
of the single ruler, the prince, was to promote the
common good. When this common good was threatened,
the prince could marshall the forces needed to
respond. This power, including political power over
life and death, Aquinas terms "perfect coercive
power."^{4} The argument ran thusly: the good of the
whole is rationally preferred to the good of the part
when the latter threatens the former.^{5} But only the
prince, or someone authorized by the prince, could
ethically intend the death of a human being for the
sake of the common good.^{6} Aquinas was quite aware
that a bad prince could abuse such power for personal
advantage. Thus he eventually argued that the public
coercive power belongs to the office, not to the
person.^{7}

As time went on, no one disputed that ordinarily
the ruler alone held competence to call the war. But
the explanation of what reasons would justify a ruler
calling the nation to war did change. In medieval
times, the explanation was that the ruler was the one
responsible for the public common good. In modern
times, the explanation became that the ruler was the
one representing the right of the people to their
common good.

This latter turn of thought grew into and out of
theories of political revolution such as those by John
Locke, Thomas Jefferson, and Jean-Jacques Rousseau.
The authority of the ruler to call a war came to be
seen as derived from the authority of the people to
appoint and to change the ruler, and revolution is one
means to effect such a change.

This connection alerts us to an important
historical fact. The tradition of Justified
Revolution, both legally and ethically, has developed

independently of the Just War tradition. There is little direct reflection on this fact, and probably a major cause is precisely the problem of "competent authority." Of course, this does not mean that thought on competent authority in revolutionary war was previously absent. Writers in the Middle Ages frequently studied principles in respect to Tyrannicide.

1. Human rulers and human laws, which are for the purpose of the public common good, are falliable and sometimes unjust, i.e., not for the public welfare.
2. There is a higher law than human positive law.
3. One should expect some failings in the best of laws and the best of rulers; and one should expect the majority of the laws and rulers not even to achieve the rank of best; yet one should still tolerate them for fear of something worse taking their place; hence: the moral rule of PRUDENCE is primary above Justice in any ethics of rebellion.
4. However, when the injustice hurts the public common good in a prolonged and systematic manner, it is to be resisted in proportion to the need, even though great care must be taken as to the means used, again, lest something worse take the place of the present injustices.
5. The means used can move into those of physical violence, perhaps even the killing of the ruler.
6. There is too great a danger that selfish or evil people will take advantage of the option of #5 (since they more often than good people would benefit from disruption of the social order) ever to let the judgment of when it is that the people must turn to resistance of violence rest in the hands of "private persons" in the state.
7. There are those in the society who are to judge for the public the prudence and the justice of the ruler, the laws, and the option for resistance or violence on the part of the people.[8]

Early in the modern era, John Locke distinguished degrees of gravity in "tyranny," which he defined as the exercise of power beyond what was morally right. These degrees were: occasional lapses; sustained harassment of individuals; widespread invasion of public liberties; and "a long train of abuses, prevarications, and artifices, all tending the same way, (which) make the design visible to the people,..."[9]

Locke considered each citizen competent to judge to which degree along the scale above the government had come. This is a personal judgment of actual tyranny. But Locke did not give just any individual, or private group, the right of rebellion. This would open to anarchy and confusion. Actual rebellion is only a right of the body of the people.

Consonant with this he distinguished "consent to be in a society," and "consent to this particular government."[10] Only the people as a political entity may rebel against a particular government. And this is only ethical if the government itself has been at war with the people to the degree of the "long train of abuses," etc. (One may compare today's model of "structural injustices" as the "original violence.") Thus, the people are "warring back" (= re-bellare). But they are still a society.

According to Thomas Jefferson, governments are instituted to secure the rights of the people, and they derive their just powers from the consent of the governed. Whenever any form of government becomes disruptive of these ends, the people (note again, not private groups) have the right to alter or abolish it and institute a new government. And again, prudence dictates this will not be done for light and transient causes. But "when a long train of abuses and usurpations (= an overreaching exercise of power), pursuing invariable the same Object evinces a design to reduce them under absolute Despotism, it is their right, it is their duty, to throw off such Government."

In sum, early modern thought rather consistently held that the people, as a whole, have the authority to call a revolution if the rulers act (the societal structures perform) consistently against their common good. But we must note that these modern analyses assume a bourgeois-democratic society already in place, whereas many contemporary revolutionary situations have developed in societies not in such socio-political structures.

There has been a development of thought on the leadership in revolution for those societies which do not have bourgeois-democratic structures. Nevertheless, there has been consistent attention to the principle that it is the people as a societal whole, and not some private group, that are to make the revolution. The justice of the cause can be determined by private individuals, but to act on this just cause is only proper to the people as a unity.

Marx had held that the necessary conditions for a revolution that would successfully achieve a humanistic, socialistic society were that there had to be in place and institutionalized a political structure of representative government and an economic structure of industrialized capitalism that produced new wealth. But in bourgeois social relations, these structures would serve the interests only of the ruling bourgeoisie. To ignite the revolution, the proletarians would finally see the structures as not serving their universal human consciousness. So they would take over the structures, impose their universal class interests for an interim (the "dictatorship of the proletariat") until a new consciousness formed in all people, and then have the state, which is the power structure that always serves whatever is the ruling class, wither away. The leaders of the proletarians would be from the proletarians themselves. The articulation of their cause might well come from former bourgeoisie (like Marx himself) who, for various reasons, came to join the revolution. But these articulators would only articulate, they could not invent or supply ideas for the agent of the revolution.

Lenin faced the problem of how does one have a revolution when the two structures of representative government and industrial capitalism are not in place. His answer was a vanguard party which would champion the interests of the proletariat for a time, by substituting its power for the continued absence in the proletariat of a universally humanized consciousness. In lieu of the "dictatorship of the proletariat" which Marx envisioned as the stage needed to humanize the political and social structures after the people had taken power, Lenin envisioned the "dictatorship of the party".

Mao theorized that if one is to advocate revolution in backward countries, one must accept an independence from objective economic conditions for the consciousness of those who spearhead the revolution. This revolutionary group will possess the truth concerning what the people "really want," even though the people as yet do not know this. In other words, the revolutionary group (Lenin's vanguard) can be identified with the true or ultimate will of those who make up the theoretical revolutionary class. And the only means that the actual revolutionary group can use to move into political power is military violence. "Political power grows out of the barrel of a gun."[11]

Mao introduced the practice of long term revolutionary war, in which regular army units employ the tactics of "irregulars" (partisan units usually found fighting in parallel with the regular forces), and classical full frontal assaults are launched only when the situation demands.

He also introduced a new dimension to ideological theory with his initial identification of the peasantry and the vanguard party called for by Lenin. Even though Mao soon abandoned this identification in practice, the shift from restricting the agent of revolution to the urban proletariat and opening such agency to peasants in pre-industrialized countries proved a quantum leap in revolutionary theory. It has proved most successful when the vanguard party keeps to Marx's principle that theory can best be made revolutionary in practice when it is done in terms of the real needs of the people in the struggle.

The vanguard organization leads the struggle, and its mobilizing ideology elicits a spirit of self-sacrifice, discipline, and cohesion among the party. Such an organization works to ensure that it enjoys substantial support among the population by processes of education, politicization, and selective use of terror.

Fidel Castro and Che Guevara furthered this development of thought with the foco insurreccional theory. Guevara concurred with the voluntarism of Mao, but rejected the Leninist notion that a vanguard party had to work with those people that would make up the actual agents of the revolution. In place of the vanguard, Guevara proposed the foco which consisted of a military group starting the revolution in one place. As the proletarians and peasants saw that this revolutionary military group was fighting their enemies, they would form _focos_ elsewhere and eventually generate a full scale revolution.[12] Che's theory envisioned a small, independent group, fighting on its own, and thereby inspiring other small groups to do the same, with the eventual creation of a revolutionary army large enough to be successful.

The _foco_ theory holds that, for Latin American revolutions, the basic terrain should be in the countryside; revolutionaries need not and must not wait until all the objective conditions are right to launch their struggle, since the _foco_, the mobile focal point of insurrection, is able by its very existence to create them.[13] The revolutionary group was to head straight into armed struggle without any significant mobilization of the population, especially the urban population. (This caused Guevara problems in Bolivia, since there the guerrillas never obtained popular support.)

The theory was not well accepted by the Soviets, since it advocated a guerrilla force emerging out of the local conditions independently of any Communist party already established in the country. It also assumed that only immediate military violence could effect a socialist revolution in the lesser developed states.

The _foco_ approach worked for Castro in Cuba. But it failed in attempts after that to culminate in a successful revolution in Venezuela and Bolivia. The Soviets, therefore, persisted in their "peaceful influence" strategy in Latin America. But they were staggered in this strategy in the early 1970's by right-wing triumphs in Chile, Uruguay, Argentine, and Bolivia. The Sandanista victory in Nicaragua attained along the lines of Castro and Guevara has forced the Soviets to rethink their position. And their tardiness has made Castro the accepted leader of revolutionary thought in all of Latin America.[14]

Carlos Marighela, in Brazil, decided to turn to the "base," or proletarian and peasant level, instead of a vanguard level of party elite, and to take up urban guerrilla terrorist tactics rather than a rural _foco insurreccional_ strategy.[15] A "base" was made up of a small number of people in a neighborhood area who would meet together to discuss and analyze their shared social problems. They would thereby "raise their own consciousnesses" and thereafter elect some practical guerrilla type of military action suitable to their local urban situation. This "urban guerrilla" strategy generally did not work well, but it signaled the turn from terrorism as an adjunct to guerrilla strategy to terrorism as itself the form of the war.

Let us stipulate that there are countries wherein the "structures of society" (i.e., its ways of doing things in dimensions that are pervasive in society, e.g., its legal institutions, its educational institutions, its economic institutions) systematically work against the common good and yet are to the material benefit of those in social power.

The problem in contemporary revolutionary war is to discern who really speaks for the people. [One might here think of Amilcar Cabral in Guinea Bissau, the petit bourgeois leaders in Peru, the Tupamaros in Uruguay (all in the 1960's), the United Front in Nicaragua in the 1970's, and the various rebel forces presently in El Salvador and Guatemala.] This is complicated by the Leninist premise of the need for a vanguard party, which premise has been developed by Cabral into the need for catechesis and by the Latin Americans into the need to "raise consciousnesses." Today most revolutionaries themselves do not think they represent the present will of the people during the earliest phases of a revolution. And if we consider that the concept of class struggle implies that not all the people support the revolution, it is not especially clear who counts as making up "the people."

In such situations, who has the authority to "call a revolutionary war"?

Historically, the boundaries for an answer usually have been argued for in "consequentialist" terms. For example, if simply anybody could call for violent revolution, the chances are that those with evil reasons would be likely to do it more quickly and more often than good persons, since they suffer from both good and evil regimes. Also, the social order would be likely to continuous turmoil. And finally, the likelihood would be that it would fail or not improve the situation, because of the complexities of a social revolution, and the outcome would be worse for the people than the prior tyranny.

These are all arguments from prudence, which the medievalists and generally the moderns up to our time held a higher social virtue than justice. But to say why not just anybody may call a revolution does not say who does have the authority.

The modern theories of revolution remained rather vague on the question. Quite probably they understood that in their times, unless there was majority support for a revolution, the authors would fail and be punished as seditioners, and that this would limit those who would dare the attempt. (Harington's quattrain fits this time.) But today experience indicates that this is not true in countries with those types of government which have succumbed to revolutions. [I here disagree with Michael Walzer.[16] There is at least a pragmatic difference between totalitarian and authoritarian governments. The former never have suffered a successful revolution, since, as Gerard Chaliand notes, they do not hesitate to use all tactics necessary to suppress it.[17]] And theoreticians of revolution assume that, in the phases prior to any continuous armed hostilities, support will be minimal. Today's typical revolution, e.g. Guinea Bissau, Nicaragua, El Salvador, Guatemala, is not a spontaneous levee en masse in which some incident sparks a massive response. Rather, a revolutionary movement, if it is to be successful, at least in capturing governmental power, must plan on a long, slowly developing dialectic with the people's and governmental responses.

The question today also encounters a change in the specific purpose for many revolutions. Heretofore revolutionary agents conceived of their social union and perhaps even the social institutions as fundamentally sound but presently suffering from some obstructive dysfunction, such as a tyrannical monarch. The aim then was to restore the body politic to its innate but obscured justice.

In contrast, many today conceive of their social union as deformed and their social institutions as fundamentally anti-human, as "oppressive." They intend to liberate the society by establishing institutions that will function for the human benefit of all and which will re-form the social union itself. With a new consciousness, they find heretofore accepted institutions to be oppressively unjust and no longer tolerable. Earlier thought on the need for competent authority to call a war was related to the idea that violence in society is bad because it fundamentally disorients the behavior of others in the society. But, as Jon Gunnemann notes, the contemporary revolutionary sees violence as a means to reorient behavior into a new consciousness.[18]

By calling for change by appeal to a new consciousness of liberation and humanization, many contemporary revolutionaries claim to act in the name of the people, or for the true will of the people. But they anticipate this and only involve the people in terms of catechizing or raising consciousness to gain support which, by the very need for such efforts, is assumed to be as yet deficient. We may stipulate that the revolutionaries have a sincere social consciousness and are not motivated toward banditry. But sincerity is not sufficient criterion for authorization in these societies.

Legal thought does not help us much.[19] First of all, International law does not avert to the justice or to the representative character of existing regimes. All regimes, no matter how unjust or unrepresentative, benefit from the UN Charter, Article 2(4), prohibiting the threat or use of force against the territorial integrity or political independence of another sovereign state. Also Article 51 authorizes collective self-defense, thereby permitting intervention on behalf of an established regime when its civil war is linked with direct or indirect foreign intervention amounting to interstate aggression. It would seem that a revolutionary group has no standing under either article.

Even if we hold that the right of self-defense resides primarily in the people and only secondarily in the governmental regime, it is rarely possible, except in colonial revolutions, to equate the people with a revolutionary movement and its forces, notwithstanding the latters' claims to be representative.

Legally, no matter what the degree of plausibility to claims of representative character, the revolutionaries must acquire a degree of international personality before they can be treated as a legal "belligerent."

Moreover, the basic interest of a regime combating revolutionaries is usually best served by denying them belligerency and treating them as criminals and disturbers of the peace. Likewise, accordance of belligerent status by third parties is largely a matter of convenience and political advantage. So neither action need be in reference to standards of justice.

Until recently, it was usual to require four conditions of guerrillas before they acquired belligerency status. (1) They had to be under responsible command; (2) they had to wear a distinctive and discernible sign; (3) they had to carry their arms openly; and (4) they had to conduct their operations in accordance with the laws of war. There was no relaxation of these conditions in deference to the "cause" involved. (However, citizens who engaged in a _levee en masse_ were required to meet only the last two conditions.)

In the 1974-77 Geneva Conference on the Reaffirmation and Development of International Humanitarian Law Applicable in Armed Conflicts, some effort was made in Protocol II, Article 1, to extend conventional benefits of the law of war to civil war when the revolutionaries are "dissident armed forces or other organized armed groups which" are under "responsible command." It was also specified that such were expected to "exercise such control over a part of [the disputed] territory as to enable them to carry out sustained and concerted military operations and to implement this Protocol" (that is, abide by their duties as belligerents in a war).

This last requirement usually is irrelevant for revolutionary forces, who often do not control much territory for any length of time, especially in phases one and two of the Maoist revolutionary cycle. Much depends on the geographical and social characteristics of the country involved. "Sustained and concerted military operations" may be maintained without long-term control of territory, which may not even be an objective until quite far along.

266

To complicate matters, the Protocol II of 1977 was somewhat muddled by Protocol I, Article 1(4), which would give privileged belligerency status to national liberation movements engaged in wars against "colonial" or "racist" regimes or "alien" occupying powers. This provision, specifically aimed at South Africa and Israel, qualifies such national liberation movements as belligerents without any requirement that they meet the substantial conditions of Protocol II, Article 1. Its effect is to give authorization to certain groups who claim to struggle for "liberation" of the people, which authorization is to be based exclusively on the cause for which they "struggle." (Neither of these Protocols has as yet achieved wide acceptance.)

How do these proposed additions to international law blend into the ethical problem of competent authority? The Protocal II would be of little help in early phases since the legal criteria pertain only after a certain level of success. If taken as an ethical guide, this would mean an effort became ethical if it succeeded, but unethical if it failed. This would return us to Sir John.

Could there be help from Protocal I, 1 (4), with its allusion to certain privileged causes? Perhaps at times, but it does not seem to apply, for example, in Latin America. And one thing seems sure. Revolutionary war competent authority is a separate question from the alleged justice of the cause.

In his intuitive way, Michael Walzer has an interesting suggestion for our question. "(I)t is not when the guerrillas look after the people that they acquire war rights, but when the people 'look after' the guerrillas.[20]

Two brief comments are in order. Guerrillas may become authentic representatives of the people when the people begin to "look after" them. But not all those the people begin to "look after" become authentic representatives in the sense of authorized revolutionaries. One might think of Bonnie and Clyde.

Moreover, even if Walzer's suggestion helps clarify an answer, which I think it might, we still face a problem similar to that Sir John gave us. Are the revolutionaries on moral ground in the interim before the people look after them? And what if many of the ordinary people turn against the revolutionaries because of their tactics?

Perhaps we should now see how important it is not to force a just war category univocally upon a revolution. Like all content-directive principles, the principles for a justified revolution must come from induction guided by formal ideals, such as the competent authority requirement. Many people trying to act well have made individual judgments in contemporary situations that the cause is sufficient to call a war of revolution. Their societies do not have bourgeois-democratic structures. They have decided they can, and thus they should act for the common good. In accord with prudence and fidelity, such authors of revolution try to fill out their competency requirement by organization, the exercise of control through responsible subordinates, some political and military success, and a credible willingness to accept the duties as well as the rights of belligerency under the law of war. We can make an induction from the multiple contemporary decisions to call revolutions and conclude that what counts as ethical authorization may be something quite developmental, not something completely present at the start.

B. Just Cause for Revolutionaries

The element of causa belli is consistently required by Just War authors from Cicero to contemporary positivists. On this element there is formal agreement, even though there has been obvious content-directive disagreement between the theorists as to what would count as a justifying cause.

The basic concept is that there must be a serious value threatened in the situation that is higher on a common good hierarchy than the disvalues involved in taking military action. This grounds the ius ad bellum level of "proportionality," and reflects the hierarchy of values essential to the principle of the double effect. Historically such items as protection from already initiated military aggression, restoration of rights wrongfully denied, reestablishment of just order, and reestablishment of secure balance of power have been claimed as just causes by different theorists.

268

As for revolutionary war, the Natural Law tradition recognized two causes as sufficient for armed resistance against an incumbent regime: self-defense and reaffirmation of the sovereignty of the people.[21] That is, if the regime consistently and fundamentally oppresses the common good or basic rights of the people, or if it consistently and fundamentally acts in ways contrary to the legitimate exercise of its power, the people are justified in reclaiming authority in the society. Today one could interpret "regime" as "the institutions of power."

Yet in a sense, many contemporary revolutionaries have teleological goals more than they have immediate causes. They often gain support by mediating their goals through present causes of dissatisfaction. But one sees that the immediate causes of themselves could never validate the intended continued control by the revolutionary party once political control has been gained. The common assertion is that "the revolution is an on-going process" to a "truly free, just, and human society" which once for all will resolve the major social problems. One gains awareness of these long-range goals by means of a "new consciousness," which in turn demands as a moral necessity the total redoing of the personal life-styles of the people as well as the institutional structures of society.

To identify what counts as a candidate for an ethical cause of a revolution, one must first understand the kind of revolution one studies. Some revolutions may be simply a way to bring about political change worthy of the people as they are. Herein the agents conceive of their social union and even their social institutions as fundamentally sound but presently suffering from some obstructive dysfunction, such as a tyrannical monarch. Their cause is to restore the body politic to its innate but obscured justice.

In contrast, many today conceive of their social union as deformed and their social institutions as fundamentally anti-human, as "oppressive." They intend to liberate the society by establishing institutions that will function for the human benefit of all and which will re-form the social union itself. With a new consciousness, they hold all heretofore accepted institutions to be oppressively unjust and no longer tolerable. The cause is therefore just because the new institutions expressing the new consciousness are intended to be more just and less oppressive than the present ones.

It is to these goals of new institutions and new consciousness that the revolutionary groups appeal to validate their continued control once they have achieved political power. In the earlier revolutions, once political control had been wrested from those in power who were oppressing the people or abusing the power, the ones who took over would quickly move to put the people back in charge. Now, those guided by Marxist-Leninist theories require an "interim" period in which to purity structures and raise consciousnesses.

Besides sufficient injustice, the "just cause" requirement also involves an ad bellum proportionality between the probable good and the probable evil brought about by a revolution. The Scholastic Natural Law tradition is quite grudging in its acceptance of the right of internal armed resistance. The inclination is to presume that the probable good will not outweigh the probable evil.[22]

But if one conceives of revolutionary change in terms of liberation and humanization, the matter of ad bellum proportionality is quite otherwise. There is claim to a new consciousness of what society must become if there is to be complete and perfect "justice" and "peace." With such a purely formal style of defining the goal of revolution, there is not content specification as to what will count as satisfactory intermediate steps. (This of course, is not true to Marx's own thought. He, like Hegel, insisted that not all change was of necessity an advance and that real advances must be incremental and not "shot from a pistol.") Many contemporary revolutionaries reject any proportion requirement either ad bellum or (as we will see) in bello. Many Leninists connect the open-ended cause of justice with in bello tactics, and argue that any tactic is justifiable. The open-ended ad bellum end justifies any in bello means. No cost is too high, no war is too long for the revolution's utopian success.

Unfortunately, experience of the twentieth century insurgency victories does not bear resemblance to the classless utopias for which the revolutionary wars are fought unless one accepts that any change in power counts for "justice," "democracy," or the

270

"overthrow of oppression." This especially is true when the teleological goal of a perfect society implies an on-going revolution to change all aspects of personal as well as social life. The "interim" period after the revolutionary group has taken political control must have specifics by which to evaluate how things are progressing. This requirement simply takes the new revolutionaries at their word: the interim period is part of the revolution. Therefore, the ethician cannot ignore the requirement to specify the goals so as to permit examination of the proportionality of the evils that occur and the good of the goals causing the war. (Obviously the ethician will require standards for in bello proportionality also.)

The third element in just cause, the "solid likelihood of success," favors the revolutionaries. If they have a legitmate claim of self-defense, the tradition exempts them from any precise application of this element. So they can choose to continue to fight for as long as necessary to overthrow the regime. Yet one must keep in mind that seizure of political power alone does not count as success for their teleological goal.

The intermediate stage of seizure of political power can be pursued by insurgents almost indefinitely with very modest means. This is especially true today given the willingness of outside states to aid in insurgency wars. The insurgents usually can claim in good conscience not only the probability but the certainty of success politically even if not militarily. The only required condition for all this is that their foe is a Western democracy or a regime supported primarily by a Western democracy.[23]

The fourth requirement of just cause, the exhaustion of peaceful remedies, has little relevance to an insurgency. It presumes again that the war is a last resort to rid the evils and restore an otherwise adequate set of social institutions. Thus, it ignores what many present revolutionaries actually intend. It also conceives of violence as primarily disorienting the behavior of others in the society. But the contemporary revolutionary intends to reorient behavior in a new consciousness. Of course, conspicuous refusal to permit the people to settle issues peacefully by expressing their preferences may be evidence of the illegitimacy of either party's claim to represent the people. However, one should recall that the incumbent regime need not be just or be representative to be in legal authority. And what can count precisely as a valid expression of the will of the people in most countries of the world is such a problem that most "elections" are prudently looked on with caution and skepticism.

Additionally, the requirement of exhaustion of peaceful remedies would require reasonable responses to bids for a negotiated settlement from either side and/or third parties. But this, too, is a subject that must be dealt with cautiously and realistically, since initiatives for negotiations and peaceful settlement may be spurious and injurious to the security of a party entering them in good faith with an adversary seeking unfair political and military advantages.

C. Right Intention for Revolutionaries

The first component traditionally involved in right intention requires that a belligerent limit itself to pursuit of the avowed cause of the war. However, in contemporary revolutionary war, the teleological goal means that it is necessary to achieve complete control of the political, economic, and social system. Limitation to such total control is no limitation at all.

The second traditional component should be more likely to foster restraint on zeal in revolutionary war. This is the intention of reconciliation leading to a just and lasting peace. If each side sees its enemies as people it wants to live with in peaceful cooperation and not as enemies it wants to conquer and rule, right intention may be achieved. (This will have effects on how the war is carried on, the in bello dimension.) This seems to run against much present emphasis on class struggle. The emphasis often reduces the options for future attitudes of the conquered enemy to those of conversion or elimination.

Anticipation of reconciliation may also reinforce the third component of right intention: freedom from hatred and the desire for vengeance.

The requirement obviously faces a psychological problem for participants during the time of actual belligerency, especially if one side has provoked righteous anger. But it seems pragmatically verifiable if the animosity does not continue long after the war ends (e.g., attitudes in U.S. toward Germany and Japan after World War II), or opens to overt behavior during the war that goes beyond its political bounds (as will be delineated on the _in bello_ level discussion). Unfortunately, the character of modern revolutionary war is often quite the opposite of such a spirit, especially with the use of ideological catechesis to galvanize a mass movement.

II. IUS IN BELLO Requirements

A single, cold passion for the revolutionary cause must suppress within him all tender feelings for family life, friendship, love, gratitude, and even honor. For him there exists only one pleasure, one consolation, one reward, and one satisfaction --- the success of the revolution. Day and night he must have one single purpose: merciless destruction. To attain this goal, tirelessly and in a cold-blooded fashion, he must always be prepared to be destroyed and to destroy with his own hands everything that hinders its attainment.[24]

Three factors complicate the analysis of _ius in bello_ elements in a revolutionary war. First, the legal regulation of revolutionary war is in a primitive state compared with the developed _ius in bello_ for international conflict. Even the 1977 Geneva Protocols are superficial and incomplete, primarily because of Third World pressures during the conference. These nations did not like the prospect of restricting means typically employed, and so they avoided the issue by not treating many of the usual _ius in bello_ subjects in Protocol II.

Second, _ius in bello_ insurgency carries those problems with it that stem from the tendency of the parties to take the attitude that the superior justice of their _ad bellum_ goals justifies almost any effective means.[25]

Third, given the realities of the situation, revolutionaries might be limited as to what strategic and tactical options they may adopt if they are to have any chance of success.

A. In Bello Proportionality for Revolutionaries

We noted above the difficulty revolutionaries have in accepting ad bellum proportionality because of the characteristic way they have of phrasing their ends (causes) in utopian or open-ended ways. It logically follows that they will be even more hard pressed to discern proportionality in the conduct of the war, except insofar as such proportionality contributes to the success of their war. For example, they rule out those tactics that would tend to undermine their support by the people. However, this makes the tactics wrong because of their political consequences, not because they are disproportionate for valid military goals.

Still, the usual form of the principle, "only such force is ethical which is truly necessary for military success," is hard to apply in revolutionary war, because purely military success may not be congruent with the political, economic, and social successes that are equally if not more important in such conflicts. This especially is true when the enemy is a Western democracy or a developing country aided by Western democracies vulnerable to media and other criticism. For example, it is strategic for revolutionaries to single out the most positive programs, their key personnel, and the beneficiaries of those programs for violent attack. For it is detrimental to the revolutionaries' interests and propaganda for the counterinsurgents to be seen as making positive, successful efforts on behalf of the people.

Consequently, it is a major problem here to discern the concrete way to measure the relation of the use of military force to the complex political goals of the revolutionaries. Since the military goals may or may not be essential to the political goals for today's revolutionaries, it is incumbent that the political goals be made concrete enough to permit a reasonable person to judge to some extent the limits of proportionality. This requirement cannot be satisfied by goals phrased only in ideological terms.

By "ideological terms" here I mean those terms, such as "liberation" and "humanization", which have generally favorable emotional connotations, but which have idiosyncratic references for the revolutionaries because of their prior selection of some particular socio-political theory. As will be discussed further in the next chapter, the only standard by which one can reasonably test the validity of a cause or goal is in reference to items that are valued by some general consensus. Even if the words used in an appeal are the proper ones, the meanings of the words must also be similar as understood by the revolutionaries and by the outside evaluators.

As the means to these political goals, the rebels do have strategic military goals. These include the weakening of the enemy's forces and the undermining of the people's confidence in the government. The tactics to achieve these will change as the war goes on, but initially they involve attacking whenever or wherever an opportunity is found.

B. In Bello Discrimination for Revolutionaries

Since the major objective for revolutionaries is to control the population in a political sense, the rationale for who fits into the set of those who are noncombatants undergoes radical shifts.

Whole groups of people who are noncombatants, and consequently usually considered illegitimate targets under traditional ius in bello standards, are held to be proper targets under revolutionary logic. Since the war is primarily a political war and is waged "on behalf of the people," it follows that those who disagree, oppose, or hesitate as neutral are classified as enemies of the people. There is no basis for immunity as there is no way to be uninvolved and qualify as not ("in") harming ("nocent").

Also, since according to Marxist theory the war is a class war, those who belong to the "oppressor" or to the "exploiter" class are class enemies without more, and they merit direct and intentional attack, whether they carry arms or not.

Finally, in early phases, the strategy essentially includes efforts to subvert the people's confidence in the government. This involves doing those actions that will convince the population that no one is safe anywhere as long as this government is in power." Tactics are selected that will cause terror and will elicit a violent response from the governments with the hope that such will engender fear and bitterness against the government.

The revolution also undermines categories of discrimination with its terrorism in early stages. One of the most common early strategies is to "refuse to accept a single identity," and thereby make it quite difficult for the counterinsurgent forces to distinguish combatant and noncombatant. The guerrillas defend this strategy by insisting that the war is a people's war. The only army involved is the army of the oppressors. The people are defending themselves. If you want to fight against us, the guerrillas say, you are going to have to fight against civilians, for you are not at war with an army but with a nation. Therefore, you should not fight at all, and if you do, you are the barbarians, killing the old, the women, the children.

The guerrillas' strategy is thus to place the onus of indiscriminate warfare on the enemy. (Recall how well they succeeded in the Vietnam War.) The guerrillas themselves then have to discriminate to some extent to win the hearts of the people. And it is much easier for them to discriminate than it is for the government forces.

Any regime will view insurgent operations against it as illegal and will view the participants as criminals, accrediting no legitimacy to their struggle. It is not surprising, therefore, that all insurgent warefare is defined by its opponents as terrorism and the active participants as terrorists. But it is not helpful for moral analysis to confuse terrorist tactics in revolutions with that type of war, which will be discussed in the next chapter, consisting almost exclusively in the targeting of civilians in a "class" manner.

Frequently insurgent organizations employ terrorist methods because they cannot secure any popular support from the population they claim to represent. Such groups then claim responsibility for terrorist acts and make claims that such are "military targets," showing a sensitivity to the limits of moral targets in warfare. As noted earlier, even revolutionary groups who do have, or reasonable hope to gain popular support often employ terrorist methods, at least in early phases. For example, beginning in the late 1950's, the Vietcong waged a campaign aimed at destroying the governmental structure of the South Vietnamese countryside and, between 1960 and 1965, assassinated some 7500 village and district officials, including public health officers and clergy.

The systematic terrorizing of populations is a strategy that can be used in different types of war, and by both established governments and well as by revolutionary movements. Its purpose is to destroy the morale of a nation or a class, or to gain attention; its method is the random murder of people and the destruction of civic facilities. Randomness is the crucial feature if the immediate goal is to spread fear and insecurity. This would not be the case if the immediate goal was to establish the revolutionary organization itself and to provoke government retaliation. With the latter intention, the assassination of specific people identified in some way with the regime, the party, or a policy is the strategy.

Such terrorizing of ordinary men and women takes its heritage from the domestic tyrant, as Aristotle wrote, "The first aim and end of tyrants is to break the spirit of their subjects."[26] It only emerged as a strategy of revolutionary struggle after World War II. Before then, those who were called "terrorists" usually held to a code whereby they sharply distinguished legitimate and illegitimate targets for their attacks. The former consists of officials who are somehow the political agents of the regimes considered oppressive. Even though war conventions and international law consider such officials nonmilitary, if there truly is unjust oppression by a government of its people, such officials may not be without guilt.

The war convention and the political code have a similar structure: the distinction between officials and citizens parallels that between soldiers and civilians. The logic behind the distinctions in respect to military acts and terrorist acts is the distinction between aiming at particular people because of actions they have done or are doing, and aiming at whole groups of people, indiscriminately, because of who they are. The first kind of aiming is appropriate to a limited struggle directed against regimes and policies. The second reaches beyond such limits; it threatens whole peoples, whose individual members are systematically exposed to violent death at any time simply because they share what they cannot avoid, a collective identity.

Nevertheless, traditional war ethics distinguishes the legitimate vulnerability of the soldier and the political official. Assassins of political figures, even if these were involved in a perceived oppressive tyranny, have never been treated in common moral judgment as soldiers. There may be cause, in the early stages of revolutionary war, to attack middle and upper level officials of an oppressive government. But the most that could be justified would be attacks on those who individually have carried on continuous and gross abuses against the people. It would not be moral to attack some official simply because that individual was an official. (The assassination strategy of the Vietcong was wrong, even though it was successfu.) There might be good reasons for individual officials to cooperate materially with an oppressive regime.

Finally, those under attack are likely to believe that compromise with the terrorists is impossible. Terrorism is associated with the demand for unconditional surrender.

NOTES

(1) That there were no revolutions in premodern times, see the evidence of Yves Congar, "The Sacralization of Western Society in the Middle Ages," in Roger Aubert, Sacralization and Secularization, Concilium Vol 47 (New York: Paulist, 1969), 66-70.
(2) See Karl Griewank, Der Neuzeitliche Revolutionsbegriff (Weimar: Hermann Bohlaus Nachfolger, 1955), 171-182; for a slightly different analysis of Hobbes' contribution to transforming the concept of political revolution see Mark Hartman, "Hobbes's Concept of Political Revolution," Journal of the History of Ideas 47 (1986), 487-495.
(3) Summa Theologiae II-II, 124, 5, ad 3.
(4) Summa Theologiae II-II, 65, 2 ad 2; 67, 4.
(5) Summa Theologiae II-II, 64, 2.
(6) Summa Theologiae II-II, 64, 7.

(7) <u>Summa</u> <u>Theologiae</u> II-II, 63, 3.

(8) Some sources: Marsiglio of Padua, <u>Defensor</u> <u>Pacis</u>, Alan Gewirth, tr. (New York: Columbia University Press, 1956), Disc. I, ch. 18; Thomas Aquinas, <u>De</u> <u>Regimine</u> <u>Principium</u>, Bk. I, cc. 3 and 6; Hubert Languet or Philippe Duplessis-Mornay ("Junius Brutus"), <u>Vindiciae</u> <u>contra</u> <u>Tyrannos</u>, Harold Laski, tr. (London: Bell, 1924); Juan Mariana, <u>De</u> <u>Rege</u> <u>et</u> <u>Regis</u> <u>Institutione</u>, G.A. Moore, tr. (Washington,D.C.: Country Dollar Press, 1948), cc. 6 and 7.

(9) <u>Second</u> <u>Treatise</u> <u>on</u> <u>Government</u>, #225.

(10) <u>Second</u> <u>Treatise</u> <u>on</u> <u>Government</u>, ##220-224; 226; 243.

(11) "Problems of War and Strategy," <u>Selected</u> <u>Works</u> II, p. 224, (Peking: Foreign Language Press).

(12) See Sheldon B. Liss, <u>Marxist</u> <u>Thought</u> <u>In</u> <u>Latin</u> <u>America</u> (Berkeley, University of California Press, 1984), ch. X.

(13) Debray describes the <u>foco</u> as "a united vanguard, honest, intransigent, nonsectarian, without any preconceived model, ready to take the most unconventional paths to arrive at its ends, selected and steeled by the struggle; a vanguard which only the practice of <u>foco</u> guarantees." Regis Debray, <u>Strategy</u> <u>for</u> <u>Revolution</u> (New York: Monthly Review Press, 1970), p. 74.

(14) See Pedro Ramet and Fernando Lopez-Alves, "Moscow and the Revolutionary Left in Latin America," <u>Orbis</u> 28 (1984), pp. 341-364, esp. 346, 348, 350, 357.

(15) See Carlos Marighela, <u>For</u> <u>the</u> <u>Liberation</u> <u>of</u> <u>Brazil</u> (Baltimore: Penguin Books, 1971), p. 150; see also his <u>Minimanual</u> <u>for</u> <u>the</u> <u>Urban</u> <u>Guerrilla</u>. See also, Liss, <u>Marxist</u> <u>Thought</u>, p. 121.

(16) Michael Walzer, "On Failed Totalitarianism," <u>Dissent</u> 30 (1983), 297-306.

(17) Gerard Chaliand, <u>Guerrilla</u> <u>Strategies</u> (Berkeley: University of California Press, 1982), p. 9.

(18) Jon Gunnemann, <u>The</u> <u>Moral</u> <u>Meaning</u> <u>of</u> <u>Revolution</u> (New Haven: Yale, 1979), p. 12.

(19) I relay here on the summary by William V. O'Brien, <u>The</u> <u>Conduct</u> <u>of</u> <u>Just</u> <u>and</u> <u>Limited</u> <u>War</u> (New York: Praeger, 1981).

(20) Michael Walzer, <u>Just</u> <u>and</u> <u>Unjust</u> <u>Wars</u> (New York: Basic Books, 1977), p. 185n.

(21) See Aquinas, <u>Summa</u> <u>Theologiae</u> II-II, 42,2 ad 3; Heinrich A. Rommen, <u>The</u> <u>State</u> <u>in</u> <u>Catholic</u> <u>Thought</u> (St. Louis: Herder, 1945), 473-76: "the lawful defense of a body politic's inalienable right to the realization of the common good." Also, Johannes

Messner, _Social Ethics_ (St. Louis: Herder, 1949), 596-601.
(22) See, for example, Messner, _Social Ethics_, 596-601, 723-724; Pius XI, _Firmissimum_, written in 1937 on the revolution in Mexico, para. 34-36; Paul VI, _Populorum Progressio_, para. 30-31. For Aquinas' position, see _De Regimine Principum_, Bk. I, ch. 6.
(23) See Gerard Chaliand, _Revolution in the Third World_ (New York: Penguin, 1978), 37, and _Guerrilla Strategies_, 9.
(24) Sergei G. Nechayev, "The Catechism of the Revolutionary," para 5 and 6.
(25) See V.I. Lenin, "The Tasks of the Youth Leagues," in _Selected Works_, 3 vols. (Moscow: Progress, 1977), III, 410-423, esp. 417-418.
(26) _Politics_, 1314a.

CHAPTER SIXTEEN

ETHICAL PROBLEMS WITH TERRORISM

One must be careful to define what will count as terrorism in any discussion in order to preclude such casual usage that would dilute the term's specificity and thereby make the moral problems involved even more difficult to treat. People have used the term to refer to acts of armies during conventional type war, acts of governments against their own populations, and acts of guerrilla forces against government officials in revolutionary wars.

Here I want to examine the phenomenon of "a planned campaign of paramilitary types of action which is characterized by episodic violence against random targets in order to injure and territy ordinary people for political purposes while seeking to avoid military confrontation with governmental forces." For our purposes, guerrilla attacks on governmental officials would not of themselves be terrorist actions. In those cases, "the perception of the perpetrators... indicated that the victims were militarily, spiritually, or politically on the opposite side in a polarized, civil-war environment."[1]

The strategic aim of terrorism as defined here is to unsettle the everyday life of society by destroying those habitual expectations necessary for getting on with the ordinary affairs. The purpose of this strategy is to symbolize and publicize (by taking credit) the intrusion of the terrorist movement into the relation between the fundamental adequacy of the political order and the everyday life of the people.

Using the technique of terror, the perpetrators strive by force to impose the movement's will upon other people, either within a single political state or across state boundaries. It is consequently a kind of war.

What that will is varies among the many terrorist groups. Some, such as the Basque Homeland and Liberty army, the Palestine Liberation Organization, or the Irish Republican Army, are nationalist-separatist and are acting out grievances from ethnic or cultural offenses they will no longer tolerate. Others, such is the Shi'ite Muslims in the Middle East or the Sikh groups operating in India, combine a religious with a cultural motivation and seek to purify their areas of all foreign cultural and economic influence. Still others, such as the Arab terrorist groups of Abu Nidal or Abu Mussa, appear to be free lance mercenaries.

For the first two varieties, and indirectly for the third, the campaign of terrorism is a war wherein the terrorists claim the "moral high ground." They think of themselves as heroes in an epic battle against evil forces and appeal to ideals and goals that often either are culturally idiosyncratic or employ only formal terms (e.g., "justice") whose connection with the terrorists' activities is unintelligible to or disputable by to those not in the group.

Even though the tactics of episodic violence have long been associated with war actions by "irregulars," guerrillas, and assassins, in the second half of the twentieth century the strategy which employs almost exclusively the use of these tactics has become a new species of war. This new way of war takes to an extreme some characteristics of guerrilla war developed out of the thinking and practice of Mao Zedung (as suggested, perhaps, by the insistence of the Sendero Luminoso in Peru that they are Maoists).

Mao's first theme was that fighting for directly political results could sustain guerrillas even though they were numerically and technologically inferior to their military opponents. Such motivation and their occasional political successes would enable the guerrillas to survive until they eventually wore down their opponents and gained their ultimate political goals.

The second theme, joined to the political motivation of the fighters themselves, was the politicization of the general population. The movement deliberately and overtly did things to include in the struggle those people who ordinarily would be indifferent or passive bystanders. These erstwhile bystanders were to become the politically influential "audience" of the guerrilla military actions.[2] The effect of a guerrilla operation on this audience was of an importance beyond evaluation by traditional military criteria for success.

This second theme taken to an absolute extreme has become a identifying feature of the terrorist actions today. We may use it to distinguish between those whose form of warfare is carried on almost exclusively to effect this audience, and those guerrilla groups who resort to terrorism as but one of many tactics in their diversified strategy (e.g., the North Vietnamese-Viet Cong Tet offensive of 1968).

On September 13, 1970, Palestinian terrorists from the "Popular Front for the Liberation of Palestine" (PFLP) blew up four hijacked airliners in Jordan. More significantly, they blew them up in front of television cameras. This act brought the fact of terrorism to the evening television news around the world. Gerard Chaliand writes:

> The use of terrorism as propaganda stems largely from the attitude of the media in the Western democracies, which accord an often disproportionate amount of attention to spectacular acts of violence. The prevailing attitude toward information is so perverse and twisted that a gang of hijackers can draw far more attention from the world press than struggles that are operating efficiently on the real battlefield. The media never accorded the campaign led by Amilcar Cabral and the P.A.I.G.C. the importance it warranted, even though for ten years it was the most significant struggle in Africa.[3]

Mao himself rejected terrorism as herein defined, that is, random tactical violence against non-governmental targets. (Whatever Mao's reason for this rejection, two causes for it were that his war confined to China had a dominant nationalistic theme, and he counted on the rural peasants for support.) But the contemporary terrorist has moved into the targeting of "civilian" people and places by absolutizing the theme of the "effect upon the audience" as the standard for choice of operations.

The causes for this move are no doubt multiple, but an obvious one is the failure in the Middle East and in Latin America in the 1960's and 1970's of efforts by politically motivated groups to wage successful direct or guerrilla war along the lines of

Mao, Fidel Castro, or Che Guevara.[4]

An ethically significant result of this change has been to extend the set of those persons and places considered proper direct targets for military violence. By the single criterion of political consequences, any person or group or locale upon which a military attack would be "likely to appear important" to the audience intended to be politicized becomes a legitimate direct target.

> Wars reflect the age in which they are fought. Both world wars of this century reflected the industrial age. They were wars of production. The Allies ultimately produced and delivered weapons in greater volume than their opponents. Terrorism reflects the postindustrial age. An increasing portion of the economy now is devoted to the creation, collection, retrieval, transfer, and dissemination of information. Political power increasingly rests on the ability to create or control information. Terrorists are primitive psychological warriors in an information war. Terrorism reflects the current age of instant communications and rapid mobility.[5]

How might we go about moral evaluation of this new form of war? Virginia Held begins her answer with the premise that the proper approach is to accept that different moral theories may be more suitable than their alternatives for different moral contexts.[6] She means that we are judging reasonably when we employ teleological forms of justification for some areas of decision, deontological forms in other areas, and so on. [This is not quite the same as I have argued in chapter one that those in different positions in society have different values and different rankings amidst values, but it may have many of the same "good decisions" made by those in these difference positions as its evidence. Her point seems rather to be that each of us will cite criteria from divergent moral theories when we explain what counts as making particular decision a morally good decision. Each of us at one time is a utilitarian ("it's better on the whole for all affected"), at another a rational egoist ("nobody will get hurt"), at another a virtue follower ("it's just not the fair thing to do here"), and so on.]

Held calls her general method "experimental morality," by which she indicates a process of moral inquiry that preserves the distinction between description and prescription and yet is analogous to scientific inquiry. That is, "moral theories or hypotheses can be developed, and subjected to the tests of moral experience.[7] It is here, as I understand her, that Held is thinking along the lines proposed in chapter one, although she does not seem to analyze moral standards into first-level and second-level components. Her procedure is to construct moral theories from the study of past actual moral experience, to gain clarification of and coherence within the theories by philosophical analysis and discussion, and then to accept or reject the resultant theories on the basis of further ethical experience, which, as distinct from science, is that of "action, decision, active approval or disapproval."

The content of moral standards develops as present moral decisions go against various aspects of standards derived from training or theories. And for subsequent theorizing,

> We should listen to those engaged in and those affected by various acts to hear what they intend and feel and think. We should enlarge our experience beyond the academic settings of moral theory and professional discussion. What we do not experience ourselves, we should try more often to experience indirectly through literary accounts, reportage, and especially the statements of participants.[8]

By her call to listen to what the terrorists "intend and feel and think" I understand Held to indicate that the subjective convictions of the terrorists (that what they are doing is morally good) are data for the test of our prior moral hypotheses.

Held's hypotheses and testing method offers some analogies with the methodology of this book. There are in the tradition of the Just War the recognition of a standard from past consensus (individual decisions and inductive generalization), and the openness to put such a standard against new decisions in new circumstances in order to test if there is need

285

of a new consensus in the present. But there are some important differences between this and Held's approach. The tradition favors the premise that only the feelings of those participants who are, and who have evidenced themselves to be, virtuous are self-validating morally. The ethician must have some prior estimate of the moral virtue of the participants in order to know how to weigh "what they intend and feel and think" as moral evidence. The difficulty comes when terrorists have idiosyncratic ways of identifying virtuous actions. This suggests there is little likelihood that any consensus that such actions as they do are indeed ethically good will come about.

To apply her method to the question of terrorist violence, Held sets up the problem with a series of general steps. First she proposes a principle for justification of a disruptive act within a political system: "If an act not permitted by existing laws but concerning which there are strongly felt conflicting positions turns out to have results which are generally considered to contribute to the well-being of the political system, the act will be considered justifiable within this system."[9] The justification mode is in terms of future consequences of the act, which Held finds as the normal mode for political morality.[10]

Given the additional assumption that the continued well-being of that political system is at least better than its destruction (analogous to the first type of revolution mentioned in the previous chapter), the argument is deductively valid. The unlawful acts of violence will be morally justifiable by reference to consequences if they have three characteristics:

> (1) They do not lead to additional, more extensive violence;
> (2) They directly and promptly bring about political consequences which are more decisively approved within the political system than the actions were disapproved.
> (3) No effective alternative means of bringing about these consequences were possible.[11]

This last characteristic seems consonant with the in bello tradition of justifying existential evils by reference to "military necessity." But Held has not directly confronted the traditional ground for this: that to omit what was necessary militarily would be to accept the likelihood that the unjust side would win. It is precisely the terrorists' idiosyncratically religious or cultural claim of justice that throws any appeal to "necessary means" into moral doubt.

Next Held takes up the question of the violent act that may be morally justifiable but which, because the present system depends for its survival on certain configurations of prevailing power, cannot be justified within the political system itself. (This would be analogous to the second type of revolution mentioned in the previous chapter.) Here the characteristics for justification are:

> (1) It does not lead to additional, more extensive violence.
> Either,
> (2) It directly and promptly brings about consequences which are in terms of a justifiable moral system, of sufficient greater moral good than evil to outweigh the violence itself, and no effective alternative means of bringing about these consequences are possible;
>
> Or,
> (3) It is prescribed by a moral rule or principle which is valid and applicable to a situation before the individual, and no alternative way of fulfilling this rule is possible.[12]

Specifying on the third point, Held argues that we may use violence to defend outselves against those who prevent us from entering into cooperative, morally justifiable relations with other people.

Applying this approach to the specific question of the morality of terrorism, Held argues that one should not shut down reflection by a definition. If one defines terrorism in terms of systematic violence that makes no distinction that might exempt the innocent from being targets, or in terms of sacrificing all other considerations for the sake of some political end, the moral evaluation is preset.[13] She offers a *prima facie* rebuttal of such definitional question-begging by citing reports that some in Third World countries view terrorist acts as the noble acts of "freedom fighters."[14]

For further rebuttal she cites a distinction by Robert Young that terrorist acts may be intimidatory in intent but need not thereby be indiscriminate in targets.[15] Young also thinks that terrorism may be justified as a part of an ideological "program of revolutionary struggle" analogous to the justification of certain wars.

Held thus sets up her argument for a conditional approval of terrorist acts analogous to a conditional approval of any war by the just war tradition. In it she faces the hard question of targets. And she employs what she considers the normal political method of ethical evaluation: consequences.

> We might conclude that _if_ war can be justified, terrorist acts can be also, if they have certain characteristics. But if terrorism includes, not by definition but in fact, the unnecessary killing of the innocent, it is at least not more justified than war in doing so, though the scale may be smaller. And if comparable good results can be accomplished with far less killing, an alternative to war that would achieve these results through acts intrinsically no worse than those that occur in war would be more justifiable....
> We might agree that the causing of war, whether through aggression, violent repression, the extermination or expulsion of unwanted populations, or by depriving people of the means to maintain life, is the ultimate crime of violence. If war to prevent the success of those who cause war can be justified, lesser uses of terror and violence can also, sometimes, be justified.[16]

Held seems to use the consequences to test terrorism in two ways: in terms of proportionality of the existential evil weighed against the political good; and in terms of the significance of discrimination when it is a matter of the lesser evil. Both obviously are part of the just war tradition, which she acknowledges by approval of citations which state this plainly. So the question would be: is she suggesting that, according to her method of experimental development, contemporary strategies and tactics of terrorists could be justified? She could be understood in this way, because of her reference to those in the Third World who look upon terrorists as "freedom fighters," which indicates that at least some today judge such actions as moral.

To justify terrorist war in terms of the political good achieved, which is not only to be proportionate to the physical evils brought about by the terrorists but, even more, is to be achieved with even less physical evil than if the terrorists employed conventional war, is to justify terrorist war under the category of ad bellum just cause. Given a proportionate cause for war, if less total physical evils are likely by terrorist strategies than by conventional war, there would be a proportionate cause for terrorist war.

The caution here would be whether the cause was, in principle at least, of a kind open to appreciation by those with no vested interests in the struggle (the "disinterested spectator" test), or whether the cause was so ideological as to distort judgment by the terrorist. (Again, we have in the tradition that not all morally righteous feelings are self-validating.) In the latter case, the existence of the evils to be overcome might be mostly in the perceptions of the terrorists and not be convincing in moral examination.

But if that hurdle is cleared, there is still the matter of the killing of the innocent. Held writes comparatively here: "if terrorism includes, not by definition but in fact, the unnecessary killing of the innocent, it is at least not more justified than war in doing so, though the scale may be smaller." I understand this as a way to bring in the in bello category of proportionality with its aspect of the "indirect" killing of innocents. That would be the expected way to interpret the qualifier "unnecessary."

However, her way of phrasing suggests she may also be opening to direct targeting of the innocent. This seems especially possible given her emphasis in the justification on the good results that might be accomplished with far less killing than in conventional war. If one emphasizes only the consequences, and if one recalls the theme of "impressing the audience," one might offer that the tactic of the direct killing of a few innocents might achieve greater consequences for the terrorists than the direct killing of many governmental officers.

These two points of an ideology controlling the cause and the direct targeting of the innocents are taken up by James T. Johnson.[17] Writing primarily about terrorism as a tactic of insurgents, Johnson bypasses the suggestion that political officials might be arguably included in the category of combatants in a insurgency war. He focuses on the recent extension of the set of legitimate targets that makes noncombatants, however defined, not only included in the set, but even the primary targets as the strategy through which to undermine the political structures that ordinarily support everyday living. He does not find a reason to qualify rejection of this strategy.

> (I)t is the direct, intentional violence against the innocent that marks this form of the use of force as fundamentally evil.[18]

According to Johnson, such a blatant divergence from even the minimum implications of the *in bello* principle of discrimination cannot be saved by anything in the cause.

Johnson also finds reasons to reject the claim that "the overwhelming justice of the cause justifies the kinds of actions terrorists commit." He tests the claim to a just cause by "the other traditional ideas that together determine when resort to force is justified." He concludes that the idea of a justifying cause as used by terrorists cannot overcome three objections.

The first objection is that the claim to a justifying cause by terrorists today is fundamentally ideological and this kind of cause has been rejected by the tradition as sufficient for any use of force because such claims are not subject to verification. Johnson cites the consensus that developed on this point in the sixteenth-century wars of religion.[19] The standard by which to test the validity of causes includes the requirement that the reasons are in principle open to judgments by third parties standing outside the conflict. I might add here, as earlier noted, that worthy sounding terms to express attitudes claimed by any group do not, without more, justify their actions. A group may claim to be struggling for "peace and justice," but what counts as such remain so amorphous as to condone any and every means. This relation between end and means indicates that the concept of the end ("peace and justice") is without content and can either justify any means or justify no means. Vocabulary becomes the opiate of the partisan.

The second objection is that a claim to have just cause presupposes an authority able to determine when an injustice is present that affects the community for whom the authority acts, and the authority must truly derive status from the community on whose behalf the claim is made.[20] But terrorists are often a small cadre, cut off from the community for which they claim to act.

The third objection is the apparent absence of right intention in terrorists' activities. The desires to harm, take revenge, and eventually dominate that all are expressed with "implacable animosity" seem irreconcilable with anything in the tradition concerning this third ad bellum requirement. With many of the terrorists' causes, the grievances are from offenses considered to be transcendent, and so the costs to be imposed on the enemy are seen as having no limit.

These terrorists campaigns, sometimes now labeled "low-intensity warfare," have thrown off balance those who confront them, in reference to the appropriate means to respond, or even the need to respond. This ambiguity in their opponents is not unwelcome to the terrorists.

> They hope that the legal and moral complexities of these kinds of challenges will ensnare us in our own scruples and exploit our humane inhibitions against applying force to defend our interests. Ambiguous warfare has exposed a chink in our armor.[21]

The other side of the moral problem of terrorism, consequently, is the justification of the response to it. Because of the uniqueness of this kind of low-intensity warfare, the political and military dimensions of response are more overtly connected that in conventional wars. To take direct action against those responsible for past acts of terrorism is risky. To take direct action against those judged to be planning future acts of terrorism is even more risky. But if to refrain from taking such action does not seem to induce terrorists to curtail further terrorism, such refraining does not seem to fulfil the duty to protect the citizen victims.

Any direct action against terrorists will cost lives, and, given present terrorist proclivity to take up residence in the midst of those who are only passively involved, such action quite likely will cost innocent lives. This must be evaluated under in bello proportionate risk of indirect killing.

Another risk in direct action is that the state acting against terrorists will, at least in the eyes of some, be seen as the culprit. So there will also be a political task of international explanation.

A third risk in direct action is that, because of the nature of the terrorist kind of warfare, it is not usually possible to wait until all the uncertainties of a situation are settled. But the risks in delay may outweigh the risks in taking action.

The ambiguity of this kind of warfare confuses those citizens who must support the governmental action. So it is imperative for governmental leaders to educe and support full public debate on the moral and strategic issues involved in response to terrorism. They must clarity how terrorism is a kind of war, and they must clarity how there is little likelihood of a quick resolution. Many countries have as part of their culture the attitude that all problems can be resolved by discussion or by direct action. As a result, the people with such a culture are unprepared for international situations that require patience amidst ambiguity, and perseverance in the wake of slow developing results of policy. This is especially important if accomodation that promises some relatively permanent solution is judged unlikely.

NOTES

(1) Michael S. Radu, "Terror, Terrorism, and Insurgency in Latin America," Orbis 28 (1984), 35. For a more general typology that includes "functional terrorism" by revolutionary groups against public officials and "repressive terrorism" by governments

against its own people, see Hippchen and Yim, Terrorism, International Crime, and Arms Control (1982), ch. 7; Grant Wardlaw, Political Terrorism (Cambridge: Cambridge University Press, 1982) For an extensive listing of definitions of terrorism, see Alex Schmid, Political Terrorism: A Research Guide (New Brunswick: Transaction, 1984).
(2) See Brian Michael Jenkins, "New Modes of Conflict," Orbis 28 (1984), 9.
(3) Gerard Chaliand, Guerrilla Strategies (Berkeley: University of California Press, 1982), 30.
(4) See Gerard Chaliand, Revolution in the Third World (New York: Penguin, 1978), 39-50. However, the United Front-Sandanista success in Nicaragua caused the Soviets to upgrade the Castro-Guevara strategy; see, Pedro Ramet and Fernando Lopez-Alves, "Moscow and the Revolutionary Left in Latin America," Orbis 28 (1984), 341-364, esp. 346, 348, 350, 357.
(5) Jenkins, op. cit., 10-11.
(6) Rights and Goods: Justifying Social Action (New York: The Free Press, Macmillan, 1984).
(7) "Violence, Terrorism, and Moral Inquiry," Monist 67 (1984), 622.
(8) ibid., 623.
(9) ibid., 611.
(10) ibid.
(11) ibid., 612.
(12) ibid., 614.
(13) She cites Paul Wilkinson, "The Laws of War and Terrorism," in The Morality of Terrorism: Religious and Secular Justifications, eds. David C. Rapoport and Yonah Alexander (New York: Pergamon Press, 1982), 310-311; and Michael Walzer, Just and Unjust Wars (New York: Basic Books, 1977), ch. 12.
(14) Here she cites John Dugard, "International Terrorism and the Just War," Stanford Journal of International Studies XII, 21-37.
(15) Robert Young, "Revolutionary Terrorism, Crime and Morality," Social Theory and Practice 4 (1977), 287-302, at 288.
(16) Held, "Violence, Terrorism, and Moral Inquiry," 620. Discussions in the United Nations by members of the "third world" have often been along these lines. See Abraham D. Sofaer, "Terrorism and the Law," Foreign Affairs 64 (1986), 901-922.
(17) Can Modern War Be Just (New Haven: Yale, 1984), 60-63.
(18) ibid., 61.
(19) See his discussion of the rejection of religion as just cause that would justify the extreme violence

that actually took place, in *Ideology, Reason, and the Limitation of War* (Princeton: Princeton University Press, 1975), 168-171, 214-219.

(20) On the extension of the idea of right authority to guerrilla warfare and terrorism he cites Michael Walzer, *Just and Unjust Wars*, 184-188.

(21) See George Schultz, "Low-Intensity Warfare: The Challenge of Ambituity," U.S. Dept. of State, Current Policy Paper, No. 783, an address given January 15, 1986, 1.

CONCLUSION

THE TRADITION AND TODAY

The ethician has no license to invent ethical norms, either formal or substantive. On the contrary, the ethician tries to articulate the intelligibility within the moral judgments of people who already are trying to do the right thing. The actual ethical judgments made by people in the world are the ethician's data.

It has been proposed in this work that these data from individual ethical judgments show variations in analogous situations, and that these variations correspond to the presence or absence of societal duties. These societal duties so affect valid ethical judgments that an action that may be required or at least permitted for one with certain of these duties could be wrong if done by one without such duties. The reverse may also be true.

Consequently, the data for a study of international ethics include not only the immediate and particular judgments but also the societal duties operative in the interpretation of the international situation.

It has also been a thesis of this work that the history of international ethics is an important part of the ethician's data since this history helps clarify how societal duties affect the interpretation of international problems. At the very least, historical study shows how often in the past the above distinction has been made between personal ethical standards and the ethical standards of someone acting in a societal role, from the leader down to the plain citizen.

The validity of this distinction for the moral thinking of governmental leaders has always been joined to the special obligations these leaders have to the common good of their own people. These special obligations have never meant a moral indifference toward the existential good of other states. Indeed the tradition, at least since Cicero, has insisted on a universal extension of the moral significance of people's social existence. But the necessity of societal institutions if certain human values are to be realized has meant that the security and enhancement of such institutions is a societal value and the basis for special obligations for office-holders.

This indicates that political ethics, and a fortiori international ethics, do not derive their substantive, second-level principles from the same sources as does personal ethics.

The traditional starting point for any problem in international ethics has generally been to accept that all people and all states deserve moral respect. Consequently, in those decisions wherein the affirmation of the more important values of one's own state means the present negation of the values of another state, such a negation must be done reluctantly and only as much as necessary, since one still acknowledges and respects the existential values as they pertain to other states even as one negates them.

To say that the primary duty of state leaders is to their own country is not to say that these leaders have no duties to other states or to the people of other states. But it is to say that there is a hierarchy of duties that must be followed in decisions.

The presence of the other duties means that not just any actions can be done to carry out the higher duties. But the reality of the higher duties means that there is an objective ground for decisions in times of conflict.

Moreover, one accepts that the position that the values affirmed are more important is only relatively objective. That is, ranking the values affirmed to be of higher importance is correct from a polis-centered analysis of the human situation and is not the result of arbitrary whim, yet ranking them higher is proper to one who has duties as leader of this country and not that country.

In this study's attention to history as data in international ethics, I have argued specifically that categories from the Just War tradition are still most helpful. International dealings seem to occur along a spectrum that has war between states as one extreme end. In the one direction, this model of a spectrum affirms that questions of reasonableness and morality do apply to war. In the other direction, the aptness of this model is evidenced as the attitudes these Just War categories express in their formal aspect continue to be ones that people insist are germane to all international decisions, even those outside war.

Moreover, while it is not surprising that the substantive, or second-level, principles of earlier times are not applicable without modification, we have seen that this does not make them otiose. On the contrary, how people expressed their formal moral attitudes in specific kinds of circumstances, and how they developed, modified, or changed these expression are significant guides in our new circumstances.

In addition, so often in framing substantive principles for international ethics there has been appeal, usually without explicit indication, to the principle of the double effect. Whenever in the history of the tradition the ethical problem was expressed in terms that noted a limited range of alternatives and, consequently, an unavoidable conflict between states, the consensus on the standard most regularly emphasized that it was correct for the state to act for its own common good with the subsumed but regretted negation of the existential values of others. It is striking that seldom has there been a principle in the consensus expressing the utilitarian greatest happiness criterion with its presumption that a leader's decision, to be moral, must show an egalitarian ranking of states' interests.

Once again I aver that ethicians acting properly do not invent principles. People really do use the principle of the double effect. The ethician does one's best to articulate what is involved.[1] What the ethician finds is that, when people see that any of their alternatives in a situation will involve the negation of certain existential values for human beings, people quite ordinarily make their decision in terms of "the more important existential value," with a regret for the necessary existential evil done and an attention that proportionality is respected.

The formal categories within the Just War tradition have particularized matters that must be satisfactorily handled if states are to be ethical in those conflicts that use military power. But again, historical study shows that the proper methodology for gaining substantive content to these categories involves recalling earlier consensus plus a set of individual decisions in historically new conditions.

It is here, according to the argument in this work, that the contemporary problems of nuclear weapons, intervention, revolution, and terrorism intersect with history and methodology. Neither bare appeals to past standards nor vacant appeals to the formal categories are adequate.

There are as yet no consensus principles for these contemporary problems. The tradition has been operative in the several decisions by office-holders and in the appeals for justification, but the ranking of values, itself an essential for the principle of the double effect, remains debated. This especially seems the case in the problems of nuclear weapons and terrorism.

Whether historical precedents of ethical principles are on a par with contemporary judgments or whether the precedents enjoy a presumptive status is itself an interesting question. The tradition itself opts for the latter alternative. But, of course, to have that fact settle the matter would be to beg the question. Still, history gives us reason to think that the contemporary problems may not be as qualitatively new as they sometimes seem.

> People make their own history, but they do not make it just as they please; they do not make it under circumstances chosen by themselves, but under circumstances directly found, given, and transmitted from the past.[2]

> Men make history, and not the other way 'round. In periods where there is no leadership, society stands still. Progress occurs when courageous, skillful leaders seize the opportunity to change things for the better.[3]

> I shall be content if those shall pronounce my History useful who desire to give a view of events as they did really happen, and as they are very likely, in accordance with human nature, to repeat themselves at some future time———if not

exactly the same, yet very similar.[4]

NOTES

1) See Meaning and Reason in Ethics, rev. ed. (Washington: University of America Press, 1979), 72-79.
2) Karl Marx, The Eighteenth Brumaire of Louis Bonaparte (Moscow: Progress, 1967), 10.
3) Harry S Truman, This Week, February 22, 1959.
4) Thucydides, History of the Peloponnesian War, I, i, 22.

INDEX